A Tradition Reborn:

From the Old Latonia Race Track
to Turfway Park Racing and Gaming

A 140-Year History

A Tradition Reborn:

From the Old Latonia Race Track to Turfway Park Racing and Gaming

A 140-Year History

Robert D. Webster
and Dr. James C. Claypool

Foreword by Hall of Fame Jockey Steve Cauthen

Cover concept: Robert D. Webster
Cover artwork: Zachary Wood -- ZW Designs

On the cover: Background image is of the Old Latonia clubhouse and grandstands.
Inset is a portion of the front of the new Turfway Park Racing and Gaming.
Quote on the back cover: Aaron Spurlock, long-time mutuel department manager.

Special thanks to Jan Hawk, Karl Lietzenmayer, and Pamela Webster, editors

Also by Robert D. Webster:

(Author)

A Brief History of Northern Kentucky

The Beverly Hills Supper Club: The Untold Story Behind Kentucky's Worst Tragedy

The Balcony is Closed: Northern Kentucky's Long-Forgotten Neighborhood Theaters

Northern Kentucky Fires: A Summary of the Most Memorable Fires of the Region

(Contributor)

Northern Kentucky Heritage Magazine

The Encyclopedia of Northern Kentucky

Also by James C. Claypool:

(Author)

The Tradition Continues

Kentucky's Bluegrass Music

Rascals, Heroes, and Just Plain Common Folk

Kentucky Patriot Doctor: The Life and Times of Alvin C. Poweleit

(Editor)

The Diary of a Serviceman: Robert Ralph Hartman

The Encyclopedia of Northern Kentucky

The Story of Gallatin County, Kentucky

A Bicentennial History of Covington, Kentucky

CONTENTS

Foreword

By Hall of Fame Jockey Steve Cauthen

Since it opened in 1883, and until today, a span of 140 years of Thoroughbred excitement, Northern Kentucky's premiere racecourse has produced more than its share of historic events. Kentucky Derby winners, Hall of Fame jockeys, and noted trainers and owners have all competed there. Over the years, millions of people, some famous but many just ordinary folks, have come to enjoy both great and run-of-the-mill horse racing. Songs have been written about the track, and major motion pictures have featured it.

Always on the cutting edge, Latonia/Turfway Park produced the $2 bet, the largest United States mutuel payout ever, and the nation's first sports book, all of which and more are chronicled in this book. Stories of fame and fortune, as well as tragic mishaps on the track, are articulately outlined in this year-by-year narrative record. In addition, over 200 images will take each reader back to the days of the Old Latonia Racecourse and allow those who visited what is now referred to as "Old Turfway" to reminisce. There are also many photos to show readers what the new and improved Turfway Park offers.

Today, Turfway Park is an exciting blend of casino-style gaming and Thoroughbred horse racing located in a beautiful new $150 million dollar facility, thanks to its new owners, Churchill Downs, Inc. Based on recent statistics, the future looks exceptionally bright for both.

Local historian and respected author Bob Webster, who brought us the true story behind the Beverly Hills Supper Club disaster, teamed with Dr. Jim Claypool, renowned expert on Thoroughbred horse racing in Kentucky, to pen a book sure to put a smile on the reader's face. It certainly did mine.

Chapter One

The Original Latonia Race Track:
The Most Beautiful Racecourse in America

By the time Kentucky joined the Union in 1792, horse racing had already become quite popular in the New World. In every town across the American colonies, people knew who owned the fastest horses… and who were the quickest riders. We remember from our school days the heroic journey of Paul Revere and his speedy ride to warn that the British were coming (though the tale is historically inaccurate).[1] But even before the American Revolution, many colonial settlers boasted of their horse's speed and endurance, only to be challenged by other villagers. Due to such informal dares, horse racing became the first "organized" sport in the United States.

The first widespread racing included short sprints with what were – and still are – called quarter-horses. Quarter-horse tracks are a quarter-mile long and are straight shoots. Rather than animals whose abilities lay with long-duration rides, horses had to be fast sprinters to be in any way competitive. By the late 17th century, horse races were being held up and down the colonies, typically on Saturday afternoons and often in front of courthouses, churches, or taverns. Large gatherings of men, women, and children generally accompanied these popular contests. In his *Racing in America*, John Hervey describes the quarter-mile contest as "…one of the most picturesque and vivid aspects of turf sport ever seen in this or any other country." Another writer called it "…a rough and tumbled affair with jockeys trying to foul their opponents and unseat their rivals."[2] Quarter-horse racing became so popular that, for safety reasons, it was banned on some of the busier avenues and permitted only on designated streets. An example of this was in Lexington, Kentucky, where during the late-1790s, such dashes were replaced by three- or four-mile heat races conducted on the outskirts of town. And according to the late Northern Kentucky historian, John Burns, Cincinnati's Race Street was so named because of the many exciting contests held up and down that straightaway.[3] In 2023, Quarter-horse racing remains popular in many parts of the United States.

Thoroughbreds

Arabian blood arrived in Virginia horse racing after 1732 when Samuel Gist of Hanover County imported *Bulle Rock*. Immediately, there was a quick rise in the overall quality of the racing stock in the colonies. Fairfax Harrison's research in 1928 shows the names and pedigrees of 50 English stallions and 30 mares imported to Virginia in 1774. All descended from three Arabians around the beginning of the 18th century. The first Thoroughbred of English stock to appear in Kentucky was *Blaze*, arriving in 1797.[4] Today, all authentic "Thoroughbred" horses must have unbroken bloodlines stemming from these three original English mares and Arabian stallions.[5]

By the 1750s, the aristocracy of the American colonies began to take an even greater interest in Thoroughbred horse racing, and many owners imported animals from only the most prestigious bloodlines. As pioneers slowly settled in what is now Kentucky, they brought their horses, of course... not only for work but for pleasure. As a result, by 1800, 92 percent of Kentucky taxpayers owned a horse, and the average owner had more than three.[6] Jusst like in the original 13 colonies, friendly wagers between horse owners soon became commonplace in Kentucky.

Colonel William Whitley

One early Kentucky frontiersman, Colonel William Whitley of Lincoln County, organized a comprehensive system for these impromptu dares between settlers. At his Sportsman Hill estate, Whitley is credited with building the first circular racetrack in Kentucky.[7] By 1800, the sport of horse racing had spurred the building of crude tracks in Georgetown, Danville, Shelbyville, Versailles, Winchester, and Maysville.[8]

Courtesy: Guardian of the Wilderness Road

Whitley had fought against the British Army in the American Revolutionary War and, in doing so, despised the British and many of their traits. Because of this, Whitley suggested two extreme "opposites" to the sport of horse racing when developing his rules and regulations. First, he decided that racing would be run counterclockwise rather than clockwise, as in England. Second, races would take place on dirt rather than on grass. Both of Colonel Whitley's non-English regulations were soon implemented across the United States as the "American" way to race Thoroughbreds.[9]

Kentucky – "The "Horse Capital of the World?"

Indeed, horse racing in Kentucky has a long and rich history. The words "Kentucky" and "horses" are almost synonymous. In the 2020s, Kentucky Governor Andy Beshear proclaimed the Commonwealth the "undisputed horse capital of the world."[10] However, that slogan may need to be revamped. Dick Hancock, President of the Florida Thoroughbred Breeders and Owners Association, trademarked that catchphrase on behalf of Ocala and Marion County, Florida, in the 1990s. And concerning the total population (all breeds), Texas and California lead the way with 678,000 and 642,000 horses, respectively. Florida is a distant third with 300,000, followed by Oklahoma, Illinois, Ohio, and Colorado. Kentucky comes in eighth place with only about 150,000 horses of all breeds.[11] That being said, while other states can boast of a higher number of horses overall, Kentucky, by far, leads the nation in Thoroughbred breeding, with more than 8,000 registered foals being born in the state each year, representing about 40 percent of the annual North American foal crop. Therefore, with no uncertainty, Kentucky can be described as "The Thoroughbred Capital of the World."

Other Kentucky "claims to fame" are the American Saddlebred and Standardbred horse. Developed into its modern style in Kentucky, the American Saddlebred was the "officer's mount" during the Civil War. Since then, this breed is often seen in pleasure riding and is the typical "saddle-seat" horse. The Standardbred is a pleasure and competition harness racing horse. Both species are now found worldwide, although predominantly in the United States.

Kentucky Racetracks Open

While the first "homegrown" Thoroughbred racecourse was laid out in the Bluegrass State in 1789, thirty-nine years later, in 1828, the Association Track opened in Lexington. It was the first track in Kentucky to conduct Thoroughbred racing by Whitley's written rules and a formal governing body.[12] While several smaller operations opened in the following years, the next racecourse of significance did not open for nearly 50 years.

On May 17, 1875, a new racetrack opened in Louisville, Kentucky, for its first official day of racing.[13] However, the name later known worldwide would not be attached to the track for over a decade. Colonel Meriwether Lewis Clark, the grandson of the famous explorer William Clark, traveled to England and France in 1872. Clark attended the Epsom Derby in England, which sparked his dream to create an even more spectacular horse racing event in America. Upon his return, he put his vision into motion, intending to showcase the Kentucky breeding industry. He leased 80 acres of land from two of his uncles, John and Henry Churchill, and after selling membership shares, he constructed grandstands, a clubhouse, a porter's lodge, and stables. Clark created three primary races for the opening meeting: the Kentucky Derby, the Kentucky Oaks, and the Clark Handicap. The winner of the first race that day was *Bonaventure*. However, the day's feature race, the Kentucky Derby, was won by a three-year-old chestnut colt named *Aristides*. A crowd of more than 10,000 witnessed 15 Thoroughbreds contest that 1-1/2-mile-long event. It was not until 1883 when that landmark racetrack took the name Churchill Downs, and *Leonatus* won the first Kentucky Derby under the new track name.

Present to witness *Aristides* race to victory in 1875 in the first-ever Kentucky Derby was 14-year-old, Matt J. Winn. Later as a professional tailor, one of Winn's clients, Louisville horseman William E. Applegate, who was then 40 percent owner of Churchill Downs, convinced Winn to invest and join the partnership. In 1938, Matt J. Winn became president of the corporation, and later, he would significantly impact horse racing in Northern Kentucky.[14]

4

Northern Kentucky Gets into the Action

The tremendous success of the Louisville and Lexington tracks prompted a group of Northern Kentucky businessmen and politicians to organize a similar Thoroughbred operation to serve racing enthusiasts in the uppermost counties of the state. In 1882, T.J. Megibben (Track President and Racing Judge), Major Elias D. Lawrence (Racing Secretary), Colonel Robert W. Nelson (horseman), Frank P. Helm (attorney and Covington City Councilman), and local judges George C. Perkins, Walter W. Cleary, and John Taylor formed the Latonia Agricultural and Stock Association, which obtained a charter to race Thoroughbred horses. Taylor was the son of Colonel James Taylor and grandson of the prominent landowner and founder of Newport, Kentucky, General James Taylor. The city of Taylor Mill, Kentucky, also found its name from this noteworthy family.

When the investors began searching for the ideal spot for a state-of-the-art horse racing facility, the clear choice lay just south of Covington, Kentucky, only five miles from neighboring Cincinnati, Ohio. Acreage was cheap that far out of town, and much of the property in question was owned by the Taylor family, which assuredly helped in the decision-making. The parcel was nice and flat, nestled between the hills of what is now Fort Wright and Taylor Mill. Another benefit, major highways such as the Covington-Independence Turnpike (now KY 17/Madison Pike) and Taylor's Mill Pike (now Ky 16/Taylor Mill Road) ran nearby, as did the Kentucky Central Railroad and the Cincinnati and Lexington Railroad. The 109 acres (later increased to about 172 acres) were in the little town of Milldale. When Milldale annexed neighboring Rosedale to the southeast, the city's population grew to over 5,000.[15] In 1894, the entire area was incorporated as South Covington, but that term was never used. Instead, the name "Latonia" was borrowed from a nearby mineral spring water spa. Latonia Springs, which at one time included a multi-story hotel, was located at today's

Sketch of the Latonia Springs Hotel

5

Madison Pike and Highland Pike, where a United Dairy Farmers currently stands. A member of high society in the mid-to-late-1800s would have often traveled to Latonia Springs to relax and drink the so-called miracle water.

In the late 1800s, Germans and the Irish made up a large portion of Latonia, Covington, and neighboring Cincinnati's population. Church festivals, family outings to amusement parks such as the Lagoon in nearby Ludlow, Kentucky, and Cincinnati's Coney Island, and gatherings at local beer halls or taverns were essential to community social life. Of course, picnics and boating on nearby rivers and lakes were also common. So was gambling. Gambling was an integral part of the recreational activities of the Irish and German Catholic communities. Card playing at saloons, fraternal clubs, and private homes; bingo; dice; and lotteries run by churches were accepted parts of everyday life. Neighborhood bookmakers, typically set up at corner taverns, also afforded men a popular and convenient way to bet on sports. These were more reasons why Northern Kentucky, with its highly relaxed attitude towards gambling, was chosen as the ideal location for a new horse racing facility.

While the location for the new track was ideal, so was the timing. Since the American Civil War, the upper South had experienced a noticeable spurt in sporting interest... best exemplified by the first Kentucky Derby in 1875 and the success of America's first professional baseball team, the Cincinnati Red Stockings of 1869.[16] But the city of Latonia was far from a thriving mecca for recreational sports and gambling in the late 1870s. There were only a few businesses in town, primarily servicing workers on the nearby railroads. That all changed in the early 1880s when rumors of a new Thoroughbred racetrack surfaced. While the track was being built, several new businesses were established at the five-way intersection just to the north. The success of these establishments skyrocketed, of course, once the racetrack was fully operational. Banks, groceries, bars, apartments, drugstores, jewelers, and hardware stores lined present-day Decoursey Avenue at the busy crossroads later known as Ritte's Corner, so named for Walter Ritte, proprietor of one of the earliest saloons there.

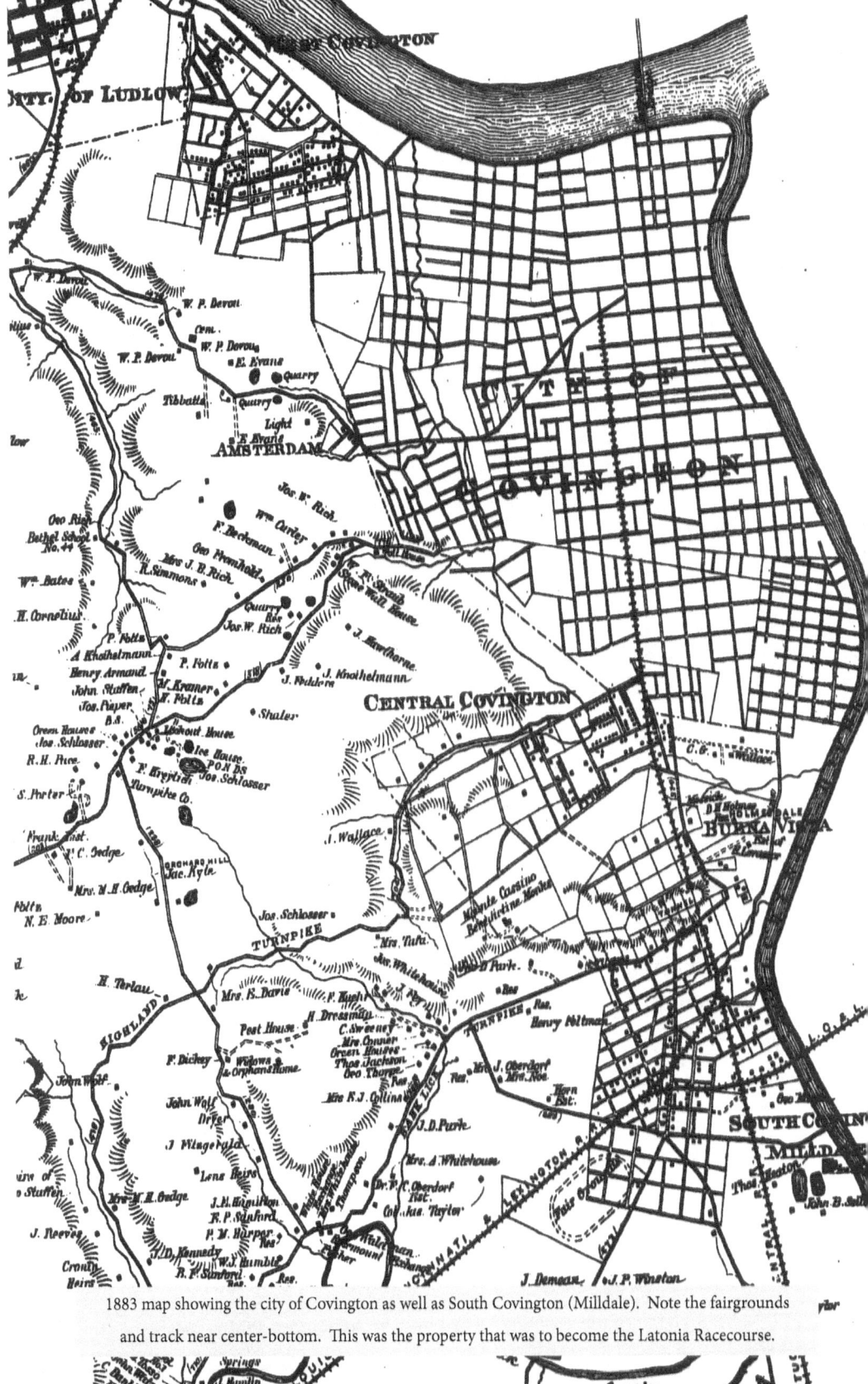

1883 map showing the city of Covington as well as South Covington (Milldale). Note the fairgrounds and track near center-bottom. This was the property that was to become the Latonia Racecourse.

The Latonia Race Track

On June 9, 1883, the new track's much-anticipated opening day saw the muddy dirt roads leading out of Covington jammed with carriages and riders on horseback. Out-of-town fans were transported to the region by the Kentucky Central Railroad, which had its terminus at the corner of Pike and Washington streets in Covington, and the Louisville and Nashville Railroad, which departed from Pearl and Butler streets in Cincinnati every half-hour. Horse-drawn omnibuses carried the patrons from the stations to the track. Of course, both depots could be reached by streetcar but, all things considered, it took tremendous effort to get to the new and somewhat remote attraction. Many latter-day references cite its location as the intersection of Winston Avenue and West 38th Street, which is technically correct, but misleading. Winston Avenue, from present-day McDonalds to Howard Litzler Drive, would have been home to the racetrack's barns or "backside." The grandstands and public viewing areas were on the west, the railroad-track side of the property. The public entrance was on the north.[17]

The original Latonia Race Track consisted of a massive wooden grandstand and clubhouse, a mile-long dirt racing oval, horse barns, and a landscaped infield decorated with flowers and shrubs. The infield would eventually feature a large, manufactured lake in the center. Co-author and acclaimed historian Jim Claypool beautifully described the pre-race activities of Latonia's opening day:[18]

"On opening day at Latonia, a cloudy Saturday dampened by a persistent day-long mist, a crowd estimated at over 8,000 assembled. The first race was scheduled for 3 o'clock and, during the two or three occasions that the sun appeared before the inaugural race, the fans responded with hearty cheers. As Mr. Currier's band played music that one scribe complained was 'pleasant but 25 years outdated,' the surreys, omnibuses, day carriages, hacks, and road carts arrived and were positioned in a long queue so that the fun seekers could both socialize and yes, if they so wished, view the races. Women were clad in fashionable clothing with wasp waists and plethoric bustles. At the same time, the men, sporting walrus mustaches and Santa Claus whiskers, wore toppers and derbies, skin-tight trousers, and flowing ties. If not seated in their conveyances or picnicking nearby, the women sat in a special grandstand pavilion while the men roamed more freely."

The first race on the card was a mile-long event, and 16 horses were called to the post. *Markland*, a brown colt owned by Colonel Jack Chinn and G.W. Morgan of Harrodsburg, Kentucky, finished a full length ahead of *Rena B* to become the first ever winner at Latonia. *Markland's* owners received $300 for their effort, while *Rena B's* interests received $100. The second race was the first running of the Clipsetta Stakes, a race which, until 1994, was run annually as part of the modern-day Turfway course's regular stakes series. The five-furlong (five-eighths of a mile) race for two-year-old fillies offered a purse of $750, with $600 going to the winner. A brown filly, *Eva S.*, held off *Mona* to win by a length.

The featured race on opening day was the 1-1/2-mile Hindoo Stakes. The unusual name was borrowed from the 1881 Kentucky Derby winner. While this race became Latonia's yearly premier event, the name was changed in 1887 to the Latonia Derby. The field for the first Hindoo Stakes included the top three finishers of the 1883 Kentucky Derby, which had just been held a few weeks earlier in Louisville. The fact that three "Derby" horses raced on Latonia's opening day, coupled with the fact that Isaac Murphy, a black jockey with the all-time winning percentage in stakes races in America at the time, was onboard *Leonatus*, was a clear indication that the success of the new Latonia Race Track was sealed.

When the horses crossed the finish line in the first Hindoo Stakes, *Leonatus*, *Drake Carter*, and *Ragland* finished first, second, and third. That is precisely how they had finished weeks earlier in the Kentucky Derby. Ultimately a winner of $21,435 in eleven career starts and the best three-year-old racing, *Leonatus* earned 10 straight victories in 1883, starting with the Kentucky Derby and peaking with his remarkable seven-day triple at Latonia. His wins at Latonia were huge sporting news, and they immediately helped draw national attention to the new Northern Kentucky track. The final day of racing at Latonia's first meet was held on June 16, 1883. However, that day ended in sadness when *Snowbok* stumbled and fell while attempting to clear the fourth hurdle.[19] Select hurdle races and steeple chasing continued at the track until around 1909.

The autumn season of 1883 witnessed even greater success at the racetrack. The highlight was the two-year-old Maiden Stakes run on September 17. In this race, the following year's Kentucky Derby winner, *Buchannan*, finished second, one of five times he

Leonatus

did so as a two-year-old. At the Kentucky Derby, he rallied from eighth place in a nine-horse field to become the first of three Derby winners for jockey Isaac Murphy. Black jockeys were prevalent at southern and midwestern racecourses in the post-Civil War era, and the Latonia track was no exception. Isaac Murphy (1861-1896) and several of his peers dominated Latonia's stakes races, winning with such regularity that they were typically preferred over their white contemporaries. Rather than in the Deep South, where African Americans usually worked in the cotton fields and plantations, black men in Kentucky typically performed their duties on the horse farms in Central Kentucky. From there, these men made the natural transition into jockeys and horse trainers. Not surprisingly, the first three Kentucky Derby winners were trained by black men.

Courtesy: Los Angeles Sentinel

Isaac Murphy

The magnificent Latonia Race Track played host to more great Thoroughbreds in the following years. *Joe Cotton*, the third of four Kentucky Derby winners bred by A.J. Alexander of Woodford County, Kentucky, won the 1885 Hindoo Stakes. Other Kentucky Derby "starters" at Latonia were *Irish Pat, Keokuk, Bersan, Lord Coleridge, Blue Wing* (second in the Kentucky Derby behind the incredible *Ben Ali*), *Lijero*, and *Montrose*. Other famous "winners" at Latonia during the period include *Silver Cloud, Libretto*, and *Kingman* (Isaac Murphy's third, fourth, and fifth victory in the stakes recarded "The Latonia Derby."

The Latonia Oaks was established in 1887 and featured still more distinctive Thoroughbreds. Seven winners of the Kentucky Oaks in Louisville (*English Lady*, 1890; *Souffle*, 1896; *Lady Schoor*, 1901; *Easter Stockings*, 1928; *Rose of Sharon*, 1929; *Suntica*, 1932; and *Fiji*, 1934) also won the Latonia Oaks. Run continuously until 1910, renewed in 1920, and suspended in 1939, the Latonia Oaks became another nationally recogonized event.

By 1888, the new Northern Kentucky track was strong enough… and had its own identity… that the name of its most prestigious stakes race was changed. No longer the Hindoo Stakes, the inaugural running of the newly christened "Latonia Derby" on May 26, 1888, was the talk of America's racing community. The heavily favored *White* finished in a dead heat with long shot *Los Angeles* in the race. Instead of following traditional customs and splitting the purse, *White's* owner demanded an immediate run-off between the two horses. *Los Angeles'* owner agreed and went to place a significant wager on his horse. His thorough-bred easily beat *White*, finishing a full three lengths ahead. *Los Angles* became the first of four fillies, along with *Gowell* (1913), *Handy Mandy* (1927), and *Fiji* (1934), to win the Latonia Derby during the 55 years (1883-1937) it was run.

During the racing card on May 28, 1888, thirteen pickpockets were arrested at the track and held in the Latonia jail. When they appeared before Justice McLaughlin the following day, only 10 remained as three escaped their confinement. Those remaining were fined $30 and costs and locked up in jail until after the meet. To some, these events were evidence that the racetrack had already begun to attract thieves and an assortment of other unsavory people. To others, it was evidenced that the City of Latonia needed a new and bigger jail.

On October 6, 1888, twenty-one horses went to post in Latonia's second race on the card. This was the largest field to start at any American racetrack that year. And the list of impressive horses grew longer before the decade ended. *Hindoocraft*, a son of 1881 Kentucky Derby winner *Hindoo*, won the Latonia Derby in 1889. *Spokane*, another Kentucky Derby-winning horse, won a two-year-old maiden race at Latonia the same year. And Isaac Murphy rode to victory on *Riley* in 1890, another Kentucky Derby winner.

By the 1890s, the Latonia Race Track's success had an enormous impact on its neighboring town. Massive crowds gathered at Latonia Park, where pro-prietor William Deschler advertised accommodations for picnics, weddings, and ball parties. Beer and wine were available at the park, conveniently located on Taylor's Mill Road near the Licking River ferry. Trackside, there were crap games and chuck-a-luck contests before and after the races, and admission to the grand-stands remained at one dollar... or just two dollars for the paddock. The Latonia Distillery hawked its fine rye and bourbon whiskey at the track and several fash-ionable watering holes. John Moss, the local postmaster, offered an assortment of books, stationery, newspapers, and cigars from his home at the corner of Taylor's Mill Road and Southern Avenue. Dr. R. Lee Bird also set up practice at Ritte's Corner, and John and William Zoller worked nearby as blacksmiths. The track, its magnetic forces at work, had undoubtedly started to impact and help shape the community.

The Biggest Horse Race in the Country

The Latonia Race Track also witnessed considerable changes in appearance in its first decade. The original grandstands had been demolished in a windstorm in 1887. They were quickly replaced by an iron and stone structure, described in the *Kentucky Post* as "...a national model not exceeded by any on the North American Continent."[20] The track had also been refitted with concrete sidewalks, improved drainage, a modern bar, restaurant facilities, telegraph offices, and luxurious private suites for the use of club members. The original 200 stables in 1883 had been expanded to 700, with more planned. And modern betting sheds, constructed in 1890, easily accommodated 100 bookmakers. Latonia stakes races, which in 1883 had averaged $750 each, were now never under $1,200, and some, such as the Latonia Derby, reached $5,000 or more. The summer meeting, which once began in June and lasted only seven days, now started in May and lasted 30 days.

Most impressive, by the late 1880s, the Latonia Derby was the biggest horse race in the country, much bigger than the Kentucky Derby in Louisville. There were management changes as well. Track president Megibben passed away and was replaced in 1890 by Colonel Robert Nelson of Newport, Kentucky, one of the founders. Another change came in 1892, when the Latonia Jockey Club was incorporated with $250,000 in capital stock by a group of investors headed by William E. Applegate, with Cary Applegate, Daniel Enright, and C.J. Enright, known as the "Applegate Syndicate." Before his involvement with Latonia, Applegate had purchased Churchill Downs in 1894 and was instrumental in many changes there, including the reconstruction of the grandstands to include the now-iconic "twin spires."[21]

As the town of Latonia expanded and interest in the Latonia Race Track grew, the decision was made to extend electric streetcar service from inner-city Covington in 1893. For the first nine years of the track's existence, train service had increased from the terminals in Cincinnati and Covington, but getting to the racetrack was still quite challenging. When the first streetcar arrived at the race-course in Latonia, it foreshadowed the time when the Old Milldale #43 trolley car brought a steady stream of fans down the streets of Covington to Latonia in numbers quite astounding. By the 1920s, police officers had to stand at nearly every corner leading to the track to direct traffic. With easier accessibility, attendance at Latonia significantly increased. Records were set and re-set yearly, with some events witnessing as many as 10,000 spectators.

By the turn of the century, racehorse owners made it their standard operating procedure to rotate their best animals between Kentucky's three major racetracks. As a result, several state highways were renamed to indicate the fastest or easiest routes between those three cities, making things much clearer to the average motorist. The 3-L (LLL) Highway was christened around 1915 and was named for and connected Louisville, Lexington, and Latonia.[22] From Churchill Downs in Louisville, interested parties were taken through Shelbyville, Frankfort, and Versailles to Lexington and the Association Track. After racing there, they would travel through Paris, Cynthiana, and Falmouth – on their way to the Latonia Race Track. The 3-L name was officially discontinued before 1940, but folks throughout Kenton County and much of Northern Kentucky still affectionately refer to what is now Madison Pike as the 3-L Highway.[23] So important was this road to the success of the racetrack that a historical highway marker was erected in 2022 to commemorate the old, two-lane highway. The sign can be found on a section of the original 3-L, about one-half-mile south of the intersection of Madison Pike and Dudley Road in Fort Wright.

Courtesy: Robert Webster

An essential new organization appeared on the American scene in 1894. Based in New York, The Jockey Club exercised various legislative, executive, and judicial functions, including writing, enforcing, and interpreting the rules of American racing. It also licensed jockeys and trainers, appointed officials, and allocated racing dates. Eventually, many of these powers passed to state racing commissions, including Kentucky. But initially, failure to meet The Jockey Club's rules meant a racecourse could be declared "an outlaw track." Indeed, racing had been spread topsy-turvy across the nation since the Civil War and was long overdue for regulation and reform.[24]

Other Area Tracks

The great success of Kentucky Thoroughbred racing in the late-1800s soon spawned the opening of several other operations in the region. Each, however, failed in comparison to the success of Latonia. The Gentlemen's Full Racing Park in the Cincinnati suburb of Oakley opened in 1896 and closed in less than a decade. The Queen City Racetrack opened along the Licking River just south of Newport, where Newport Steel would later operate for decades. While Queen City catered to cheaper horses and smaller purses, one of the nation's top riders, Jimmy Winkfield, frequently raced there. Winkfield

Courtesy: The Wall Street Journal

Jimmy Winkfield

won the Kentucky Derby twice (1901, 1902) and had 220 wins in 1901. Also in 1896, the Electric Light Jockey Club, one of the first lighted tracks in the nation, opened just east of the Latonia Race Track in Rosedale. However, bankruptcy was filed during that track's second year of operation. It never reopened.[25]

Starting around 1898, the magnificent Latonia Race Track experienced its "heyday" years. Incredibly, five more Kentucky Derby-winning horses ran at Latonia between 1898 and 1906: *Plaudit,* 1898; *Lieut. Gibson,* 1900; *Judge Himes,* 1903; *Elwood,* 1904; and *Sir Huron,* 1906. And in 1906, Latonia conducted 106 days involving 699 races, with purses totaling nearly $331,000, placing it once again among the nation's leaders relative to total purse distributions. Between 1902 and 1905, interests tied to Judge George Perkins, another of the founders from 1883, obtained control of the track when the Applegate syndicate could not pay off the notes. Harvey Myers and Joseph L. Rhinock, Kentucky congress-man and former Covington Mayor, paid Perkins $88,416. This represented the principal and interest on the unpaid Applegate loan putting Rhinock and Myers, along with Jerome "Rome" Respess, in control. "Rome" Respess would become a breeder and trainer of champion Thoroughbreds at his Highland Stock Farm in Boone County, Kentucky.

By this time, a big issue throughout Kentucky was competition from tracks in the same region created by overlapping racing dates. Finally, the Kentucky tracks left the Western Turf Association, which had failed to solve the issue. They joined the newly-formed American Turf Association, the brainchild of Louisville native Matt J. Winn. Winn had recently rescued the financially troubled Churchill Downs in 1902. Winn guided the new organization, but the group was short-lived. In 1906, the Kentucky Racing Commission was formed, and all licensed racing in Kentucky has since been subject to its rules.[26]

One of the most critical long-term issues for the racetrack came with the establishment of the new city of Latonia. As early as 1897, the city attempted to annex the remainder of the old town of Milldale. Had this occurred, the racetrack would have been subject to municipal taxes for streets and improvements. The city's initial attempt to annex failed, but in 1904, when it absorbed the town of Rosedale, Latonia's aggressive mayor, J.T. Earle, went after the racetrack again. Earle, a railroad agent, bank president, and part-time politician with big dreams, launched a four-year crusade to bring the track under the city's authority. The battle, fought over fences, property rights, licenses, and even an idea to build streets straight through the middle of the track, took a new direction when on

February 20, 1906, the Latonia city council passed an ordinance annexing all race-track property.[27] Proclaiming victory, Earl announced plans to tax and license businesses directly or indirectly associated with the racetrack. As a spokesperson for the new Kentucky Law and Order League, he said he would lead efforts to declare the new Kentucky Racing Commission illegal, thereby creating a condition he speculated might end horse racing in the state. Neither plan worked. The courts kept Latonia Race Track away from the city's jurisdiction, thanks mainly to the courtroom skills of track lawyer and vice-president Harvey Myers. The Racing Commission went about its work unconcerned about threats from the mayor of what was then only a fourth-class city. By 1908, it was the City of Latonia's turn to face hostile adversity. Mayor Earle and his council were suddenly caught up in a political struggle with its much larger neighbor, Covington. In a complex series of events, Latonia was entirely annexed to Covington in 1909. Mayor Earle and his cohorts were retired and silenced.[28]

Courtesy: www.nkyviews.com

Aerial view of "Old" Latonia property

By 1912, five more Kentucky Derby-winning horses appeared at Latonia: *Pink Star,* 1907; *Wintergreen*, 1909; *Donau*, 1910; *Meridian*, 1911; and *Worth,* 1912. "Rome" Respess, mentioned earlier, owned *Wintergreen*. In 1911, the

$225,385 distributed at Latonia led the country, with Churchill Downs far behind at $176,960. More astounding, on June 17, 1912, Latonia gained an element of everlasting immortality when the track paid out the highest mutuel ever paid at a North American racetrack. The 941-1 long shot, *Wishing Ring*, won the sixth race. The win rewarded four bettors (Sam Freedman, a whiskey salesman from Cincinnati; E.B. McClure of Mt. Vernon, Ohio; H.F. Conn of Louisville; and Mrs. F.B. Laws of Glencoe, Illinois) $1,885.50 each for their $2 bets.

While Thoroughbred horse racing was always the featured attraction at Latonia during the "hey-days," other popular events were also held at the beautiful facility. In 1908, Latonia patrons helped welcome the fascination and incredible speed of the new "horseless carriage." Indeed, auto racing was held on Latonia's mile-long dirt track during horse racing's off-season, and nationally famous drivers such as Barney Oldfield even raced there. Auto racing was a colossal hit, and the crowds were enormous. The sport was so successful that an auto racetrack named the Rosedale Speedway was proposed along the Licking River nearby. While construction began there in 1909, the project was never completed.

Courtesy: "Old Latonia: America's Most Beautiful Racecourse"

Automobile racing at Old Latonia

Besides automobile racing, air shows became all the rage across the country. In the fall of 1909, the famous Curtiss and Willard Company brought their flying machines to Latonia. The event brought just as many spectators as did the

Two views of the spectacular air shows at the Latonia Race Track

Latonia Derby. One of the planes even made two loops around the nearby Holy Cross Church steeple. In the event's first year, Orville Wright was present in the infield to advise the many participants. Air show tournaments were repeated for several years at Latonia.

It was no surprise that Latonia was chosen as the location for successful auto races and air shows. By now, Latonia was known as one of America's most beautiful racecourses due to the meticulously landscaped infield and grounds, the 400-foot-long grandstands and a massive Victorian-style clubhouse. United States Speaker of the House, Covingtonian John G. Carlisle, stated it was by far the finest racing facility he had ever seen. Shortly after his visit to the area, former President of the United States, Rutherford B. Hayes, visited Latonia and was equally impressed.[29] The Northern Kentucky racetrack became so popular nationwide that in 1912, Hollywood movie makers came to the tiny burg of Covington. Here, they filmed a movie titled *Winning the Latonia Derby*. In newspaper headlines, filmmakers called the event "The Greatest Race in the History of the American Racetrack."[30] Later, in October 1916, a Labor Day celebration brought more than 30,000 people to the Latonia Race Track infield. There they witnessed a vaudeville show and professional motorcycle races, participated in foot races, listened to political speeches, judged the prettiest baby contest, and in the evening, dined and danced.

Public officials from the halls of Congress to the lowest municipal officer were numbered among those drawn to the spectacle of horse racing at Latonia. Among the many celebrities was Alice Lee Roosevelt, daughter of President Theodore Roosevelt. While she was often in town to visit poetess and college friend Julia Dinsmore, Alice also made a memorable trip to the Latonia Race Track by invitation of the Longworth family of Cincinnati, famed for their Rookwood pottery and wealth. A Longworth son, Nicholas, a Republican congressman and later Speaker of the House of Representatives, was courting the President's daughter at the time. News reporters were everywhere

Courtesy: Long Island Press

Alice Lee Roosevelt

during her visit, and national attention was again shown to Latonia, Kentucky.

"Two dollars across the board, please."

The most important contribution from the original Latonia Race Track to American Thoroughbred horse racing likely came in 1911. Before that time, wagering at racetracks involved a bet between individuals or through auction pools. Bookmakers challenged this when Latonia opened in 1883, and bookmaking won out as the standard procedure for placing a wager. Colonel Lewis Clark installed pari-mutuel machines at Churchill Downs, and Latonia followed suit in 1897, but they never caught on. Advertised as a system that provided bettors a better chance to win, the new pari-mutuel system involved clerks handling, posting, and paying bets. Betting pools included win, place, and show bets in denominations of five dollars or multiples thereof. Track officials regulated payoffs and divided the monies among all winners after subtracting the track's modest 5 percent commission. In contrast, bookmakers took at least 15 percent commission on bets, paid the racetrack $100 for each racing day they worked, and after about $50 in expenses, took about $50 profit home.

Unfortunately, bookmakers or their friends often entered horses they owned or controlled into races that these horses had no chance of winning, and bookmakers would pocket all the money bet on them. Concerned by this and rumors that some races were fixed, Churchill Downs switched to pari-mutuel betting exclusively, and Latonia followed in 1909. However, Latonia's owners took matters a step further. In 1911, Latonia lowered the standard $5 mutuel bet to $2 and offered the same for place and show betting. The $2 bet and the "$2 across-the-board" wager were thus born. That system spread from Latonia to become the national standard in Thoroughbred horse racing... and remains as such today. This caused Northern Kentucky's Latonia Race Track to become even more well-known on the national scene.

By the end of the 1912 season, Latonia had continued as one of the country's most successful racetracks. That same year, however, a group headed by Louis A. Cella, owner of Douglas Park in Louisville, merged with Matt J. Winn to form the Louisville Racing Association. Winn had been in control of Louisville's Churchill Downs almost from its beginning. Seeing Latonia's potential, the Cella group enthusiastically purchased the Northern Kentucky track. Cella quickly sent his Douglas Park general manager, John Hackmeister, to run the show. Unfortunately, Cella and Winn had butted heads numerous times, and the last thing Cella wanted was to again fall upon Winn's wrong side. He instructed Hackmeister not to compete with Winn and his Kentucky Derby in any way, shape, or form. And Hackmeister followed Winn's orders precisely.

Latonia desperately needed an independent board of governors... and a general manager whose singular purpose was to improve the track's position within the racing community. In contrast, this is precisely what Churchill Downs had in Matt Winn, tireless general manager of the Louisville track, from 1902 until he died in 1949. Matt's overall dealings included facilities stretching from New York to even Mexico at one time or another. His passion, however, was, without doubt, his beloved Kentucky Derby.

Still, Latonia continued with great success over the next few years. In 1913, in only 42 days of racing, Latonia awarded purses totaling $217,735 -- the most in the country once again, and $90,000 above Churchill Downs. Latonia had joined Belmont Park, Aqueduct, Saratoga, Pimlico, and Churchill Downs to be ranked in the top five of all American racetracks. Only at these five locations did the nation's top-quality horses race. And two more Kentucky Derby winners ran at Latonia: *Donerail*, 1913, and *Old Rosebud*, 1914. Amazingly, while training at Latonia, *Old Rosebud* was made to pull a sulky in a harness race. It is hard to imagine a modern Thoroughbred who had won the Kentucky Derby being made to do the same.

Unfortunately, tragedy struck the famous Northern Kentucky racetrack twice over the next two years. In April 1914, a lantern exploded while a trainer was tending to a sick horse in barn #18, immediately setting the structure ablaze. While several horses were rushed to safety, eight quality

Donerail at the Latonia Derby

Thoroughbreds were killed, including *Wintergreen*, the 1909 Kentucky Derby winner. The other horses that succumbed to the fire were *Baby Doll*, *Belle of Bourbon*, *Carleton Club*, *Congressman James*, *Kisland*, *Pink Coat*, and *Red Star.*

Jockey Carl Ganz

More heartbreaking is the story of jockey Carl Ganz. The Louisville *Courier-Journal* of October 12, 1915, had this headline and tragic statement: "Carl Ganz is Seriously Hurt. Today's racing at the Milldale track was marred by an accident that may prove fatal to jockey Carl Ganz of Louisville, one of the best-known and most popular riders of the present-day turf." It was the opening race on the card that day, a mile dash with 13 maidens starting. Just past the first turn, Ganz's mount, *Beach Comber*, broke down, throwing the 21-year-old fan favorite to the ground. He was rushed to a nearby hospital with a severe skull fracture but never regained consciousness. Ganz was the 1913 Kentucky Oaks winner and one of the sport's top riders. Incredibly, Carl's brother Roscoe rode *Donerail* to victory in the Kentucky Derby the same year Carl won the Kentucky Oaks. However, record books indicate the Derby winning jockey as Roscoe Goose. Carl rode under the surname Ganz, the German version of Goose, to avoid confusion with his brother.[31] Of Carl Ganz, the *Courier-Journal* stated, "In the passing of jockey Ganz, the turf loses one of its best riders, who has done much for the sport in Kentucky. Ganz was known all over the land for his spirited riding, his judge of pace, and his wonderful finishing qualities."

While the Latonia Derby remained America's most prestigious contest for several more years, Matt Winn hit full steam with his plan to make his Louisville race the best in the country. Before 1916, horses that won the Derby in Louisville were frequently shipped to Latonia, where they contested for its Derby six weeks later. After 1916, however, only five Kentucky Derby winners raced at Latonia. Winn started his big push by convincing his friend, Harry Payne Whitney, to enter a horse in his Louisville race. Whitney was from New York and, after inheriting over $12 million because of his wealthy father's death, bought 614 acres along Paris Pike near Lexington and started a successful stud farm. His claim to fame was likely as the owner of *Upset,* the only horse ever to notch a victory over the incredible *Man o'War.* When Whitney's *Regret* won the 1916 Kentucky Derby, he proclaimed in a quote reported nationwide, "I do not care if she never wins another race. I am satisfied that she has won the greatest race in America."[32] Whitney eventually entered 19 horses in what soon became the pinnacle in Thoroughbred races. While Latonia Derby's purse was… once again… the highest in the nation for three-year-olds, it would be the final time the famous Latonia Derby bested the Kentucky Derby.

Courtesy: New York Times

Photo from the 1913 Latonia Derby

The Latonia Race Track continued with successful meets, however. Another Latonia highlight came in 1917, when local bettors witnessed the racing career of a true legendary Thoroughbred. *Exterminator*

23

Exterminator

Courtesy: www.pressdirects.com

enjoyed an incredible nine-year career, but his maiden race was at Latonia on June 30, 1917. *Exterminator* raced 100 times, winning 50, placing in 17, and running third 17 times. He won at distances ranging from six furlongs to 2-1/2 miles, even at age four. He was America's top handicap and money winner for four consecutive years (1919 through 1922) and had over $252,000 in lifetime winnings. At Latonia, *Exterminator* started eight times, winning four races, placing twice, showing once, and finishing off the board only once... late in his career at age seven. *Exterminator* died in 1945 at age 30 and, in 1957, was one of the first horses inducted into the Hall of Fame.

The downfall of the Latonia Race Track began when it was sold again in 1919. This transaction gave ownership to the Kentucky Jockey Club, the most influential racing syndicate ever formed in Kentucky. Initially, the organization also planned to purchase Churchill Downs and the Association Track in Lexington. However, when they learned that the Cella Syndicate was willing to part with Douglas Park in Louisville, they bought all four facilities. Matt Winn was immediately made a partner in the new organization. Douglas Park was turned into a training facility, and in 1933 the Association Track, open since 1828, failed and closed permanently.

At Latonia, the new owners' first move was to replace Hackmeister with Matt Winn, who would split his time between Latonia and Churchill Downs. Winn's first move was to introduce a new "top" race at Latonia. The Latonia Championship ran uninterrupted from 1919 to 1939 and replaced the Latonia Derby as the track's premier contest. Winn's ulterior motive was undoubtedly to downplay the popularity and prestige of the Latonia Derby. Many insiders, especially those in Northern Kentucky, foresaw the track's future demise with Matt Winn at the helm.

Even with the new management, many more highlights were experienced at the beautiful Latonia Race Track. In the 28-day Spring Meet in 1919, $357,869 in purse monies were paid out, the highest in the nation, and the crowds were more impressive than ever. After the meet ended, a local turf writer proclaimed, "Latonia was the most popular course in America!"[33] In 1920, the grandstand and betting sheds at Latonia were enlarged and. in both 1920 and 1921, several new rows of pari-mutuels were added to accommodate crowds that on stakes days swelled to between 25,000 and 30,000. And a remarkable feat occurred at Latonia during two days of racing in the Fall Meet of 1923. On October 16 and 17, jockey Ivan Parke accumulated ten victories, which at the time was a national record.

In the following years, legendary Kentucky Derby winner *Black Gold* (1924) raced at Latonia, as did *Upset*, who took the Latonia Derby in 1922, two years after becoming the only horse to defeat the great *Man o'War*. The 1923 Fall Championship featured a thrilling battle between two-year-old champion and Kentucky Derby winner *Zev* and *In Memoriam*, owned by local brewery king Carl Wiedemann. *Zev* was beaten, much to the delight of the locals, but weeks later avenged his loss in a still-disputed finish of a match Winn had specially arranged for them at Churchill Downs. The *Zev—In Memoriam* showdown of 1923 is a standard entry in most histories of Thoroughbred racing.

A star-studded field competed in the third leg of the American International run at Latonia on October 11, 1924. The race was won by Mrs. William K. Vanderbilt III's *Sarazen*, giving the French champion *Epinard* his third straight

Courtesy: Wikipedia Commons

Courtesy: Keeneland Library

Left: *Zev*, with jockey Earl Sande. Right: *Black Gold*

defeat and proving that the American Thoroughbred was better than those in Europe. And at the 1927 Latonia Derby, *Handy Mandy* won and set a new speed record, one-fifth of a second faster than the earlier record set by *Man o' War*.[34]

The "heyday" of the Latonia Race Track continued until 1929, the same year the Great Depression began. Immediately, the size of Latonia's purses dropped, the top jockeys, trainers, and owners all left, and the overall quality of the horses diminished. That year, *Clyde Van Dusen* became the last Kentucky Derby-winning horse to ever race at Latonia.[35] However, there would still be two more incredible highlights in the track's history. First, in 1931, Latonia shined on the big screen again in Clark Gable's first-ever starring role. *Sporting Blood* featured scenes from the Latonia Race Track and Churchill Downs.[36] Secondly, 1931 is when jockey legend, Eddie Arcaro, got his start. Eddie Arcaro (1916-1997) was born in Cincinnati and started his riding career galloping horses at Latonia. At 15, he was too young to compete legally in the United States, so he moved to California and began his racing career in Mexico. Once of legal age, he came back to the United States. Arcaro won more American classic races than any other jockey in history and is the only rider to have won the U.S. Triple Crown twice (1941 on *Whirlaway* and again in 1948 on *Citation*). He won his first Kentucky Derby in 1938 (*Lawrin*) and is tied with Bill Hartack for most Derby wins with five. He also has the most wins (six each) in the Preakness and the Belmont Stakes, but it was at old Latonia where Arcaro got his start.[37]

Courtesy: Keeneland Library - Cook Collection

Courtesy: The Saratogian

Left: Clarence McCrossen on Clyde Van Dusen. Right: Eddie Arcaro

By the late-1930s, the once-thriving track was mainly used for auto races, air shows, picnics, and political rallies. On July 8, 1939, President Franklin Roosevelt made a scheduled campaign stop at Latonia to a group of over 25,000 spectators. His speech that day began with, "My friends of Kentucky, I'm glad to come to this beautiful spot today. I know about Latonia," to which he received thunderous cheers.[38]

Top: Reaping Reward wins the 1937 Latonia Derby. Bottom: President Roosevelt at Latonia Race Track

Matt J. Winn and his associates were eventually forced to act, straining to sustain Churchill Downs and Latonia in hard times. An assortment of gimmicks, such as lottery-type betting pools and lower admissions, were introduced at Latonia, desperately hoping to keep the track afloat. When that did not work, post times were changed to late afternoons and evenings to attract fans who had completed their workday. Free admissions and clip-coupon novelties were also introduced. But the Great Depression was too much. Not even the grand Latonia Race Track could escape its wrath. Old Latonia became a "ghost town."

The last Thoroughbred meet at Latonia was held on July 29, 1939.[39] There was a packed house for the track's final card. *Catalonia* became the last winning horse to cross the finish line.[40] The last significant event ever held at the racetrack was the Kenton County Centennial

Courtesy: Blood-Horse Magazine

Catalonia

in the summer of 1940. The event started with Eleanor Roosevelt pushing the ceremonial button at the White House. The Latonia racecourse property was sold to the Standard Oil Company of Ohio (SOHIO), who later sold it to developers. The Latonia Shopping Plaza opened on the site in the mid-1960s. In 2023, McDonald's, Big Lots, a vacated Burlington Coat Factory, and more than a dozen other retail stores, restaurants, and industries stand on the site.

The grand and beautiful Latonia Race Track had lived an extraordinary life. It placed Latonia, Kentucky on the map and secured in the history books some magnificent Thoroughbred champions. Racegoers and horsemen alike from all over the nation were drawn to it. Incredibly, between 1883 and 1939, horses competing at Latonia were among the finest nationwide and included 27 Kentucky Derby winners and many top finishers of other prestigious national stakes races.[41] Today, all that remains are the fond memories of those fortunate enough to have enjoyed "a day at the races" there or who had been inclined to accept a position of employment at the track. Unfortunately, like the track, those lucky individuals have also gone to the grave.

There are a few reminders of the historic racetrack still standing, however. The original paddock remains as part of Mueller Roofing Company. The structure can be found southwest of West 43rd Street, between Boron Drive and the railroad underpass. A sign on the roof states, "Mueller 1875." In addition, several "jockey's houses" still stand. These homes were built specifically for jockeys, meaning the size of the doorframes, countertops, etc., were all constructed with the rider's height in mind. These quaint homes can be found along Cottage Avenue, just off West 33rd Street in Latonia. Also left are the photographs, many preserved in this book and other publications, as well as those uploaded to the Internet.

Longtime track employee James Robertson summed up his fond memories of the historic racetrack in a wonderful documentary titled *Old Latonia: The Most Beautiful Racecourse in America* by filmmaker Cam Miller. "Old Latonia was more than a racetrack. It was a slice of Heaven on earth. And the town where she sat was like no other."

Courtesy: Kenton County Public Library

A field of Thoroughbreds race down the track at "Old" Latonia

Courtesy: Kenton Co. Library – H.E. Ashby

Courtesy: "Old Latonia" Documentary

Courtesy: "Old Latonia" Documentary

Courtesy: "Old Latonia" Documentary

Courtesy: www.nkyviews.com

Courtesy: www.nkyviews.com

Courtesy: Kenton Co. Public Library

Courtesy: www.nkyviews.com

Courtesy: Kenton County Public Library

Courtesy: www.nkyviews.com

Opposite page, top left: Employees at Old Latonia Racetrack in 1931; Right: Dozens of newsmen crowd to capture the start of a race; Middle and bottom photos: Two views of "Crossing the finish line."

This page, upper left: View of the judges platform; Right: A large crowd is gathered on the apron; Middle row, left: Another view of a jam-packed apron; Right: View of the Victorian-style Clubhose from the grandstands; Above: Popular photo of Latonia Race Track utilized as a postcard; Left: View of the grandstands from across the lake.

Postcards from the Jim Claypool Collection

Top (left to right): The iconic Victorian Club-house, with the grandstands in the distance; A typical crowd seated in the grandstands and gathered on the apron;

Second row: A rare view from the back of the grandstands; The "ladies" section of the stands;

Third row: Thoroughbreds prepare for the be-ginning of another event; A massive audience in attendance for a series of races;

Fourth row: A great view of the finish line; General view of the Latonia Race Track;

Immediate right: Automobile races at the magnificent Latonia Race Track;

Courtesy: Kenton County Public Library

Courtesy: Kenton County Public Library

Top: Crowds overflow from the grandstands at Latonia Race Track;

Bottom: Fans stand shoulder-to-shoulder on the apron and against the rail to watch exciting races.

NOTE -- It always shirt and tie, and usually a full suit, for the gentlemen. And for the ladies, only the finest and fanciest of apparel would be found at the race track. Also note on the previous page (right-hand column, second postcard from the top) women were seated in a separate section from the men.

FIFTH RACE

$25,000 Added—THE LATONIA DERBY—$25,000 Added

Forty-seventh Running of the Latonia Derby. For three-year-olds. By subscription of $25 each; $250 additional to start. $25,000 added, of which $4,000 to second, $2,000 to third, $1,000 to fourth. The Winner, if also the Winner of the Kentucky Derby, to receive $5,000 additional. Non-winners of a three-year-old race of the value of $20,000 allowed 5 lbs.; non-winners of a three-year-old race of $5,000 allowed 8 lbs. Maidens allowed 12 lbs. Acceptances to be named through the entry box the day before the race at the usual time of closing. The owner of the winner to receive a Silver Trophy.

CLOSED FEBRUARY 6, 1929, WITH 134 NOMINATIONS

ONE MILE AND ONE-HALF

Track Record—Handy Mandy (3), 109 lbs., 2:28¾

	Owner Trainer Jockey Equip. Wt.	Ticket No.
	Jacques Stable—J. Johnson w, b (Jacques Cohen) Tangerine. Green Four Leaf Clovers.	
1	ESSARE .... 121 B c, 3, Light Brigade—Wistaria	4708
	R. T. Wilson, Jr.—T. J. Healey w, b Old Gold. Green Chevrons, Collar, Cuffs and Cap.	
2	AFRICAN .... R. Leonard 118 Ch c, 3, Olambala—Grace Foster	4700
	Audley Farm—Kay Spence w, b, bd (B. B. Jones) Purple. Lavender Sash and Cap.	
3	THE CHOCTAW....... H. Philpot 118 B g, 3, Rouleau—Miss Marcella	4705
	Harned Bros.—J. Reed w, b American Beauty. White "H" Front and Back. White Cap.	
4	BORIS ....L. Pichon 118 B g, 3, Craigangower—Ecatarina	4706
	Herbert P. Gardner—C. Van Dusen w, b Black. Light Blue Sleeves.	
5	CLYDE VAN DUSEN............ C. McCrossen 126 Ch g, 3, Man o' War—Uncle's Lassie	4701
	Desha Breckinridge—C. C. Van Meter w Blue. Gold Belt and Cap.	
6	LORD BRAEDALBANE......... .. W. Crump 118 Br g, 3, Whisk—Home Star	4704
	C. C. and G. Y. Hieatt—A. D. Steele w, b Old Gold. Gold Bars on Black Sleeves. Black and Gold Cap.	
7	BEN MACHREE......... K. Noe 113 B f, 3, Playfellow—Sweet Brier	4702
	Basil Manor Stable—Owner w, b, bd (W. F. Polson) Orange and Black Stripes. Orange Sleeves and Cap.	
8	BUDDY BASIL .... D. Dubois 118 Ch c, 3, Basil—Eris	4707
	Hal Price Headley—W. W. Taylor w, b Navy Blue. White Sash, Collar, Cuffs and Cap.	
9	†PARAPHRASE .... 118 B c, 3, Supremus—Parody	4703
	Hal Price Headley—W. W. Taylor w, b Navy Blue. White Sash, Collar, Cuffs and Cap.	
10	†AMSTERDAM .... W. Fronk 118 B c, 3 Archaic—Balmacara	4703
	† HAL PRICE HEADLEY ENTRY	4703

1 38 60 44 42 16 21

CAUTION *060 6 36*

Be sure that the number of your ticket corresponds with the mutuel number of the horse on program. Errors can not be corrected after a race starts.

Left: Program page from 1929 at Old Latonia, showing *Clyde Van Dusen* finishing second. He was the last Kentucky Derby-winning horse to race at Latonia;

Right: Front and back of a 1930 tote ticket;

Opposite page: Maybe the most recognized and copied photo of the Old Latonia Racecourse. This view is of the Clubhouse and Grandstands.

Chapter One Endnotes

1. In reality, Revere was captured along the way. It was William Dawes and Dr. Samuel Prescott who completed the task of warning the colonists. See https://www.paulreverehouse.org/the-real-story. It is only through the poem by Henry Wadsworth Longfellow that Revere became famous.

2. *Ibid.*

3. "Horse Racing in Northern Kentucky," Robert D. Webster with James C. Claypool, *Northern Kentucky Heritage Magazine, Vol. XXVIII, No. 2.*

4. Historical Marker Database, "Beginning of Horse Racing in Kentucky," retrieved on July 7, 2022.

5. "Horse Racing," James C. Claypool, *The Encyclopedia of Northern Kentucky*, Paul A. Tenkotte and James C. Claypool, editors, pages 460-461.

6. *"How Did Central Kentucky Become Horse Racing Country?"* slate.com/articles/news and politics/ex-plainer/2010/04, retrieved October 1, 2018.

7. Historical Marker Database, "Beginning of Horse Racing in Kentucky," retrieved on July 7, 2022.

8. *Ibid.*

9. "Horse Racing," Claypool.

10. Beshear made this comment in a Press Release titled "State's Thoroughbred Breeders' Incentive Fund Awards Nearly $15.9 Million to Kentucky Breeders," on February 14, 2022, see: khrc.ky.gov/Documents/KBIF2021.pdf.

11. "Horse Racing in Northern Kentucky," Webster/Claypool.

12. "Horse Racing," Claypool.

13. Churchill Downs website.

14. *Ibid.*

15. "Latonia Racecourse," James C. Claypool.

16. *The Tradition Continues, the Story of Old Latonia, Latonia, and Turfway Racecourses,* Jim Claypool, Hayes Publishing, Ft. Mitchell, KY, 1997, page 2.

17. James C. Claypool, "Old Latonia Race Track (1883-1939)," *Northern Kentucky Heritage Magazine, Vol. XI, No. 1,* page 1.

18. *Ibid.*

19. *Ibid.*

20. *The Tradition Continues,* Claypool, page 21.

21. William E. Applegate, Wikipedia.com, retrieved on July 3, 2022.

22. "Horse Racing in Northern Kentucky," Webster/Claypool.

23. *Ibid.*

24. James C, Claypool, "Old Latonia Race Track (1883-1939)," *Northern Kentucky Heritage Magazine, Vol. XI, No. 1.*

25. Webster/Claypool.

26. *Ibid.*

27. Karl J. Lietzenmayer, "Earle, Last Mayor of Latonia," *Northern Kentucky Heritage Magazine, Vol. II, No. 1.*

28. *Ibid.*

29. *Ibid.*

30. *Ibid.*

31. *The Tradition Continues,* Claypool, pages 41-42.

32. *The Tradition Continues,* Claypool, page 38.

33. *The Tradition Continues,* Claypool, page 54.

34. *Ibid.*

35. *The Tradition Continues,* Claypool, page 38.

36. Cam Miller, "Old Latonia: America's Most Beautiful Racecourse."

37. Bill Christine, "Eddie Arcaro, 'The Master,' Is Dead at 81," *Los Angeles Times*, November 15, 1997, retrieved on June 11, 2022.

38. *Ibid.*

39. *Ibid.*

40. *Ibid.*

41. *Ibid.*

Chapter Two

The "New" Latonia Race Track

In the larger picture, the loss of the Latonia Race Track in 1939 took a backseat to worldwide events. When Germany invaded Poland on September 1, 1939, attention was taken away from the sport of Thoroughbred horse racing and was placed on what would soon be World War II. Additionally, while anti-German sentiment was raging nationwide, its share in Northern Kentucky was among the largest due to the high concentration of German immigrants in that region.

Meanwhile, the Latonia Race Track had closed, not because of the war or any related event, but because the track's owners had decided it was unwise and unprofitable to keep it open. In reality, that conclusion had been 10 years in the making. It began with the economic conditions created by the Great Depression, which started in 1929, and accelerated when the quality of racing and the size of the purses offered at Latonia began a steady decline in the early 1930s, from which the track never recovered. Management was also an essential factor. During the 1930s, Matt Winn and The Jockey Club he represented were forced to make a hard business decision. Finally, in the late 1930s, Winn had to choose between Latonia, a marginal enterprise on the decline, and Churchill Downs, home of his beloved Kentucky Derby. Winn's decision to concentrate on the Louisville track was no surprise.

Polk Laffoon and Maurice Galvin, two others connected to The Jockey Club, also need mentioning. Laffoon, Latonia's president until it was reorganized and linked to Churchill Downs in 1937, was no more than a figurehead president. Still, he brought prestige and influence to his association with Latonia. His horse, *Deadlock,* had finished fourth in the 1922 Kentucky Derby, making him a prominent horseman in his own right. A successful Northern Kentucky businessman and the owner of two area farms, Laffoon had also been chairman of the Kentucky Racing Commission since 1929. From 1931 to 1935, he relied heavily upon help for Latonia from his cousin, Governor Albert Benjamin "Happy" Chandler. And being one of the state's top Democrats, he balanced Maurice Galvin's Republican ties.

Of the two men, however, Maurice Galvin was more deeply involved in the running of the Latonia Race Track. Galvin was one of Northern Kentucky's most powerful politicians and, although a Republican in a state where Democrats dominated, had been able to wield considerable influence at the local and state levels. Some of his power was based on his connections to The Jockey Club and his position as vice president of Latonia. More importantly, however, Galvin was another friend of "Happy" Chandler, Kentucky's freewheeling Governor from 1935-1939, who, although a Democrat, took political positions similar to those of Galvin and other bipartisan politicians in the state. Galvin was known to ask Chandler to help Latonia get and maintain favorable racing dates. He counted on Chandler's support, as Galvin tried to make a go of it at Latonia during the difficult years of the middle- to late-30s. Maybe the most critical detail in this whole mess... Maurice Galvin also did legal work for the large Sohio petroleum refinery next to Latonia. This tie was the final puzzle piece concerning Latonia's closing and sale. Galvin's relatives, as well as a former clerk in his law office, believe that sometime during 1939, Galvin either approached Sohio or vice versa, and preliminary discussions were started concerning the possibility that the Latonia Race Track property might be sold to Sohio. They also believe that Galvin was instructed to proceed immediately when Galvin informed Winn and the other members of The Jockey Club of his discussions.[1]

Statistics show that Latonia was not the only Kentucky racetrack to suffer during the Great Depression. Tracks in the Commonwealth fell even further behind their competitors nationwide in the 1930s by whatever measure, be it purse distributions, profits, attendance, or even the quality of racing. In general, it could be regarded that if not for Winn and the popularity of his Kentucky Derby, Churchill Downs might very well have ended up in the same predicament as Latonia.

Other matters are linked to Latonia's demise, of course. Several new tracks had opened in America, many of which were in far more populated regions. For example, throughout the 1920s, trainloads of Chicagoans had come to Latonia with money to wager at the famous racetrack and spend in local retail stores. The Depression and the rise of tracks nearer to the Windy City ended that pilgrimage.

It is tempting to consider the theory that if Latonia could have held on until 1941, WWII and the economic recovery it spawned, coupled with Latonia's access to cheap public transportation during wartime gas rationing, might have been enough to ensure the track's recovery. After all, speculation might continue that these same conditions contributed to the survival of Cincinnati's River Downs and other struggling racetracks. The argument ends there, however, because Matt Winn had no interest in sustaining or reviving racing at Latonia unless a considerable profit was to be made. And in the end, the most significant gain was realized by selling the beautiful racecourse to Sohio.

In the end, Latonia closed in 1939, even though track management heavily advertised the upcoming 1940 season. On March 24, 1942, the historic property was sold for $263,000. Dismantling of the grandstands, stables, and other buildings began almost immediately. The demand for aviation fuel, at a time in the war when the outcome was still very much in the balance, made the loss of an old and unprofitable racetrack seem insignificant. Still, thousands lamented the loss, if for no other reason than that "Old Latonia," as it would soon be known, was one of the last survivors of an age gone by. And in the collective minds of those who still mourn the loss of Old Latonia, the historic track is, as it should be, still remembered for its joy and innocence. The men who established the course at Milldale in 1883 were men of the old school of gentlemen who saw horse racing not as the big business it later became but instead as a sport that they, by founding the track, made accessible to one and all. The bottom line is that the "call to the post" was silent in Northern Kentucky for two decades. A Kentucky Historical Highway Marker was later placed at the corner of 38th and Winston to commemorate the magnificent racetrack and its legacy.

Top: 2023 view of a portion of the Old Latonia Race Track property. The site is now home to Big Bob's, Big Lots, a McDonalds, a bank, and a few other establishments

Middle: American Legion Hall, situated at 38th and Winston in Covington (Latonia), where a Kentucky Historical Highway Marker stands.

Bottom: Close-up view of the marker.

Horse Racing Leaves Northern Kentucky

Live horse racing was gone from Northern Kentucky. Yet, the availability for the local bettor to place wagers on horse racing flourished in the region for several decades. Many chose to visit Keeneland or Churchill Downs and their pari-mutuel tellers. Others traveled to the nearer but less prestigious River Downs on the outskirts of Cincinnati, Ohio. A silver dollar deposited into the turnstile gained each patron a general admission ticket to the track. Visits to racetracks were among the legal ways… but far from the most popular methods for bettors to place a wager on a horse race. Bookmakers at Latonia were present from the very day it opened in 1883. But from the 1920s, the number of those individuals increased dramatically, both because the track was in its heyday and just as much due to the Prohibition Act, implemented in 1920, which seemingly made circumventing the law in vogue.

Where there was money, there was crime. When the Latonia Race Track opened in 1883, crime in Northern Kentucky was small and unorganized. By the early 1930s, however, that all changed, and it changed in the most extreme fashion imaginable. Cleveland's Mayfield Road Gang, once the largest organized crime syndicate in the Midwest aside from the notorious Chicago Mafia, entered Northern Kentucky and soon controlled a massive web of illegal gambling operations for over three decades. Newport, Kentucky, for example, only a stone's throw from Covington and Latonia, its neighbors to the west, was once known nationally as "Sin City," for it was often claimed that any vice a man desired, if he could afford it, he could find it in Newport, Kentucky.[2]

Unlike many similar regions across the country, Northern Kentucky became a magnet for organized crime. The blame can be traced back to 1803 when a United States military arsenal was erected on Newport's west end at the confluence of the Licking and Ohio rivers. Once occupied, soldiers were drinking, gambling, and committing acts of violence, often just for amusement. The sudden assembly of hundreds of young men was immediately followed by an infestation of somewhat enterprising young women to service at least one of the soldiers' needs. In a *Kentucky Post* article, writer David Wecker summarized the city's early history this way: "Newport was a frontier, a lawless slip of territory at the edge of civilization; a place where drinking, prostitution, gambling, gunplay, and all-around carousing was the natural order."[3] By 1811, soldiers outnumbered white males in town 157-37; by 1812, thousands of militiamen were coming and going through the Newport Barracks. In 1815, the Army handed out $75,000 in back pay to soldiers mustering out and let them loose in Newport to celebrate.[4]

Linked with Newport's early history, the simple makeup of the region played an equally significant role in how Northern Kentucky became a mecca for gambling. Much of the area comprised German and Italian immigrants and some Irish – mostly Catholics. The Germans brought their beer-drinking and sporting traditions. Then there was the Catholic Church's practice of lotteries and festivals to raise money for their charitable giving. At summer festivals and many church-sponsored events, men drank and placed wagers in the name of the fundraiser of the time. Before long, these same citizens found it only natural to enjoy other forms of vice, such as betting the ponies and engaging in friendly poker games, all in the back rooms of their favorite corner saloons. A collective mindset developed that gambling, per se, and drinking, per se, were OK. Even in 2023, you will find that is still the mindset in the region.[5]

With the introduction of the Volstead Act in 1920, there was no way Northern Kentuckians were going to give up their drinking… and their gambling. Neighborhood bars continued to supply their "regulars" with illegal alcohol smuggled in, mainly from Canada through runners in Detroit. Soon, George Remus, later known as the "Bootlegging King," organized a network of dealers and suppliers for the entire Midwest. Born in Germany and raised in Chicago, Remus later moved to Cincinnati, where he made headlines for killing his wife during broad daylight in Eden Park. When Prohibition was repealed, illegal gambling operations soared. Every saloon had slot machines, and most had table games such as blackjack and roulette, all hidden in a back room or secret basement club.

When the Cleveland Syndicate moved in, they took over everything. Their standard procedure was to find a successful bar or club, offer the owner a somewhat-reasonable purchase price but allow him to stay on as manager, while they reaped all the profits from the new operation. Most owners quickly obliged, and those who did not found their club engulfed in flames the following morning.[6] By the late 1930s, more than twenty illegal gambling clubs existed in Campbell and Kenton counties, such as the Flamingo, Bluegrass Inn, Grandview Garden, Sportsman's Club, and the two most successful clubs: the Lookout House and the Beverly Hills Country Club. Before 1960, the number of such clubs had grown to more than fifty. Superstars in the entertainment world, such as Milton Berle, Phyllis Diller, Jerry Lewis, Dean Martin, Marilyn Monroe, and Frank Sinatra performed at fancier clubs like the Lookout House and the Beverly Hills. Sadly, the Beverly Hills (then the Beverly Hills Supper Club) would experience a tragic fire in 1977, later discovered to be mob-related, that killed 169 and injured dozens more.[7]

At every club and corner saloon, there were plenty of bookmakers to accept bets from patrons. And if not in person, wagers were taken over the phone. It was said that when Newport's Merchant's Club was later razed, more than 100 telephone lines were found to exist in the building.[8] One can only imagine the smoke-filled hidden rooms where these bookmakers plied their trade. Through a series of events, too many to mention, illegal gambling clubs were all but erased in Northern Kentucky in the early-1960s. There were no more facilities where patrons could walk in and play the slots, try their hand at blackjack, or spin the roulette wheel right out in the wide open. As far as horse racing is concerned, the clean-up in both Kenton and Campbell counties made bookmaking less public and wide open, but it certainly did not eliminate it. And while many thought the Mafia was gone from Northern Kentucky, it were not!

Meanwhile, from 1945 to 1960, the majestic sport of horse racing experienced dramatic change nationwide. "Modernization" and "larger" were the sport's new bywords. The money involved, the sheer number of horses, races, owners, breeders, and even the number of racetracks increased, as did betting and attendance. On September 22, 1945, Belmont Park in New York, for example, had its first $5 million day, while the Kentucky Derby in 1946 paid a record gross purse of more than $124,000, including the first million-dollar Derby handle of $1,202,474, an astonishing 55 percent above the 1945 bets. Modernization came when the filming of horse racing was introduced, allowing a permanent record of the race, and allowing stewards to review the film to verify a winner. Another change came in the form of horse transportation. While once it was railroads that allowed the shipment of horses from track to track, air travel became available in the late 1940s, and Thoroughbreds could race at tracks from coast to coast. The filming of races and unique air transport methods were derived directly from technologies introduced in the war.

After Latonia's closure in 1939 and before 1959, there were many changes throughout the Northern Kentucky region as well. Especially after WWII, there was an explosion in new housing, and many families moved to the suburbs. Cities such as Fort Mitchell, Lakeside Park, Taylor Mill, Erlanger, Elsmere, and Edgewood started experiencing rapid growth. Still, houses were being built street by street rather than in massive subdivisions. Downtown Covington remained the major shopping rendezvous for residents, especially those in Kenton County. With places such as Coppin's department store and Eilerman's clothing store at Sixth and Madison, Egelston-Maynard's, a block to the north for sporting goods, a half-dozen shoe stores, Lang's Cafeteria and Woolworth's lunch counter, people came to Downtown Covington from far and wide. Few considered a trek across the river to Cincinnati for such things at that time and, of course, there were no shopping malls even being considered. Covington and Latonia were also home to several movie theaters such as the Kentucky, Liberty, and Madison for entertainment, Devou Park, the Twin Oaks golf course, and YMCA, and for recreation, and grocery stores such as Kroger and Remke. The Latonia Bakery (Emerson's Bakery in 2023) has been a staple near Ritte's Corner since it opened in the 1930s, and other "mom-and-pop" operations were scattered throughout the region. The Dixie Highway from Covington to Erlanger was once known as the "Gourmet Strip" because of the many top-notch culinary choices. The White Horse and Town and Country (Park Hills), the Lookout House and Oelsner's Colonial Tavern (Fort Wright), Greyhound Tavern (Fort Mitchell), Retschulte's Five Mile

House (Lakeside Park), the Cabana Club and Colonial Cottage (Erlanger), and Doc's Place and the Swan (Elsmere), are just some of those long-lasting eateries.

Horse Racing Returns to Northern Kentucky and the Track that Never Was

The birth of New Latonia and Turfway Park (and eventually Turfway Park Racing and Gaming and Newport Racing and Gaming) began in the mid-1950s. Incredibly, the outcome started with the announcement that a new harness-style track would be built outside Florence, Kentucky in rural Boone County. For those unaware, harness racing involves a horse pulling a rider sitting in a small seat known as a sulky rather than a traditional horse and jockey. And, unlike

Courtesy: Wikipedia Commons

Thoroughbreds or quarter-mile sprinters, these horses are known as pacers or trotters. First-time spectators might be reminded of the exciting chariot races of ancient Rome, as seen in such films as *Ben-Hur* and *Gladiator*.

A typical harness-style race

The construction of the "Kentucky Raceway" was announced in November 1955 by Edward Price, a Cincinnati-area importer and head of the Kentucky Harness Racing Association. The track would be located along US 42, about two miles west of the main intersection of what is now considered Old Florence (off present-day Evergreen Drive, where the Saddlebrook subdivision stands). Kentucky Raceway, which operated in 1956 and 1957 and later from 1963 to 1965, had a seating capacity of 6,000, accepted bets by pari-mutuels, and purposely set race dates not to conflict with the Thoroughbred meets at Cincinnati's River Downs.

The "New" Latonia Race Track

After the announcement of Kentucky Raceway, a group of men in rural Kenton County devised their plan for what would be called the New Latonia Racetrack. On January 13, 1956, the *Cincinnati Times-Star* newspaper announced that a $4 million Thoroughbred racetrack was to be built near the intersection of Nicholson Pike (now Walton-Nicholson Road/KY 16) and the Independence Turnpike (now Madison Pike/KY 17), about two miles south of the city of Independence. Rel "Robert E. Lee" C. Wayman, a local real estate broker, owned 110 acres; Newman Armstrong, former Kenton County detective, 18 acres; Vermont Rankin, 13 acres; and Harris Myers, 10 acres. Architectural drawings indicated an ultra-modern clubhouse with a seating capacity of 4,800 that included terrace dining and moving stairways. The fireproof grandstands would seat 7,200. The local investors submitted a request for racing dates from the Kentucky Racing Commission, but the Commission took no action regarding the project. In addition to the disastrous setback from the Racing Commission, the group experienced strong opposition from a very well-organized group of Kenton County ministers and clergy, especially the Baptists. However, just as Wayman and his associates in rural Kenton County were giving up on their dream, another group of investors had teamed up with a similar vision.[9]

On July 25, 1956, Matt Winn Williamson, the grandson of the late Matt J. Winn, organized a group of investors and formulated plans to build their version of the New Latonia Race Track. The idea was born during a meeting at Ben Castleman's White Horse Tavern in Park Hills. Castleman would achieve fame as a local horse owner and breeder, and more will be discussed about him later. Williamson, like his grandfather, worked the press to his advantage whenever possible. In this case, he purposely concealed the names of those involved until the last minute and greatly enhanced the preliminary details of the project. Newspaper accounts revealed, "...local, Lexington, and Cincinnati capital is interested in establishing a high-quality horse racing track in the Boone County area of Northern Kentucky. The investors are of the highest character and have pledged upwards of a quarter-million dollars to purchase a tract of land situated mainly on Price Pike, west of Florence, with a connecting road to Donaldson Highway in nearby Erlanger."[10]

One week later, those plans came to fruition when the Kentucky Jockey Club, Inc. acquired title to 473 acres on Price Pike at $1,000 per acre. Most of the property, 400 acres, was purchased from Walter Scott, 40 acres from M.W. Morris, and 33 acres from Michael O'Hara. Included in the purchase was a two-story colonial home in a tree-shaded setting, which became the original track office.

Nearby was a lake, around which the track would be built. Architect Bill Burke drew up the plans, and construction was to begin that November. Boone County administrators and state engineers constructed a connector road from Dixie Highway to Price Pike and eventually to Donaldson Road to accommodate the expected large crowds. Since the new thoroughfare led to the new Latonia Race Track's racing turf, it was named Turfway Road.[11]

Caroline Williams sketch of the Scott Farm

Matt Winn Williamson was named president of the newly formed Kentucky Jockey Club and became the organization's primary spokesperson. On October 24, 1956, he announced that the track would be built on an entirely new theme. Central to this plan was building the clubhouse and grandstands together in a single unit, with the clubhouse embracing the upper level and the grandstand the lower floors, allowing fans in both areas to have equal views of the finish line. The plans called for stables to accommodate as many as 1,000 Thoroughbreds and automobile parking for up to 12,000 patrons. A 7/8-mile grass course would be built within the planned one-mile dirt track. When fully operational, the grandstand structure would seat more than 7,000 fans, with another 1,000 seats available upon grass terraces on the apron.

As terms of the purchase were revealed, so were the participants of the new organization. Besides Williamson, the incorporation included Attorney Joseph B. Arnold, Richard R. Dupree, Jr.; H.P. Morancy, secretary of the Kentucky State Racing Commission; James Paddock, Louisville businessman and horse owner who later replaced Williamson as president; and Warren Wright, Jr., owner

Courtesy: Kenton County Public Library, with special graphics by the author

Courtesy: The Jim Claypool Collection

Top: Aerial photo of Florence, Kentucky before the completion of I-75, Houston Road and Turfway Road;

Middle, left: Only a portion of the large crowd assembled for the official groundbreaking ceremony; Matt Winn Williamson is shown scooping the initial spade full of dirt; Middle, right: Equipment from Carlisle Construction standing at the ready;

Bottom: Large billboard announcing the upcoming "New Latonia Race Track."

of Lexington's famed Calumet Farm.[12] Since it was estimated that it would take $5 million to complete the project, the club established that sum as its debt limit and authorized capitalization of 3,000 shares of no-par-value stock. A day later, on July 26, Matt Winn Williamson appeared before the Kentucky Racing Commission and presented a request for a license to operate a race meet in the fall of 1957.[13]

Florence, Kentucky in 1956 was almost entirely rural and was relatively remote. It was typical of small-town America and was probably not unlike Milldale when the original Latonia opened in 1883. The business core was situated along the Dixie Highway (US 25) near the crossroads of other two-lane highways leading to Burlington and Louisville. In fact, the tiny hamlet was once known as "Crossroads." The new road connecting Dixie Highway to the facility assisted motorists but, still, the attraction would not be easily found by many. The proposed Interstate 75 changed all that a few years later. A "cloverleaf" interchange was to be constructed along the Donaldson Connector in Erlanger, allowing motorists much better access to the new racetrack.

However, financing for New Latonia was a tremendous problem from the beginning. The corporation had been hastily formed with high hopes and ambitious plans. Groundbreaking was scheduled for November 1, 1956, but delays came immediately. The much-publicized event eventually came on November 5. Press releases stated that construction would continue uninterrupted for an August 25, 1957 grand opening. Work on the steel-structured grandstands was said to begin in April. In the meantime, the racing ovals were to be shaped and prepared, parking grounds laid, footers for the 25 fireproof barns poured, and other preliminaries completed.

It all sounded good, but none of it happened as scheduled. The winter weather in Kentucky could and did cause severe delays. Most of the original capital was dissolved because of the many problems, and the prime contractors, the Lutz-Abrams Company of New York, were stymied. Meanwhile, several local subcontractors walked out, irritated due to slow pay. If things were not bad enough, that is when Wayne Carlisle, later owner of a hugely successful construction company but then a young man operating a dirt scraper, uncovered two iron coffins. One contained the body of a man and the other a fashionably dressed woman. Work was immediately stopped. Officials were called in, but no one could identify the remains. So, a new grave was dug near the horse barns, and the bodies were reinterred, and there they remain to this day.[14]

Problems for the New Latonia Race Track were far from over in February 1957, when the Kentucky Racing Commission met to approve or disapprove Williamson and the Kentucky Jockey Club's proposal to race Thoroughbreds at the new Boone County track. They were granted race dates to stretch from August to October 1957. However, at the same meeting, attorneys representing the Northern Kentucky Turf Association (parent company of Kentucky Raceway) demanded that the Commission award them Thoroughbred racing dates as promised, provided they meet all requirements by the Commission. On May 9, 1957, the Turf Association was granted 25 race dates for 1957, September 7 through October 5, at their oval near Florence. With no live Thoroughbred horse racing in the region since 1939, suddenly there were two such racetracks just in Boone County.

Thoroughbred racing at Kentucky Raceway turned out to be a disaster. Despite the Association's promise of compliance with the Commission's recommendations, horse racing there, in the one month it

The Kentucky Raceway

was conducted, could be described as "bottom-of-the-barrel." The facilities were utterly inadequate. It was a black eye for Thoroughbred racing in Kentucky.

Back at new Latonia's construction site, progress was slow, and in 1958, work nearly came to a complete halt. On March 21, 1958, Williamson went before the Commission to announce that the Kentucky Jockey Club wished to relinquish the racing dates they had been awarded. The facility would not be ready. Instead, he asked for dates in 1959. With the embarrassment of the Kentucky

Raceway disaster still fresh, the Commission told Williamson that he better have Latonia ready for racing in 1959, or there would never be racing permitted there.

It was no secret about the financial situation at Latonia. By September 1958, the owners were entirely out of money, and the facility was far from completion. Only the outline of a racing surface had been carved at the time, and the only other completed work was the footers for the massive grandstands. It was public knowledge that the Jockey Club was broke, but an incredible story broke in the *Kentucky Post and Times-Star* on September 27, 1958, possibly the answer to their prayers. John B. Kelly, Sr., an East Coast millionaire and the father of Princess Grace of Monaco, was going to invest and help rescue Latonia.[15] Kelly, who at the time was president of Atlantic City Racetrack in New Jersey, was a longtime friend of Williamson. Bob Hope and Frank Sinatra were other investors in the Atlantic City track. Kelly's involvement generated a new wave of enthusiasm and excitement. Another article proclaimed that with Kelly's involvement, there had been several indications that the track, which had been abandoned since early spring, would get its running surface ready for Thoroughbreds before the scheduled meet.[16]

Earlier in the week, Williamson had announced that the track would be ready by August 1959 and that the Kentucky Jockey Club had regrouped. George Fabe, a partner in Fabe Construction Company of Cincinnati, was now involved. Fabe stated that Bishop International Engineering Company of San Francisco had replaced the New York contractor and that bids for the uncompleted areas of the project would be accepted immediately. The final chapter in the building of New Latonia had begun, but it still did not go as smoothly as Williamson or Fabe had hoped. There were more delays, shoe-string financing, and a desperate race to meet the Commission's mandate of an August 27 completion. Nearly $1.5 million had already been spent, and it would take another $2.5 million to complete the project. General contracting and subcontracting had been turned over to Frank Bishop, a prominent horse breeder drawn into the enterprise by Williamson, who was at the time a partner in Bishop's California breeding farm. The final cost of the New Latonia project was estimated at $5 million.

When the morning of August 27, 1959, arrived, so did the construction crews. Dozens of workers performed the finishing touches and cleaned up debris until the scheduled first post time of 2:00 p.m. There was no time for a dry run or to double-check electrical systems. Weeks of publicity paid off, however. Horace Wade, who had served as racing director and publicity director of Gulfstream Park in Florida, assumed Latonia's publicity duties and carried them out perfectly. In a well-orchestrated press release series, Wade announced that Latonia had been "Built for the future and inspired by the past."[17]

Opening Day

The stage was set for Latonia's opening day. Newspapers warned that, although the opening was scheduled for Thursday, a weekday, a large crowd was expected. To accommodate fans, maps showing the roads leading to the track were published in many newspapers, usually with a reminder that when the new interstate highway being constructed was completed, probably in 1960, it would run within a half-mile of the site, with exits at crucial roads leading to the new track. The Greenline Bus Company announced a unique service to the racetrack that would take fans directly to admission gates. The Ohio Bus Lines scheduled a run out of Dayton with stops at Miamisburg, Franklin, Hamilton, Mount Healthy, and thence to the park for only $3.00, admission included. Across the river in Indiana, the Anderson Ferry also advertised special arrangements for race fans.

Several newspaper articles preliminary to opening day focused on memories of Old Latonia. Pat Harmon of the *Post and Times-Star*, and other local sportswriters, told the stories of the great races at the old track, listed the famous jockeys, trainers, and owners seen there, and spoke glowingly of the promise held by the new track. Every writer seemed to look for angles and ways to tie the old with the new. One of the best articles was one where W.J. "Rusty" Marlman was interviewed. Marlman, a Covington native, owned a small stable and had been recently racing in Chicago. When he brought 11 horses to race at the new Latonia, it was written that "one of the real old-timers from the heyday of Old Latonia has come home to race again."[18]

At 2:00 p.m. on August 27, 1959, the Inaugural Meeting began at new Latonia with clear and sunny skies and temperatures in the 80s. While there was a shortage of mutuel clerks, most fans did not seem to care. They were apparently caught up in the excitement. Traffic was a mess along Donaldson Highway and Price Pike, the two main arteries into the park, but somehow, a crowd totaling 11,117 packed the grandstands, with Governor A.B. "Happy" Chandler in a front-row seat. As fans filed through the admission gates, they received a clear, 12-ounce souvenir glass with green lettering displaying the Jockey Club logo and a sketch of the new facility. Admission to the grandstands was $1, and $3 to the clubhouse. Parking was 50 cents or $1 for valet services.

The new Latonia featured a five-level, self-contained building anchored by a grandstand with a clubhouse on the top. The structure provided two floors for grandstand seating, a mezzanine, the clubhouse level, and a private room called the Latonia Club. The clubhouse was a modern design and had an area for terraced dining. The Latonia Club, a secluded, members-only spot, was furnished with plush carpeting and luxurious lounges. Each main level had a promenade overlooking the paddock and walking rings. The maximum capacity was said to be 20,000.

The opening day card featured nine races. Two had purses of $2,000, the others around $3,000, and the opening day feature, the Quickstep Handicap, a 6-furlong sprint for 3-year-olds and up, was a $10,000 event. News photographers, given free reign of the property, decorated the sports and society pages with their handiwork the next day. In contrast, Jack Pille, the official track photographer, walked out and took a shot of the finish of the first race, then a posed photo of the horse and jockey, and afterward went back to the photographer's room on the lower level and waited for the next race to end... a routine he continued to follow at Latonia for the next 23 years. Pille became a fixture in Kentucky horse racing as the track photographer at Keeneland, Churchill Downs, and Latonia during the '50s, '60s, and '70s, and at Keeneland in the '80s. He worked on a handshake and never concerned himself with someone infringing his copyright or publication payments. He died in 1989.[19]

All items on this spread courtesy: Jim Claypool Collection

Opposite page: "New" Latonia -- Opening Day program, souvenier glass (front and back), and promotional magnet asking patrons to "Come back to Latonia;"

Bottom photo: Aerial photo of the grandstands before the windows were added;

This page: "$2 to win on #3 Tote ticket for the 7th race on August 27, 1959; Above: The first winner at "New" Latonia;

Bottom photo: A jam-packet grandstand.

Historian, Thoroughbred fan, and this book's co-author, Jim Claypool, described the first race at new Latonia this way: "When Carroll Burns, the starter, set the horses off in the first race, there was excitement and applause. Twelve two-year-old fillies rounded the last turn and headed down Latonia's 970-foot stretch toward the finish line. The vast assemblage of fans roared and cheered loudly when, from the top of the stretch, jockey George Hettinger guided his mount, *Scotts*, to a lead that had widened to a convincing four-length triumph by the finish. In every way, it was the perfect opener. Not only had the race gone off without incident but judging by the large crowd gathered near the winner's circle, the race was regarded as quite an exciting event."

However, *Scotts'* owner and trainer became the real story after the race. The storyline was almost too good to believe. The owner/trainer of the horse to win the inaugural race at new Latonia was William Boganowski, a former jockey at Old Latonia. The new track was said to have been built to serve tradition, and that it did. It was all smiles when Hettinger and Boganowski were awarded a silver trophy by Leslie Combs II, chairman of the Kentucky Racing Commission, for winning the first run at modern Latonia.

History was called again a few races later when "Happy" Chandler, serving a second term as Kentucky's Governor, was present in the winner's circle to present a trophy... just as he had done many years before at Old Latonia. This time, however, the ceremony took an unusual turn. Chandler, frequently impetuous when on center stage, handed the trophy to Fred Evanger, owner of *Coltrane*, before the race had been declared official. Moments later, the objection sign flashed on the infield tote board. And after several minutes of film review, a foul claim was allowed, and *Coltrane* was disqualified. Undaunted, Chandler regained possession of the trophy and awarded it to *Mr. Fantastic's* owner, Seely Killpatrick.

The final races of the track's first day were uneventful. A total of 65 Thoroughbreds had raced on opening day at Latonia; none would go on to have particularly spectacular careers. The jockeys were of a higher caliber. Clarence Meaux, a respected handicap rider; James Combest, a job rider

56

from the Illinois circuit; and William A. Peake, who had many wins at numerous New York tracks that year, were included. Future Hall of Famer Don Brumfield and Walter B. Williams, former contract rider for the Darby Dan Stables, were also on the card that day. Two solid local riders were also present: Phil Borgemenke, later an official at Latonia and Turfway Park, and William D. Lukas, the leading rider that year at River Downs in Cincinnati, Ohio.

Present at Latonia's opening day was 24-year-old Dan Coletta. A young school teacher during the day, Coletta had taken a part-time job as a mutuel teller at River Downs on weekends during live racing. The meet had closed there for the season and, when he heard the Florence, Kentucky racetrack had opened, he applied there. "It was my first day of work – opening day in a brand-new facility. The place was packed," he recalled. "Back then, there were separate lines for purchasing tickets and cashing in. There were windows for $2 bets, $5 bets, $10, and combination wagers. Ten-dollar tickets were yellow, with blue trim. Combination tickets were green. There was a change person too; someone who would walk back and forth behind the line and give change – extra money – to the tellers who needed it."[20] Coletta stayed with the Latonia/Turfway Park for over 60 years and was still working part-time at Turfway Park Racing and Gaming when this book was published in 2023.

The second day of racing saw an estimated crowd of only 3,202. Saturday's attendance increased to over 7,000 but, still, a pattern was quickly developing. Over the years, Latonia enjoyed a good turnout on Saturdays, but only mediocre attendance on all other days. In the overall scheme of things, Latonia had assumed the position in Kentucky and the region of a second-class operation. Statewide, attendance and mutuel totals put Latonia far behind Churchill, Keeneland, and Ellis Park and only slightly higher than Louisville's Miles Park, considered the rock bottom in the state. Regionally, Latonia was behind River Downs and Beulah Park in Ohio, and only similar to Raceway Park in Toledo, Ohio, and Wheeling Downs in West Virginia, both of which were minor tracks with racing ovals of less than one mile. Something would have to change.

The New Latonia opened with an overall 'unfinished" appearance. The original design called for a glass enclosure of the entire grandstand, but that would not be completed for several years. Most racetracks are designed with outside rails, but someone initially forgot to provide those for Latonia. Only days before the first meet, Father Middendorf, the priest in charge of the adjacent Catholic Marydale Retreat, questioned why there was no outside rail to prevent horses from getting loose and entering his property. At overtime rates, the Stewart Iron Works company in Covington fabricated and installed the fences just in time for the first race.

The situation with stalls, one of the prime concerns for horsemen, illustrates this "half-assed" and "band-aid" approach to the facility's planning. With 1,300 applications for stall space accepted during the Inaugural Meet, only 680 were available. Horsemen were sent to distant stabling facilities, some barely standing. One would assume those horses stabled right at the track had a great advantage. And while the accommodations at Latonia looked new and modern, they were not well designed. The stalls were made of prefabricated concrete with no ventilation, causing them to become thermal "hot boxes" in the August and Sep-

Early photo of the New Latonia Race Track grandstands, prior to the addition of glass windows

Courtesy: Kenton County Public Library

tember sun. In the following two years, permanent wooden structures began to spring up. Before they were completed, desperate measures were needed to tide things over. Temporary tents were installed for the stabling of horses at first. Most incredible, football players from nearby Boone County High

Bill Perry

School were recruited by Bill Perry, a local horseman and part-time track official, to sledgehammer holes in the walls of the concrete stalls so that air could circulate.

Aesthetically, modern Latonia was no prize winner. The half-finished grandstand area, little more than the skeleton of what had initially been planned and with no glass front, had been painted one coat of battleship gray, and it was many years before a second coat was ever applied. On the third floor, nearest the original track offices, was a huge unfinished area only used for storage. Years later, it was fitted with pine paneling and opened for betting. The dining area, which would later be improved and greatly expanded by the general manager, Paul Mooney, was a simple two-row arrangement and significantly curtailed Latonia's ability to offer promotional events and cater to private groups.

Of all the embarrassing planning errors and premature opening mishaps, the infield lake caused the most confusion. From the first day of operation to today, horse riders and patrons alike cannot understand the situation. The water feature was outlined in the shape of Kentucky and was intended to pay tribute to Old Latonia's magnificent infield lake. However, once dug into the earth, it was discovered that the grandstands and main structure would have to be built on the southwestern side due to the sun's location, presenting spectators with an upside-down view of the lake. Add to this, the persistent traffic slowdown created by narrow two-lane roads leading into the track and a myriad of other minor issues which, at times, seemed to be increasing in almost geometric proportions, and the overall conclusion had to be that "all was not right" at modern Latonia.[21]

The general state of affairs at Latonia was no secret. Knowledgeable observers, especially those familiar with the Kentucky racing circuit, stated openly that it would take a tremendous effort from Latonia's management and corporate directors to sustain the enterprise. And they were right. Simply put, Latonia had been underfinanced from the start, and its principal shareholders were strained heavily to get the facility open, let alone keep it afloat.

At the end of the Inaugural Meet in October 1959, the fate of modern Latonia teetered precariously. Threatened with permanent loss of its racing dates if it did not open before the year ended, Latonia opened on time, but barely. The glitter of opening day and the sheen of a facility featuring an ultra-modern design had initially helped hide the racetrack's flaws. As the season progressed, however, Latonia's shortcomings started to show. Corners had been severely cut, finishing touches had been hastily applied and, overall, problems in the planning, design, and construction had begun to surface. Most importantly, there was no money left to fix them.

After the first meet ended, Latonia's financial strain came to a full boil. Matt Winn Williamson, president of the corporation and whose brainstorm produced the racetrack, had pledged much of his assets to help cover construction, including his Old Westport Place, a vast horse farm in Anchorage, Kentucky. He would eventually lose the farm when it was sold to cover unpaid bills and satisfy a bond for Walter Scott, who had owned most of the property where Latonia now sat. The total financial package, a mixture of shares and bonds, was nothing more than a patchwork quilt. Harry Trotsek, a local horseman and one of the founding directors, held the track bonds. Trotsek was patient, and his patience was rewarded with preferential treatment concerning the location of the stalls he required for his stock of Thoroughbreds. With Williamson financially broke and his position at Latonia eroding, most of the burdens of sustaining the enterprise fell on James Paddock, the company's vice president. Paddock was the man who stepped forward during the track's darkest hours and helped save it. During the winter months of 1959-1960, Paddock was increasingly considered the man in charge and, others on the board, including Freeman Keys and T.A. Grissom, fully supported him. Williamson's later departure also signaled the end of involvement for both John Kelly (Princess Grace's father) and Oliver de Vanderbilt III, wealthy investors whose positions as directors had been based solely on their ties to Williamson. However, neither should be recalled as "active" board members.

Often using his own money to cover daily operating expenses, James Paddock brought Latonia a vitality and steadfast resolve that was sorely needed. He also had a clear vision of what Latonia faced, the central questions being whether the corporation could forestall its debts and whether it would be granted race dates for 1960 by the Kentucky Racing Commission. It was no surprise to Paddock when the track's creditors wasted little time pressing their case during the off-season months. In November 1959, fifty-five liens totaling over $1.7 million were filed in local courts against the corporation, driving the entity into receivership. The very existence of Latonia was now at stake. With Paddock in the lead and Williamson barely hanging on as president, Latonia's officers were suddenly in front of a court-appointed bankruptcy trustee. Luckily, John M. Robsion, Jr. was the trustee hearing the case and probably holding the racetrack's future. Robsion was a well-schooled authority on bankruptcy and corporate finance. The court's purpose was clearly to give Latonia time to work out its difficulties while providing it with experienced statesman-like leadership. With Robsion, that is precisely what Latonia got. He allowed track officials time to set matters straight while faithfully executing the court's directives.

Robsion knew the enterprise would collapse if Latonia lost its race dates for 1960. Through a series of meetings with the Kentucky Racing Commission, starting on December 29, 1959, and ending on April 30, 1960, Robsion and Paddock pled their case. They worked diligently to convince the Commission that their restructuring plan was solid as they requested race dates for the upcoming fall. At each meeting, the Commission presented challenging requirements, ranging from a detailed list of new officers to a breakdown of how the outstanding debt was to be paid. In the end, the Latonia Operating Company was formed, with Frank Bishop, T.A. Grissom, Freeman Keys, Herbert Mundy, and James

Paddock as crucial members. Matt Winn Williamson was out and would have no future ties to Latonia. Keys, a prominent Central Kentucky horseman and owner of Reverie Knoll Farm and Racing Stable, was named president. Paddock took the executive vice president role, but he ran the show. The Commission granted race dates for 1960, beginning on August 31 and ending on October 5.

Three years passed before Latonia recovered from its disastrous start. While a triumph for the company, changes in some aspects of the region's infrastructure also proved pivotal for the track's future. The much-anticipated Interstate 75 was finished and, from that point forward, Northern Kentucky, especially Florence and all of Boone County, began a never-ending growth period. Business, industry, and massive subdivisions erupted almost overnight. What was once nothing but rural pastures and farmland along US 42, US 25, and Burlington Pike became congested roadways, expanded from their original two-lane curvy paths through the country to four- and six-lane, divided thoroughfares. All of this played in Latonia's survival.

For the start of the 1960 Meet, Latonia rescheduled the race card from a 2:00 p.m. start to 10:30 in the morning. The change was made because Latonia would have competed directly with River Downs on Saturdays and Mondays. The new schedule was meant to entice patrons to come to Latonia... and stay. To encourage this further, there was free admission to those entering the track by 12:30, lunch could be purchased for $1.00, and fans were invited to watch a free water-ski show on the infield lake. There were 14 races on the card that Saturday. The weather was outstanding, and the crowd grew from 1,500 to 5,000 by 12:30, many to take in the water show and enjoy the inexpensive lunch. By the start of the final race, attendance was estimated at over 9,000. By all accounts, opening day for the 1960 season was a huge success. The entire meet, however, can be described as mediocre at best. Attendance averages were 1,500 on weekdays and 5,000 on Saturdays. Stakes purses were set at $2,500, 75 percent below the opening day card. Still, management was convinced the situation could be turned around. After lengthy deliberation and a vote by many to close, the company decided to request race dates for the 1961 season.

Aided by Robsion's unwavering endorsement, Latonia was awarded 34 racing dates for 1961, 11 of which overlapped and were in direct competition with River Downs. The overlapping dates were right at the beginning of the meet, and Latonia responded with a steady flow of advertising and press releases. Those emphasized the newness of the facility and the quality of horses that would be on the schedule. The bright sparkle and modern conveniences of the facility were linked with an admission price of only $1.00 and $2.00 to the clubhouse. Another essential piece of Latonia's 1961 success was that Don Brumfield, Keeneland's all-time winning jockey, later the winner of the 1966 Kentucky Derby and a Hall of Fame inductee, announced that he would be riding at Latonia and not at River Downs. Although Brumfield became the top jockey in the state for many years, Latonia's riding title went to Erlanger, Kentucky's Dave Oldham in 1961, with Brumfield a distant second. By the end of the meet, the competition between the two racetracks was a draw... with Latonia leading in attendance and River Downs winning with total purse money.

A significant change came to the racetrack before the 1962 season. On May 14, 1962, the *Kentucky Post and Times-Star* reported that John B. "Pat" Kelly of Louisville was named director of operations. Kelly, a former director of sales for the Kentucky Exposition Center in Louisville, was also vice-president of Mid-States Enterprises, Incorporated, listed as the new operating company of Latonia. Kelley was a true horseman, formerly a field representative for Crown Crest Farms in Lexington and general manager of the Jockey Guild of the United States. Maybe most important at the time, Kelly's college roommate was William May, the reigning chairman of the Kentucky Racing Commission.[22]

The 1962 Meet ended on October 4, with Don Brumfield winning top jockey honors with 36 wins. The mutuel handle was a record $5,052,266, an average per day of $180,437. Sadly, James Paddock, the man who sacrificed so much to keep Latonia from closing, died in 1962 and thus was denied the chance to savor the turnaround. The racetrack made a profit for the first time, and things would improve even more in the next two years.

Winter Racing's Debut

In 1964, Latonia was awarded racing dates for two meets: a 24-day Autumn Meet from September 4 to October 2 and a new Winter Meet scheduled from November 23 to December 12. The supplementary meet was undoubtedly bold, given Latonia's earlier woes. The most significant move was Frank Bishop's promotion to general manager and Bishop's hand-picked representative, Frank Tours, as executive vice-president. Tours was a public relations specialist who had worked at California's Santa Anita racetrack. The two-meet season ended up being a study in contrasts. The first was a great success and bolstered everyone's spirits; the second, the track's first attempt at winter racing, was a total disaster. Temperatures in the open-air grandstands were frigid, and no one came. Something had to be done to attract more fans during the cold-weather dual meet. Throughout the season, Tours proved to be the man in charge and should be remembered and credited as initiating the first measurable facility improvements at new Latonia. The first changes involved cleaning up the infield lake and planting marigolds. The following year, in honor of this, Latonia's new stakes race for three-year-old fillies was named the Marigold Stakes. Planting marigolds and cleaning up the lake was just the start of Tours' significant improvements to the property. Glass was finally installed on the grandstand structure facing the track, completely enclosing the entire facility. The Finish Line Lounge was also added, and closed-circuit televisions (providing live coverage of Latonia's races and replays) were spread throughout the building. By the mid-1960s, new Latonia had become successful, though still a second-rate track.

Before the 1965 season, another significant improvement changed Latonia's future. Corwin Nixon, who headed an association that operated harness meets at tracks in Lebanon and Hamilton, Ohio, was awarded a license to run a harness meet at Latonia. In preparation, Nixon's group paid for the installation of lights at the track and would continue to operate harness meets, the Latonia Trots, at the racetrack until the mid-1980s. In 1966, Latonia asked for and received 42 days of racing which were combined into a lengthy single meet beginning on

Harness racing "workouts" at New Latonia Race Track

October 31 and ending on December 24. The new, combined dates gave Latonia's management more flexibility and worked much better. Frank Tours had left the company and was replaced by Californian Louis Petteruto. Luckily for the racetrack's future, Tours had named a new publicity director before he departed. John Battaglia, a local who would later be responsible for Latonia's best growth and development, had proven himself a turf expert as a columnist for the *Kentucky Post*.

Louis Petteruto remained head of operations for only two years (1964-1965). During that time, John Battaglia began a rapid ascent that eventually saw him become the top man at Latonia. In 1966, the track raced 41 of its 42 scheduled events in an extended season. The highlight of 1966 was when *Barbs Delight* won the $10,000 Kentucky Special and went on the following year to finish second in the Kentucky Derby. Incredibly, just when things at Latonia seemed to stabilize, and daily operations were becoming orderly, Frank Bishop, who had been flying in from California regularly to observe Latonia's progress, died of a heart attack, throwing everything back into turmoil. Legally, Bishop's wife, Connie, as heir, ran things for awhile. However, she had no genuine interest in the racetrack. The future of Latonia became unclear and uncertain once again.

Latonia: Up for Sale

On December 6, 1966, the *Cincinnati Enquirer* ran a story declaring that the Latonia Race Track was up for sale. Speculation involved three groups, and among the names mentioned as being involved in one group were celebrities Frank Sinatra and Dean Martin, both regular visitors to the fancy Newport clubs during its earlier heyday and silent partners in an Atlantic City Racetrack. Another group was represented by two lawyers from New York who refused to disclose their clients. In the end, however, the sale went to the third prospective buyer. On February 20, 1967, Latonia was sold to Lou Jacobs, owner of the local professional basketball team, the Cincinnati Royals. Jacobs, it was later revealed, also headed Emprise Corporation out of Buffalo, New York, and that the sports team was just one affiliate of a major conglomerate. Unfortunately, the names Jacobs and Emprise will be later mentioned in Latonia's long history. While no price was disclosed in the sale, the property was said to have had a net worth of about $3.5 million. Latonia was now controlled by what was advertised in the daily programs as "The Latonia Official Family." Charles Triplett, an original board member, remained racing secretary, and Kenny Plattner, from nearby Camp Springs in Campbell County, became general manager.

The 1967 Meet at Latonia provided purse money substantially above the year before, with $2,500 being the norm for standard races and stakes races worth three- to four times as much. A new daily handle record was set at $337,690, a gain of approximately 68 percent over the 1963 figure, thus dramatically topping off the ongoing surge of growth and profitability that commenced four years earlier. More history was made at Latonia on September 9, 1968, the first day of the Autumn Meet, when at 7:00 p.m., eleven horses were loaded into the starting gate, and the first modern night race in Kentucky for Thoroughbreds was run. Again, Latonia was doing something unusual and bold. The race, a $2,000 claiming event for three-year-olds and up with a purse of $1,500, was won by R.W. Kemper's *Garth R.*, with Weston Soirez aboard. Night racing at Latonia, from this point on, became the norm. Since its nearest competitors (those in Ohio

Courtesy: www.nkyviews.com

1968 Fall Stakes with Barry B. Good

and Kentucky) stayed with day racing, Latonia carved out its regional niche for racing, which helped sustain it through hard times later. For many years, racing under the lights at Latonia (and later, Turfway) helped the track stay out of direct competition with powerful adversaries such as Keeneland and Churchill.

Latonia conducted 53 race days in two separate meets in 1968, with the final event concluding on December 31. The combined mutuel handles were shy of $18 million, and daily attendance averaged 5,572, exceeding the 5,000 mark for the first time. Latonia's officials asked for and received 58 days for 1969. Kenny Plattner and Pat Kelly remained the top men in charge.

Racing at Latonia from 1969 to 1971 was, as the old saying goes, "full steam ahead." Attendance and mutuels rose in all three years, and money was put back into the facility in the form of refurbished barns and a new coat of paint. Kelly also supervised the conditioning and maintenance of the racing surface, which allowed winter racing to survive and continue. However, the weather did not cooperate at times, and the resulting cancelations were eventually understood and accepted as a regular part of the racetrack business.

In March 1971, John Kelly, accompanied by board member T.A. Grissom, Latonia's track president since 1966, journeyed to San Juan, Puerto Rico to attend the annual meeting of the National Association of State Racing Commissioners. At a dinner on March 20, Kelly choked while eating a piece of meat, collapsed, and died. Back at Latonia, John Battaglia had been Kelly's protégé for several years. Holding the dual title of assistant general manager and public relations director, Battaglia moved up immediately after the unfortunate tragedy. But Kelly's untimely death was just one of two significant setbacks for Latonia at the time.

Chapter Two Endnotes

1. *The Tradition Continues, the Story of Old Latonia, Latonia, and Turfway Racecourses,* Jim Claypool, Hayes Publishing, Ft. Mitchell, KY, 1997, pages 87-88.
2. Robert D. Webster, *The Beverly Hills Supper Club: The Untold Story Behind Kentucky's Worst Tragedy*, Saratoga Press, Dayton, KY, (2012), page 21.
3. David Wecker, "Before There Was Vegas, there was Newport," *Kentucky Post*, September 4, 2004.
4. Thomas A. Purvis, *Newport, A Bicentennial History*, page 47.
5. Webster, page 1.
6. Webster, pages 12-28.
7. *Ibid.*
8. *Ibid.*
9. Claypool, page 106.
10. Claypool, pages 107-108.
11. *The Kentucky Post and Tines-Star*, March 7, 1959, page 1.
12. Claypool, page 110.
13. Claypool, pages 110-111.
14. Claypool, page 112.
15. Claypool, page 115.
16. Claypool, pages 114-115.
17. Claypool, page 117.
18. Claypool, page 118.
19. Claypool, page 121.
20. Personal interview with Dan Coletta on October 17, 2022.
21. Claypool, pages 131-140.
22. Claypool, page 146.

Chapter Three

The Mafia, John Battaglia,
and the Spiral Stakes Debut

Rumors about mafia connections had circled the Latonia Race Track from the beginning. As far back as the mid-1930s, Northern Kentucky had been overrun with organized crime, mainly overseen by mobsters out of Cleveland, Ohio. Morris "Moe" Dalitz, an original Purple Gang member out of Detroit, later headed the "Cleveland Four" and had full reign over the 50+ illegal gambling parlors in Campbell and Kenton counties. Their two most prestigious operations were the Lookout House in present-day Fort Wright and the Beverly Hills Country Club in Southgate. Other mobsters representing Meyer Lansky in New York had control over a few similar establishments in the area. Unlawful gambling in the form of roulette wheels, blackjack, and slot machines was a wide-open affair in the region, and everyone knew it was taking place. Indeed, when the Beverly Hills opened in Southgate in 1936, governors from three states attended the opening day celebrations – as willing participants of an illegal gambling club. However, by the late 1960s and Newport's so-called "clean-up," many high-ranking mobsters left Northern Kentucky and helped develop the modern-day casinos in Las Vegas.[1]

Once only rumors, the mafia's long-running tie to the Latonia Race Track became public in the early 1970s. The purchase of Las Vegas' Frontier Hotel and Casino by Howard Hughes started an investigation that would eventually bring Florence, Kentucky into the spotlight. Documents revealed that the actual owners of the Frontier had been illegally concealed. Among the many partners listed was Emprise, the current owner of the Latonia Race Track.[2] Emprise had apparently loaned a bundle of money to "front men" for the mob-related owners of the Frontier. During later congressional hearings, it was stated that Emprise owned a Detroit racetrack and was said to have loaned masive amounts of money to other horse tracks, dog tracks, and jai alai arenas.[3] Also, Emprise had arranged secret cash payments to politicians in the 1950s. Additionally, money from Emprise permitted "Moe" Dalitz to purchase the Stardust Casino from Jake "The Barber" Factor, a friend of Al Capone.

Listed in court documents were two other Lou Jacobs and Emprise counterparts known as Northern Kentucky underworld members: Samuel Kline and Sam Tucker. When Moe Dalitz moved into Northern Kentucky, he placed Sam Tucker, another Purple Gang member, in charge of River Downs Racetrack in Cincinnati and the Beverly Hills Club in Southgate, Kentucky.[4] Tucker ran an extremely successful operation at those two properties for more than 20 years. Samuel Kline founded Stern Vending Company in Cincinnati and was also part owner of Runyan Sales, the sole distributor of Lion, a Chicago-based slot machine and pinball game manufacturer. Emprise and Kline orchestrated a merger between Lion and the Bally Corporation.[5] Bally became the sole manufacturer of slot machines for casinos across the country. The company later entered the casino business. Kline, however, was forced to step down from his top post before the company's transition after admitting to the Nevada Gaming Commission his association with known mafia organizations.[6]

Emprise had numerous subsidiary enterprises, one being the food concessions business. By 1972, under the name Sportservice, it was feeding the fans of six major league baseball teams (Baltimore, Chicago White Sox, Cincinnati, Detroit, Montreal, and Milwaukee); eight professional football teams (Baltimore, Buffalo, Cincinnati, Chicago, Detroit, Green Bay, St. Louis, and Washington): five professional basketball teams (Buffalo, Chicago, Cincinnati, Cleveland, and Milwaukee): four hockey teams (Buffalo, Chicago, Kansas City, and St. Louis); and several minor league teams. For years, they also serviced patrons at the Latonia Race Track.[7] When the Cincinnati Gardens arena ran into financial trouble, Jacobs invested more money and emerged as a 40 percent shareholder. Then in 1963, the company purchased 40 percent more of the Gardens stock and 56 percent of the Cincinnati Royals professional basketball team for $402,500.[8]

With Emprise/Sportservice, their standard procedure was to offer loans to struggling businesses in exchange for a far more lucrative arrangement for themselves – nothing new for the Mob. Usually, the beneficiary of those low-interest loans came to regret the terms... but quite often, they had no choice. The Latonia Race Track contract with Sportservice gave track management an abnormally low 15 percent of the receipts. In 1960, a trustee in the track's bankruptcy case called the agreement "burdensome." The 15 percent terms allegedly were not the result of a loan to the racetrack but to Matt Winn Williamson directly. Williamson had pledged 30 brood mares to borrow several hundred thousand dollars to invest in Latonia. When Williamson defaulted on the loan, Lou Jacobs got the horses and a stake in Latonia, but Emprise later wound up with the whole racetrack. Bill Shoemaker, racing's leading jockey at the time, had a stock interest but sold out to Emprise in 1970. "Latonia is coming on and will be a great track in the future," he said. "But I don't like the people who run the track."[9]

Besides the congressional hearings, much of the above information came to light after Don Bolles, an investigative reporter for the *Arizona Republic*, wrote a series of reports about Emprise. Bolles even went to Washington, D.C., to tell a congressional committee about his findings. On June 13, 1976, Bolles was to meet with John Adamson, a racetrack owner who told Bolles he had "more information" about the questionable company. But it was a trap. Bolles arrived at the Hotel Clarendon in Phoenix and waited in the lobby. After half an hour and no meeting, he returned to his car in the adjacent parking lot. His car exploded when a remote device strapped to the vehicle's underbelly triggered six dynamite sticks. Witnesses on the scene stated that the critically injured Bolles mumbled a few words before he was taken away in an ambulance, "They finally got me... John Adamson... Emprise... Mafia."[10] With both legs and one arm amputated, Bolles died ten days later at Saint Joseph Hospital.[11]

Recently, mobsters have adapted to the times and taken their acts online. No more risking money with a brick-and-mortar business. In 2023, they are far more likely to be busted for online sports gambling. In 2008, a Queens district attorney charged the Gambino family with illegal sports and casino-style gambling operations. Online players were allowed to borrow gambling money at 200 percent interest. In 2014, members of the Genovese family in New Jersey were indicted for making millions of dollars each year through illegal gambling operations. In Europe, officials have raised concerns over the Mafia's vast amounts of money being laundered through online gambling, particularly on sites based in Germany, where there are no penalties for illegal gambling activities. And in Italy, where online gambling surged during the COVID-19 pandemic, officials investigated more than 300 individuals tied to an online gambling scheme.[12]

At casinos, racinos, and racetracks across the country in 2023, the government regulates all wagering and cash transactions, in general, the same way transactions are monitored at US banking institutions. *Title 31*, monitored by the Internal Revenue Service, minimizes the risk of money laundering in such corporations and assures the public that all bets are legitimate... that no "fixing" is taking place. Cash-for-cash transactions and winnings of more than a certain amount, generally $3,000, are logged and reported to the government. Today, the Mafia remains nationwide, and is best known for their infiltration of legitimate businesses. But their grasp on the Northern Kentucky racetrack is over. From the early 1960s to the mid-1980s, however – and unknown by almost everyone – the mafia secretly owned the Latonia Racecourse. While locals were published to be in charge of the daily operations, a significant percentage of all profits was being shoveled into the hands of the men truly in control.

The Battaglia Years

In March 1971, John Battaglia stepped in as the new general manager with new energy and a conviction that New Latonia could be much more than it was. He became the fourth general manager in 13 years. John grew up in Northern Kentucky and was exposed to the influences of both Covington and Newport during the "wide-open" gambling years of the 1940s. With Battaglia in charge of Latonia, things were amazingly uncomplicated. If one wanted a pass (which saved bettors an extra dollar or two for betting), see John. It was the philosophy of the entire Battaglia family: his brother, Bill, in publicity; his son, Mike, the track announcer; another son, Bruce, as the maker of the morning line; and his sister, Mary Ann, as an employee in the Mutuel Room. It was not the kind of racing found at the prestigious tracks on the New York, Florida, or California racing circuits… or even the sort seen at Keeneland or Churchill Downs on Derby Day. And that was just fine. It was just simple wagering for the simple gamblers.

John Battaglia received his racing experience as a groom and a short stint handicapping races in 1949 for the *Cincinnati Post*. He followed that with another job with the *Post* as a columnist and race forecaster. That evolved into morning lines and handicapping for Churchill Downs, Keeneland, Miles Park in Louisville, and Latonia. The work soon expanded to include Hialeah in Florida and Monmouth Park in New Jersey. In 1964, he became a mount booking agent for successful jockey William Harmatz at Hollywood Park, after which he was brought to Latonia in 1967. Before succeeding Pat Kelly in 1971 as general manager at Latonia, Battaglia had already managed a quarter-horse meeting held at Latonia and served as general manager of Miles Park.

John Battaglia had huge shoes to fill in John Kelley, which was a tough challenge. But he also entered an environment where the Mafia existed as silent partners. According to *Blood-Horse Magazine*, when asked about the ownership situation and the circulating rumors, Battaglia would refuse "…to comment on the bruhaha, concentrating instead on running the track."[13] When asked to make a statement, John came off in the press as simply honest yet faithful when he responded, "I don't know anything about them [meaning Emprise]. But in their dealings with me personally, truthfully, they have been just as nice as they could be."[14]

Under John Battaglia, Latonia ended the Spring Meet in 1971 with its best-ever figures, averaging 5,602 in daily attendance, grossing more than $20 million in handle, and distributing purses above $1 million over 40 racing days. Over the following four years, from 1972 to 1975, total average attendance increased in three of those years and the daily handle in all four. Battaglia was working hard, real hard. So hard that he suffered a heart attack in 1974. After recovery, John supervised backside and grandstand improvements, purse increases, and a bus shuttle service from Cincinnati during the 1974 energy crisis.

Trainers Dennis Freking or D.F. Abner usually led the victory list through this era, while Darrel McHargue, R.A. "Cowboy" Jones, and Homero Hidalgo were among the top riders.[15] A favorite at River Downs and Latonia, *Perennial* was D.F. Abner's frequent entry. Abner picked up *Perennial* at a claiming race at Latonia in 1972 for a mere $2,500. Since then, the gelding has "…won me more money than I ever dreamed he could," Abner said in a 1978 interview.[16] Almost exclusively ridden by jockey Gene York, *Perennial* was a six-year-old competing against two- and three-year-olds in 1972 and typically beat them regularly. *Perennial* and York would claim the $4,500 Wintergreen Purse at Latonia in 1975.

Annual Bean Bash

The annual "Bean Bash" began in 1974, organized by former Kentucky State Representative Bill McBee. Initially conceived as a mere political event, it became a successful fundraiser to benefit disabled children and adults in the region. The charities participating in the event at the time of this publication in 2023 include the BAWAC Community Rehabilitation Center, New Perceptions, Redwood School, and the Special Olympics of Northern Kentucky.

The first location of the Bean Bash was at the Mid Valley Pipe Line Park on Limaburg Road in Hebron, Kentucky. The bash consisted of bean soup, tomatoes, slaw, and cornbread. The Bean Bash grew in crowd size and was moved to the Latonia Race Course in the early 1980s. Initially held entirely outdoors, it was moved inside after it developed further. Events occupied multiple floors at Latonia/Turfway Park. Each Bean Bash always had a robust schedule of events. In the past, Governors, Lt. Governors, State Representatives, State Senators, and U.S. Senators attended and made speeches. As part of the entertainment, skydivers, horse races, bingo, oral auctions, silent auctions, music, kids' rooms, wrestlers, marching bands, dancers, and Texas Hold 'Em poker tournaments were included. Some celebrities who attended include Miss America's Phyllis George Brown and

Heather French Henry, singer Billy Ray Cyrus, *Survivor* contestant Roger Bingham, and Cincinnati Bengal Football players Joe Walter and Doug Pelfrey. The annual event drew thousands to Turfway Park for more than 45 years. After the demolition of Turfway Park in 2020, the event moved to the Boone County Fairgrounds.

Courtesy: Kenton County Public Library

U.S. Senator Wendell Ford speaks at a Bean Bash

The Spiral Stakes

Like so many horsemen, John Battaglia had a dream. In his case, it was to introduce a single-stakes race to the Latonia card that would put the somewhat insignificant racetrack on the map worldwide. The term "stakes" designates the highest classification in a particular group in horse racing, such as two-year-olds, three-year-old fillies, or the winners of previous select races. In the fall of 1971, Battaglia announced to his staff that a new race would be added to the stakes schedule the following spring. The race would specifically target three-year-olds preparing for the Kentucky Derby and would be called the "Spiral Stakes." It would be the first of a trio of spring events that would "spiral" horses onward to the Blue Grass Stakes at Keeneland and culminate when those horses competed in the Kentucky Derby in Louisville. The "Kentucky Circuit" – at the time – started with the Fall/Winter Meet at Turfway Park, then to Keeneland, Churchill Downs, Ellis Park, and back to Turfway Park in September.

At the time, it was hard to believe that a race from a little track like Latonia could ever produce a horse that would run in the most prestigious race in the country. But ultimately, Battaglia's vision proved successful. Over the years, dozens of horses have "spiraled" upwards to compete in Kentucky's so-called Triple Crown. Since its inception, and at the time of this publication, two Spiral winners have gone on to win the Kentucky Derby, three have won both the Preakness and the Belmont Stakes, and four have won the prestigious Eclipse Award.

Regardless, the Spiral Stakes was hardly an overnight sensation or an idea that caught on quickly. The first Spiral was carded at one mile for a modest purse of $10,000.[17] The event's first run occurred on April 1, 1972, April Fool's Day. The doubters were bemused, and the crowd was less than had been forecast because it was a bitterly cold day. The race attracted 11 horses, with the odds-on favorite being Latonia president T.A. Grissom's *Roibbean*. Only one horse, *G's Forward Thrust*, was Derby eligible. The eventual winner, however, was *Big Dot*, shipped in from Churchill that morning.

Official Spiral souvenir glass

Courtesy: Jim Claypool Collection

Battaglia was not a man to be easily discouraged, however. With the help of racing secretary Charles Triplett, who had helped create and construct the race, and to a similar extent Bill Perry, who always wore many hats at Latonia, plans were made to recruit better horses for the second running of the Spiral Stakes. The trio knew that, while the idea might eventually catch on, the Spiral would require patient nurturing to grow and blossom. Battaglia announced that the second Spiral would be split into divisions to help accommodate the nation's horsemen. On March 31, 1973, it was run in two featured races with purses raised to $15,000. The winner of the first division was *Jack's Chevron*, ridden by Billy Phelps, a Latonia regular and riding champ in meets conducted in 1965, 1967, and 1970. Mickey Solomone came up from Keeneland in the second race to ride what turned out to be nothing more than a workout, as *Bootlegger's Pet* finished 15 lengths ahead of the field.

The third Spiral, again in two divisions, took place on March 30, 1974. Eight horses went to post in each race, and enthusiasm was high as the total purses offered that day in nine races was $61,200, a new track record. In the first race, odds-on favorite *Aroyoport* was beaten by a 5-1 shot, *King of Rome*. In the second race, a strong *Aglorite*, under a patient ride from jockey John Beech, Jr., came from last place to win by a nose.

While the Spiral Stakes was beginning to see a slight momentum, the best-remembered racing event of 1974, if not the entire John Battaglia era, occurred on what appeared to be nothing more than an ordinary night during the Spring Meet. It was one of the rarest of all sporting events. It is rarer than baseball's triple play, a perfect 300 in bowling, a hole-in-one in golf, or a three-goal hat-trick in hockey. It is similar to a record-setting field goal in football or a no-hit game in baseball. While a dead heat in racing is relatively common (two horses crossing the finish line at precisely the same instant), this race took things one step further. It was the first for the state of Kentucky, caught everyone by surprise, and occurred at Latonia Race Track on Friday evening, March 22, 1974. As recalled by historian and this narrative's co-author:

"It was a cold, clear wintry night when the $5,000 allowance test for three- and four-year-olds drew a field of 10 going one mile. Temperatures were in the 30s, and a slight headwind blew down the home stretch. The crowd, down somewhat from the weekend before because a trotting track in nearby Lebanon, Ohio, had opened, was beginning to thin out by the seventh race. The field reached the post for its eventual rendezvous with racing history at 10:45 pm. In the early stages of the race, two outsiders, *Robert Henry* and *Good Groomer,* dueled for the lead, but entering the stretch, *Deleterious*, the 3-2 favorite, got through on the rail and went to the front. He stayed there until the sixteenth pole when *Quipid* caught up and engaged him in a head-to-head match for the lead. *Bob Twinkletoes* rallied on the extreme outside down the homestretch, reached the others just beyond the sixteenth pole, and suddenly, it was three heads bobbing in rhythmic union to the finish. Placing judges Bernie Burns, Frank Muth, and Leo

Courtesy: Jim Claypool Collection

Track photo of Latonia's "Triple Dead Heat"

Borgemenke, Jr. deliberated over the photo-finish for 17 minutes before reaching a decision. Knowing just how rare the event was, a spontaneous roar erupted from the crowd when the TRIPLE DEAD HEAT sign flashed on the infield tote board."

Regarding the Spiral Stakes, it was back to the drawing board. While it would take another year or two for Battaglia's work to come to fruition, progress was being made, nonetheless. The 1975 Spiral, also in two divisions, saw *Naughty Jake* and *Ambassador's Image* emerge victorious. Purses were elevated to $26,000 each, a small but significant upward move. *Naughty Jake's* win was a hard-fought one-length triumph; *Ambassador's Image* breezed to a victory by 10 lengths. While neither horse made it to the Blue Grass Stakes or Kentucky Derby, the Spiral Stakes was finally starting to receive some credit in the press. Bill Anzer, the race writer for the *Cincinnati Enquirer*, observed, "While not as prestigious as some of the other Derby qualifiers, the Spiral, nevertheless, provides a great stepping stone to the big day in May at Churchill Downs."[18]

Then came the story of *Inca Roca*. A speedy colt who, earlier in the spring of 1976, finished second to Kentucky Derby-winner *Honest Pleasure* in the $100,000 Flamingo Stakes in Florida. *Inca Roca* gave John Battaglia's Spiral Stakes its first jump-start and helped it gain nationwide notice as a legitimate Derby prep race. *Inca Roca* arrived at Latonia after being trained by Tom Skinner at Keeneland. Only one Spiral was run at Latonia in 1976, and the purse was raised to $30,000. His biggest competition was *Here Comes Jo*, a horse he had competed against twice before, with each horse winning once. Entering the stretch of the Spiral Stakes, jockey William Nemeti moved from second to the lead and never looked back. Attendance, held down by the cold and rain, was only 5,934; mutuels a disappointing $596,922. The bigger story was how *Inca Roca* finally fulfilled John Battagliare Spiral dream. *Inca Roca* shipped to Keeneland, where he ran third in the Blue Grass Stakes, becoming the first Spiral winner in the history of the prestigious Lexington race. Two weeks later, *Inca Roca,* off at odds of 67-1, ran seventh in the 102nd running of the Kentucky Derby.

The following year's Spiral Stakes, conducted on April 3, 1977, began a streak of seven consecutive Spiral victories for the Golden Chance Farm in Paris, Kentucky, with trainer William E. "Smiley" Adams and owner Robert N. Lehmann. There seemed to be a pattern during this incredible run of wins. The track was usually wet, there was often an inquiry posted, and Julio C. Espinoza was the jockey in four of the seven victories. In 1977 and 1978, with two divisions each, *Bob's Dusty, Smiley's Dream, Raymond Earl*, and *Five Star General,* each stood in the winner's circle.

In a single Spiral in 1979, *Lot o' Gold* was the victor, ridden by the legendary Don Brumfield. *Spruce Needles* and *Major Run* were the winning horses in two divisions in 1980, completing the seven-straight wins for the team of Adams/Lehmann in Latonia's Spiral Stakes. Winners at the Florence track were finally beginning to assume roles of some prominence in Kentucky's top spring prep, the Bluegrass Stakes, and had started to play a part, albeit to this point a smaller one, in the Kentucky Derby itself.

In 1977, however, significant changes were seen in the daily operation of Latonia Race Track. The Kentucky Jockey Club, now just one of a dozen or more affiliates owned by the Emprise mob, had begun to bring in their hand-picked men. David Vance was named vice president and chief operating officer, thus becoming John Battaglia's boss. Vance, perpetually dressed in expensive black tailored suits, had come from an administrative role with the professional American Basketball Association team (ABA), the Kentucky Colonels. It was with the Colonels where Vance sealed a connection with Sportservice, who controlled concessions, and with future Kentucky Governor John Y. Brown, Jr., who owned the team. Brown also owned the Louisville-based Kentucky Fried Chicken Corporation.

Vance's connection with Kentucky Governor John Y. Brown, Jr. likely figured into Emprise's decision to place him at Latonia. They hoped to ease the relationship between Latonia's outside owners and the Kentucky Racing Commission. In the Commission's mind, Vance was "clean," and he had a reputation for success. With the Colonels, Vance helped sell the team's popularity through various fan promotions and moved his way up to general manager, just in time for the end of the ABA. That league merged with the NBA in 1976, but the Kentucky Colonels were one of four teams that disbanded.

However, Governor John Y. Brown, Jr. had a not-so-clean road ahead. In 1981, Brown was investigated by the FBI for withdrawing $1.3 million in cash from a Miami bank, which failed to report the transaction as required by law. In the late 1980s, some of Brown's associates were involved in a huge Lexington, Kentucky, cocaine and gun-smuggling ring called "The Company." While Brown walked away clean, phone records show calls from the governor's mansion to several individuals eventually convicted of drug charges in connection with the investigation.[19]

David Vance's arrival at Latonia broke John Battaglia's heart since it removed him from the top spot and demonstrated a lack of confidence by his corporate bosses. While the two men got along well, Battaglia knew his time at the Kentucky track was short. Moreover, he had too much pride and confidence to remain subservient. Battaglia had a chance to move to River Downs as general manager in 1977, and he jumped on it. Later, in 1980, with a glowing recommendation from Vance, Battaglia moved on to the same position in Charles Town, West Virginia. While at the Charles Town Track, however, Battaglia suffered a second heart attack. He died after heart surgery in 1981. In 1982, in tribute to Battaglia, Latonia established an 11/16-mile stakes race for three-year-olds, run yearly, known as the John Battaglia Memorial Stakes. Like many others, jockey Bill Troilo remembers John as "...a great ambassador for Latonia."[20]

Left to Right: David Vance, John Battaglia, and David Thompson (PR Director at Latonia)

Because of the recent felony convictions against Emprise, the Kentucky Racing Commission initially denied all racing dates for Latonia in 1977. In part, rules state that no convicted felon can hold a racing license in Kentucky. After extensive appeals and hearings, a plan was put into place where a trustee was named to oversee all operations at the racetrack. The Bank of Louisville presented a voluminous financial and investigative report that supported the controversial Buffalo, New York-based conglomerate. As trustee, the Bank of Louisville was given powers to examine and investigate all pertinent records maintained by Sportservice/Emprise and their affiliated companies doing business in the state of Kentucky. After the proceedings, Latonia was awarded 114 days in 1978.[21]

While Latonia's handle was growing and attendance was up, the track suffered greatly during the extremely frigid weather conditions during the winter of 1977-1978. Across the region, more than 12 inches of snow fell between January 25 and February 10, closing schools and businesses and halting traffic on the Ohio River for weeks. On January 30, a huge ice floe knocked the massive *Showboat Majestic* and two other boats from their moorings. The $900,000 *Clare E. Beatty* was also destroyed while attempting to be salvaged near the Markland Dam. In addition, wind gusts were clocked at more than 70 miles per hour on some days. Dozens of citizens took advantage of the unusual situation by walking across the frozen Ohio River. The month-long frigid conditions caused 70 deaths in the region.[22]

Back at Latonia, the track was forced to cancel 10 straight racing days and lost more than 30 days over the entire meet. David Vance announced that Latonia needed an average of $460,000 per day in pari-mutuel wagers to stay afloat. With so many days bringing in zero revenue, the track was in dire straits. Inclement weather caused the cancellation of six racing dates in December. The Kentucky Racing Commission was kind enough to award Latonia three additional dates in January, but those were also canceled. In January, only six of the 21 assigned dates were completed. Two were canceled after the first race was finished, and thirteen were canceled outright.[23] Jockey Mike Bryan commented, "Latonia had to be a nightmare for the track crew. They often ran trotters and pacers in the summertime, so they had to take most of the cushion up because a horse couldn't pull a sulky around the track if it was very deep. They had to add dirt and sand when it was time for the Thoroughbreds to run in the winter and spring meets. Sometimes the track would be deep, the rain would come down, and colder temperatures would cause frozen clods to form. While riding, you would be beaten in the hands, face, and knees, even broken goggles. The clods would hurt some horse's eyes, and a few jocks got broken fingers. During 1977 and 1978, it was impossible to get to the track because of the blizzards. D.H. Skaggs had me gallop

Courtesy: www.nkyviews.com

Dozens of people walking across the frozen Ohio River during the winter of 1977-1978 horses in the field with 2 feet of snow. The track was shut down for a month due to the weather. Finally, the weather improved, but many horsemen had packed up and headed south. Latonia was a great place to ride. Everyone was friendly. We were all 'Race Trackers.' We were like one big family."

Courtesy: Kenton County Public Library

Man changing the letters on the Latonia sign

The Emprise/Sportservice infiltration continued in 1978 when they placed another one of their top men on the board of the Kentucky Jockey Club. Stan Phillips suddenly appeared in the racing programs replacing Paul Mooney. Phillips, an accountant from Buffalo, had been Sportservice's racetrack financial specialist and came to Latonia to help strengthen corporate profits. One successful decision was when a New York-based marketing firm was hired to develop a new campaign to bolster Latonia's image. They came up with the slogan, "Betcha Love Us!" which became the focus of an advertising blitz blanketing the local print media and radio and television airways. It worked. In 1978, the average daily mutuels handle jumped to $512,356 even though attendance figures remained static. And for 1979, the story was repeated, with crowds remaining steady but average daily mutuels hitting $536,150, the highest ever for the racetrack.[24]

Latonia started the new decade on a high note in 1980. A year earlier, Phillips became track president, Vance remained executive vice president and chief operating officer, and Stephen Baker, an accounting major and former employee at Northern Kentucky University had been hired and promoted to assistant general manager. Regular purses had risen to around $3,000, with handicaps and stakes on weeknights paying about $4,500; weekend stakes, such as the Clipsetta, going for $12,500. Brownell Combs II replaced Bill May as Chairman of the Kentucky Racing Commission, reducing some of the heat on Sportservice, although May still retained his seat on the board. Pat Lang, who served as the official track photographer for over 30 years, became the publicity director. Bill Perry, the "jack of all trades" from the early days of the facility, worked his magic in group sales; examples included busing groups in for a day or night of racing, exhibition races that featured all-female jockeys, visits by the famous Budweiser Clydesdales, and appearances by various turf celebrities such as champion jockey Steve Cauthen.

In 1981, Latonia entered a period of choppy and uneven performance that would dramatically impact its future. Attendance was solid and stable in 1981 and 1982. However, handles were inconsistent, rising 9.8 percent in the Winter/Spring Meet of 1981 but declining 4.4 percent and 6.3 percent in the September/October and November/December reporting periods. The pattern for 1982 was much of the same, up 7 percent in one and down 9 percent in another. Emprise/Sportservice was not happy with David Vance's performance or the track's success. He was told to make significant changes, or he would be out. Over the next four years, Emprise contemplated halting its funding of the Kentucky Jockey Club and the Latonia Race Track.

However, business carried on as usual, and a special day was held at Latonia on March 1, 1981. Owner/trainer D.F. Abner's *Perennial* became the winningest horse in Latonia history, surpassing *Exterminator's* 50 wins during the 1910s and 1920s. On "Perennial Day," a five-foot stainless-steel monument was unveiled in front of the grandstands, between the two public entrances. Patrons were encouraged to rub the ionized gold upturned horseshoe mounted into the obelisk for good luck. Everyone also received a tiny horseshoe souvenir with a penny embedded inside for luck. The monument and the unusual tradition remained for many years until a new track owner, Jerry Carroll, had it removed in 1988, claiming *Perennial* was just not a prestigious enough Thoroughbred for such an honor.

The 1981 Spiral Stakes was won by *Mythical Ruler*, ridden by Keith Wirth. More importantly, the prep race started to get the proper attention it deserved in the local press. Jack Murray of the *Enquirer*, mixing in a degree of skepticism while also recognizing the Spiral's growth, referred to the 1981 event as "the first leg of a so-called Kentucky Triple Crown." The race, now a stakes event of $50,000, saw *Mythical Ruler* break to the lead and never trail. Appropriately, the race was dedicated to John Battaglia, who had died the year before.

Courtesy: Kenton County Public Library

Courtesy: Kenton County Public Library

Top: Spectators on the fourth floor of the grandstands; Bottom: Large crowd pressed against the fence

Maybe a shock to Emprise, the Spiral had been well-established and started to grow. Locally, plans were formulated to make the race a community event. The model was the highly popular Kentucky Derby Festival, organized as part of the pre-race festivities during Derby Week in Louisville. David Vance, who had seen Louisville's' festival firsthand while head of the Kentucky Colonels, proposed, in 1978, a Spiral Spring Festival to be held in conjunction with and leading up to the yearly running of the Spiral Stakes in Florence. At first, it was a modest affair involving a few events, such as a beauty contest, a golf tournament, a culinary showcase, and the soon-popular Call to Post Luncheon. However, just like the race, the festival caught on slowly and snowballed. Over the years, several community leaders were named to head the special committee to discuss and prepare plans for the event. The Spiral Festival grew significantly, and at its peak, it included a health fest, men's and women's tennis classic, a select home tour, a dog shoe for "mutts," a beauty pageant naming a Spiral Queen, a classic car show, a big-band dinner dance, a fish fry, a five-kilometer run, a children's art show, a golf tournament, a Spiral Ball, and on race day a VIP tent party.[25]

Around 1980, Emprise/Sportservice, still wanting to invest no more funds at their Northern Kentucky property, pressured David Vance to pursue corporate sponsorship for Latonia's big race. During the summer of 1981, he met with two dignitaries from the Muriel tobacco company who were very interested in sponsoring the event. However, another idea surfaced at a meeting in Louisville with Stan Phillips, Latonia's president, and Victor Zast, marketing director with Jim Beam Distillers. It took several weeks for Zast, but he eventually secured the corporate backing he needed to seal a deal with Latonia officials. The first running of The Jim Beam Spiral Stakes occurred on Saturday, March 27, 1982. It was a festive affair. In the years previous, Emprise, the corporate head of the Kentucky Jockey Club, who owned Latonia and a dozen other subsidiary companies, had relabeled themselves due to the "rumors" they were mafia owned. Delaware North became the new corporate name. For the first Jim Beam, Del-

Opposite page, top: Two-page spread of the first Jim Beam Spiral Stakes program, race #9;
Botom: Cover of that program

	WIN	PLACE	SHOW

1 1/16 MILES START / FINISH

PURSE
$150,000 ADDED

9
THE JIM BEAM SPIRAL STAKES
(Inaugural Running)

THREE-YEAR-OLDS. Colts and Geldings 120 lbs.; Fillies 115 lbs. By subscription of $100 each which must accompany the nomination; $500 to pass the entry box and $1,000 additional to start. $150,000 ADDED (Plus $15,000 from the KENTUCKY THOROUGHBRED DEVELOPMENT FUND). The added money and all fees to be divided 65% to the winner; 20% to second; 10% to third and 5% to fourth. The maximum number of starters will be limited to 12. In the event more than 12 entries pass through the entry box at the usual time of closing the 12 starters will be determined at that time, with as many as 8 horses to be drawn on the also eligible. Preference will be given to those which have accumulated the highest earnings, according to the Daily Racing Form. Those which have entered and are eliminated according to this condition will be refunded all fees paid. A Trophy will be presented to the winning owner or owners. Closed Wednesday, March 17, 1982, with 95 nominations.

MAKE SELECTION BY NUMBER

Owner	Trainer	Jockey/Morn. Line

1
pp 2
RUSSELL MICHAEL, JR. — RONNIE WARREN — 12
Poplar, Avocado "LM," Avocado Stripes on Sleeves, Poplar Cap
BETTY MONEY ⌃ 115
Dk.b. or br.f.(1979), Our Native—Need Proof by Prove It
Bred in Kentucky by Mr. & Mrs. Russell Michael, Jr.
Charles Woods, Jr.  LM

1a
pp 9
RUSSELL MICHAEL, JR. — RONNIE WARREN — 12
Poplar, Avocado "LM," Avocado Stripes on Sleeves, Poplar Cap
TALENT TOWN ⌃ 120
B.c.(1979), Olden Times—Coque Blue by Daumier
Bred in Kentucky by Mr. & Mrs. Russell Michael, Jr.
Gene Solomon — LM

2
pp 1
AISCO STABLES (A. I. Savin) — SALLY BAILIE — 8
Red, Red "S" on Black Ball, Black Chevrons on Sleeves, Red Cap
FAST GOLD 120
Dk.b. or br.c.(1979), Mr. Prospector—Flack Attack
Bred in Florida by Aisco Stables — by Ack Ack
V. H. Molina — S

3
pp 3
GEORGE PAPPAS — GARY THOMAS — 20
Red and Black Halves, Red "H," Black "I," Gold Sleeves, Red Cap
Drop Your Drawers ⌃ 120
Ch.c.(1979), Raise a Cup—Drapery by Bold Eagle
Bred in Kentucky by Bradyleigh Farm, Inc.
Jim McKnight — H I

4
pp 4
BUCKLAND FARM (Thomas Mellon Evans) — JOHN CAMPO — 12
Dark Blue, White Triangle, Dark Blue Band on White Sleeves, Blue and White Cap
HIGH ASCENT 120
B.c.(1979), Irish Castle—Tache by Ambiorix
Bred in Virginia by T. M. Evans
Kenneth Skinner

5
pp 5
A. SAM COURY — BROOKS CLARIDGE — 8-5
White, Green "BC" and Sleeves Green and White Cap
TROPIC RULER 120
Dk.b. or br.c.(1979), Key Rulla—Tahini by Nako
Bred in Arizona by Stuart H. Struck
Jim Powell — BC

6
pp 6
ROBERT E. REEVES — OWNER — 30
Yellow, Black and White Diamonds, Black and White Diamonds on Sleeves, Yellow Cap
PASSEM HONEY ⌃ 120
B.c.(1979), Honey Jay—Treat Me Nice by Retreat
Bred in Kentucky by Robert E. Reeves
Vince Clark

7
pp 7
LARRY R. LEHMANN — JASPER ADAMS — 20
Gray, White "L" on Red Hexagon, Red Chevron on Sleeves, Grey Cap
GOOD N' DUSTY ⌃ 120
B.c.(1979), Bob's Dusty—Honestly by Timea Roman
Bred in Kentucky by Larry R. Lehmann
Mike Moran — L

8
pp 8
WOLFIE & SEYMOUR COHEN AND RICHARD KUMBLE — HOWARD TESHER — 3
Blue, Light Blue Yoke, White "WC," Light Blue Band on Sleeves, Blue Cap
WOLFIE'S RASCAL 120
B.c.(1979), London Company—Daisy Trimmer by Bold Discovery
Bred in Florida by Ray Amlung
Vincent Bracciale, Jr. — WC

9
pp 10
RI-MA-RO STABLES (Roberto Perez & Robert DeFillippis) — ALFREDO CALLEJAS — 8
Yellow, Red Diamond Frame, Red Diamonds on Sleeves, Red Cap
CUPECOY'S JOY 115
B.f.(1979), Northerly—Lady Abla by Alsina
Bred in New York by Roberto Perez
Angel Santiago

10
pp 11
BLAZM J STABLE (R. Masterson & Lee Kuhn) — CHARLES L. DICKEY — 20
White, Black "J" in Black Diamond Frame, Black Sleeves, White Cap
MR. WARD ⌃ 120
B.c.(1979), Ward McAllister—Mrs. G. by Gunflint
Bred in Kentucky by Lasater Farm
Kenneth Jones

11
pp 12
ROG ACRES (D. L. Rogers) — A. T. SKINNER — 6
White, White "DLR" on Red Diamond, Red and White Bars on Blue Sleeves, White Cap
SUPRON ⌃ 120
Ch.c.(1979), Olden Times—Light Frost by Bold Ambition
Bred in Kentucky by John T. Oxley
Martin Arnold — DLR

1 and 1a—RUSSELL MICHAEL, JR. Entry
⌃ Indicates Foaled In Kentucky

Scratched—STAGE REVIEWER
Selections 5—8—2

87

Courtesy: Kenton County Public Library

Courtesy: Kenton County Public Library

Top, left: Comedian Jimmy Walker entertains a Spiral crowd; Above right: Amy Francis, 10, Burlington, 5th grader at Burlington Elementary, and friend Mary Baxter, 11, Elsmere, 5th grader at Miles Elementary, enjoy the Spiral Festival Children's Art Show at the Florence Mall; Immediate right: One of the 10K Spiral Spring Marathon events; Bottom: Cincinnati Bengal stand-out and community activist Reggie Williams, Father Celsius, comedian Jerry Lewis, and Dick Cummings at a "Call to the Post" banquet.

Courtesy: Kentucky Post

Courtesy: Kenton County Public Library

Courtesy: Kentucky Post

Courtesy: Kenton Co. Public Library

Courtesy: Kenton Co. Public Library

Courtesy: Kenton County Public Library

Top: Start of the 1982 Spiral Stakes race, the first Spiral event under the long-running Jim Beam name.

Middle, left: Singer Lee Greenwood, honored Spiral guest and who is famous for his hit song "God Bless the USA," poses with popular country music singer Barbara Bushman, along with new racetrack owner, Jerry Carroll; Right: Standard starting gate signage at the Latonia Race Track during the 1982 meet.

Botom: Funnyman Henny Youngman, with David Vance and Dr. Robert Diroux.

aware North flew in several corporate officials for a round of parties that pre-ceded the race. On race day, celebrities close to Latonia's owners, including baseball great Stan Musial, were seated in a VIP clubhouse party room where "by invitation only" guests gathered to feast and watch the races. No expense was spared. Guests at the luncheon dined on succulent roast beef, ate jumbo shrimp, and had unlimited access to an open bar featuring the race's official drink, the Golden Spiral, which was amply plied with Jim Beam bourbon. The tables at the luncheon and other dining areas were decorated with yellow daffodils, the official race flower, and a Dixieland band strolled about entertaining patrons.

At race time, the weather was cold but decent. The 12 horses were ushered onto the track by a taped recording of Stephen Foster's *Camptown Rac-es*. While it was the newly named official song for the event, it left most fans confused. The song failed to evoke the emotional response and spontaneous chorus when fans sing "Weep no more, my lady" during the traditional playing of Foster's *My Old Kentucky Home, Goodnight* at the Kentucky Derby... and it never would. Still, the first running was exciting, and fans were on their feet throughout the race. They pushed against each other, crowded forward to get a better glimpse of the action, and cheered the winner as he crossed the finish line, then once again as he slowly paraded to the winner's circle. The favorite in the race, *Wolfie's Rascal*, did horribly. The second choice, *Tropic Ruler*, fad-ed to last. And the winner, the Jasper Adams longshot, *Good N' Dusty*, made those that bet him exceedingly happy by paying across-the-board mutuels of $81.60, $27.60, and $11.60. Jasper Adams was "Smiley" Adams' son, making the win quite memorable for local horsemen. The purse for the event had been raised to $150,000, and it would increase even more in the following years.

David Vance was removed as the top man in 1982. He became head of Lou-isiana Downs in Bossier City and eventually president of DeBartolo Racing, which founded Remington Park. Emprise/Sportservice promoted thirty-year-old Steve Baker to the general manager position. Given Baker's age and limited experience, this was undoubtedly a massive gamble by the Kentucky Jockey Club executives.

To some trackmen, it was inexplicable, if not downright perplexing. If nothing else, however, Baker was aggressive. Under his supervision, Latonia introduced six new major stakes races, four aimed at developing a unique niche among females. The Bourbonette Stakes at one mile and the Cincinnati Trophy Stakes at 6-1/2 furlongs were for three-year-old fillies, while the Wintergreen Stakes at 1-1/16-mile and the Wishing Well Stakes at six furlongs featured fillies and mares four-year-olds and up. The other two stakes, the Presidents and the Forego were carded at 6-1/2 furlongs for three-year-olds and six furlongs for four-year-olds, respectively.

Jockey Billy Troilo began his long and successful career in 1982. He recalls, "There were two separate barn areas at Latonia when I first arrived, one where the present backside exists and another where Target sits today. Surrounding Latonia was nothing but farmland, a couple of bars and a restaurant or two, and a hotel. The overall appearance of the facility was dirty, dingy, and cold. But the patrons were extremely supportive and enjoyed the races. Meets were Tuesday through Sunday, with races in September, as well as from November to April. The track was terrible in the winter, but September was nice. Management put a lot of pressure on riders to mount when the track conditions were bad."[26]

More innovation came to Latonia on September 18, 1982, between the running of the first and second Jim Beam Stakes. The Florence facility became the first track in America to offer inter-track simulcast wagering when it broadcast the 1982 Marlboro Cup from Belmont Park. Simulcast wagering is a broadcast of a race from one track, allowing wagering at other tracks where the signal is being received. Not only did this provide infinite possibilities for simulcast wagering nationwide, but it also meant that other racetracks could opt to broadcast races from Latonia. Simulcast broadcasting and wagering would be a godsend to the racetrack.

Still, Baker struggled as the general manager. By 1982, the economy had tanked, and after Latonia completed its four-month Winter/Spring Meet, mutuel handle and attendance was down 10 percent compared to 1981. Moreover, things did not get any better for the young executive. Attendance leveled out for the last four years that Baker headed the operation at Latonia, but the handle declined two of the four, 1983 and 1985. Additionally, this had a negative snowballing effect on purse sizes and Baker's subsequent relations with horsemen. Racing and the overall course of events at the Florence racetrack were somewhat stagnant. "Charlie" Woods from Louisville was the top jockey in the early 1980s, winning the riding title in four of Latonia's nine meets. Another standout was Patricia "P.J." Cooksey. A four-time Turfway Park leading rider, Cooksey went on to win 2,137 races in her career. Especially rewarding for local fans, on February 28, 1988, Cooksey posted her 1,203rd career win, becoming the world's winningest female jockey by the number of victories.[27] She remained in that position until Julie Krone overtook her. After winning the 1983 Hollywood Prevue Stakes at

Hollywood Park, she became only the second woman to ride in the Kentucky Derby. A year later, she rode *Tajawa* in the Preakness, the first female jockey to compete in that prestigious race.

Two more jockey-related events of the era stand out. The first occurred

P.J. Cooksey

Courtesy: Blood-Horse Magazine

on September 11, 1976, a six-furlong dash for two-year-old maidens. The unusual thing about this race involved two of the riders. By competing in this race, John Oldham and Suzanne Picou became the first husband and wife to compete against each other at any Thoroughbred track in America. Picou and Oldham had, before they were married, competed against one another a few times before, and asked to ride against each other at River Downs once married but had been denied. Latonia sought approval from the Kentucky Racing Commission and, having received it, set the stage for this historic race. The second and more publicized event involved a mother-daughter riding duo. Patti Barton and her daughter Leah placed Latonia in the record books again on December 1, 1982. That race, a $2,500 claiming event for fillies and mares, the lowest purse offered at the time, drew a field of 12 with both Barton women on longshots. Amid the ensuing hoopla, the Bartons were invited to appear on the Johnny Carson late-night show on NBC, which they did.

The second Jim Beam Spiral Stakes took place on March 26, 1983. The purse was raised to $200,000, and the race drew a card of twelve. A crowd of 12,325 filed through the turnstiles to watch the race, some waiting to arrive until conditions in the parking lots had calmed down, only to find all the lots filled beyond capacity. The nearby roadways were jammed with parked... and, in some cases, ticketed vehicles. The on-track mutuel handle was a record $1,494,138, with a total handle including simulcast and other outside wagering at $2,087,209. With the advent of simulcast wagering, Latonia suddenly had national exposure. Up-and-coming trainer, D. Wayne Lukas, shipped in a well-respected horse named *Marfa*, putting Latonia's stakes race on the national map. *Marfa* was the favorite for the upcoming Kentucky Derby, and to have that horse race in the Jim Beam Stakes was all New Latonia needed. *Marfa* won the race decisively. He later won the Santa Anita Derby and then shipped to Keeneland for the Blue Grass Stakes. There, however, he sav-aged every horse that got in his way and was disqualified. In the Kentucky Derby, he finished fifth. Still, *Marfa* was the first "Jim Beam" winner to compete in the Kentucky Derby, and af-ter *Marfa*'s win at Latonia, top horses began to ship in regularly.

Marfa, with jockey Jorge Velasquez aboard, being escorted to the winner's circle

The 1984 Jim Beam Spiral Stakes event was a glorious affair. The weath-er soared to a balmy and unusual 60 degrees, and those who failed to come early made a terrible mistake as the crowd, despite monumental parking problems and not very efficient shuttle service from nearby parking lots, swelled to 16,333. Hundreds more jumped the gates and were therefore uncounted. As with most early Beams, the jockeys had better credentials than the horses, and the 1984 race is a perfect example. Angel Cordero, Jr. and Eddie Maple, top jocks in the East, were joined by midwestern riding sensation Larry Saumell, Kentuckian Don Brumfield, West Coast rider William McCauley, and national circuit riders Jerry

Bailey and Pat Day. The co-favorites in the main event were a horse from Florida named *Vision*, ridden by Maple, and the West Coast ship-in *Lucky Lucky Lucky*, trained by D. Wayne Lukas and ridden by Angel Cordero. At the finish line, it was Pat Day upon *At The Threshold* who finished first. His win was the first of a record five victories in the Jim Beam for the talented jockey (1984, 1987, 1989, 1990, and 1992). An accurate indication the Beam was starting to bring in better quality Thoroughbreds, four horses from that year's race ran in the Kentucky Derby.

The 1985 Jim Beam was run on March 31 and had a guaranteed purse of $350,000. The top contenders were *Image of Greatness*, ridden by returning champion Jorge Velasquez, and *Banner Bob*, Kentucky circuit regular with Keith Allen getting the mount. A new-record crowd of 16,398 witnessed a close finish as *Banner Bob* beat out the other favorite. On-track mutuels were another record at $2,121,167 and the total handle, including limited off-track wagering, was $2,196,863.

While the Jim Beam was bringing in the crowds, the racetrack barely survived the other days of each season. From 1982-1986, Latonia seemed to be happy as the "second-class track" it was. Many seeds that would propel Latonia through this era and later help spur Turfway's great success were planted, just not yet harvested. Attempting to capitalize on the popularity of the Jim Beam, several more stakes were introduced in the Winter/Spring Meet of 1985-1986. The Gowell Stakes debuted in 1985, named for the horse that won the Inaugural Stakes at Latonia in 1913, and the Prevue Stakes, meant to "preview" the talents of the following year's three-year-olds. Two more stakes were added to Latonia's card the following spring. One, the Breeder's Cup Marfa Handicap, named for 1983 Beam winner *Marfa*. The second was the Latonia Breeder's Cup, carded on March 22, 1986, as part of the Jim Beam Day race program.

Polytrack

On September 7, 1985, one of the most significant improvements at Latonia made its debut. While others had installed a synthetic surface on training tracks, Latonia Race Track became the first track in North America to install the all-weather surface called Polytrack on its primary racing oval. Polytrack was first introduced in England in the early 1980s and offered several benefits compared to a traditional dirt track. The surface is safer for horses because of the unique cushioning effect. Trainers using the training track at Keeneland had reported lower vet bills and significantly fewer problems keeping their horses fit and sound.[28] Beyond the safety advantages, horsemen had been impressed with the reduced kickback, its adaptability for various training regimens, and its uniformity in different weather conditions. The visible component combines silica sand, wax, and multiple fibers; the hidden drainage component allows water to drain quickly through the surface, eliminating the freeze-and-thaw cycles that plagued the old track during its winter meets. After the installation, Turfway's track condition was always listed as "fast," no matter the weather.

With the growing success of the Jim Beam Spiral, national horse racing enthusiasts were taking notice. As a result, the 1986 Beam was broadcast live on ESPN and locally on WLW radio. It was slated as a Grade III Stakes, with a purse of $350,000. Of the 147 nominated horses, 12 were accepted and made it to the gate. *Broad Brush* stood out as the favorite, trained by Maryland-based "Dickie" Small. Maryland played a big part in that year's Beam, since the first- and second-place finishers were Maryland horses. *Broad Brush* nosed out *Miracle Wood* in front of a near-record crowd, even though the Kentucky Wildcats and the Louisville Cardinals were playing in the NCAA Men's Basketball Tournament the same afternoon.

Immediately after the 1986 event, it was time for Jim Beam Distillers to renew their contract with Latonia regarding corporate sponsorship. But behind the scenes, the future of the Derby prep race was in question, and so was the track itself. Barry Berish had replaced Victor Zast as the distiller's primary contact, and there was little doubt that Berish felt uneasy about Latonia's future. It was also apparent that Delaware North, the new name for mafia-owned Emprise – and Sportservice, the affiliate now in charge of the racetrack, were interested more in their bottom line than in putting money back into the track. Just as disturbing, Latonia management was having ongoing disputes with the horsemen regarding purse sizes of the everyday races, as well as the overall condition of the facilities. Berish was ready to back out and told Beam's upper management to withdraw the corporate sponsorship of the event. Emprise had also given up, and Latonia needed a miracle. On April 9, 1986, just two days after Latonia closed its Winter/Spring Meet, the track was sold again.

Chapter Three Endnotes

1. The first casino was the Golden Gate on Freemont Street in 1906. Others followed, but the modern-day "Vegas Strip" did not occur until the mid-1940s with the opening of the Flamingo and Tropicana.
2. Also among the owners were Anthony J. Zerilli and Michael S. Polizzi, two high-ranking members of the Detroit Mafia family.
3. "Hot Dogs, Beer, and Car Bombings," *San Diego Reader*, April 29, 2004, June 29, 2022.
4. Jason Schwartz, "Jeremy Jacobs Looks Like a Saint Compared to His Father," *Boston Magazine*, March 27, 2013, retrieved on June 30, 2022.
5. "Hot Dogs, Beer, and Car..."
6. "Suit Identifies Gambling Figures," *The Cincinnati Enquirer*, May 24, 1980, page A-4.
7. John Underwood and Morton Sharnik, "Look What Louie Wrought" (Cover Title "The Godfather of Sports)," *Sports Illustrated Magazine*, May 29, 1972, retrieved on June 30, 2022.
8. *Ibid.*
9. *Ibid.*
10. C.D. Stelzer, June 11, 1997, "Phoenix Rising," *Riverfront Times*, retrieved on June 30, 2022.
11. "Was Delaware North involved in the death of Don Bolles?" *Artvoice*, December 17, 2006, retrieved on June 29, 2022.
12. Melanie Radzicki McManus and Melissa Phipps, "10 Businesses Supposedly Controlled by the Mafia," Howstuffworks.com, updated December 1, 2021, retrieved on June 30, 2022.
13. *The Tradition Continues*, Claypool, page 157.
14. Claypool, pages 156-157.
15. Claypool, page 157.
16. "Perennial is the Abners' Old Favorite," *Cincinnati Enquirer*, August 1, 1978, page 27.
17. In Claypool's *The Tradition Continues*, he points out that in many written histories, the purse is incorrectly cited as $15,000 (page 174).
18. Claypool, page 177.
19. "John Y. Brown, Jr.," wikipedia.com, retrieved on July 1, 2022.
20. Personal interview with Billy Troilo on November 16, 2022.
21. "Racing Panel Okays Latonia For 1978," *Cincinnati Enquirer*, November 11, 1978.
22. "44 Years Ago: Relive Cincinnati's infamous blizzard of 1978," WLWT news report on January 13, 2022, retrieved on September 18, 2022.
23. "Latonia Hit by 10 Straight Zero Days..." *Cincinnati Enquirer*, January 22, 1978, page 21.
24. Claypool, page 162.
25. Claypool, page 183.
26. Personal interview with Billy Troilo on November 16, 2022.
27. Claypool, pages 162-163.
28. "Turfway Park to Install Polytrack," Brisnet Report, April 28, 2005, August 8, 2022.

Chapter Four

Jerry Carroll, Jim Thornton,
and Turfway Park

After the 1986 Jim Beam Spiral Stakes, Delaware North, formerly known as Emprise, the mafia-controlled conglomerate and Latonia Race Track owner, felt more than uneasy about the facility's future. Running the racetrack under one of their many subsidiary companies, Sportservice, they had contemplated dropping their financing of the racetrack for several years. The final straw came when they learned that Jim Beam Distillers was pulling the plug on their corporate sponsorship of Latonia's biggest event. The historic racetrack needed a miracle to continue operation, and they needed it quickly. It came in the form of Jerry Carroll.

Jerry Carroll, the eldest of two children, was born in Cincinnati, Ohio. At various times, the family lived in Aurora and Batesville, small Indiana communities located on the Ohio River and Interstate 74, respectively. Jerry spent his junior year of high school at Millersburg Military Institute, a well-known boy's academy in Millersburg, Kentucky, where he developed his first interest in Thoroughbred horse racing. Each day, he would purchase the *Daily Racing Form*, make "mind bets" at various American racetracks, and, the next day, eagerly check the results of these imaginary wagers. An avid golfer at Millersburg, Carroll often listened with keen interest as his teammates from farming communities in the Central Bluegrass talked about horses their families or neighbors had bred, raised, and in some cases, trained and raced.

Sometime during his high school years, Carroll and some of his classmates journeyed to River Downs in Ohio for his first day of racing, and he was hooked. He began to perfect his understanding of the horse industry by visiting Calumet and Claiborne, two of Kentucky's most prestigious horse farms. During this same period, Carroll made his first trip to the Latonia Race Track in Florence. In love with the sport, he vowed to own a Thoroughbred and to win a race someday. But life and other passions would come first. In 1962, Carroll finished high school in Aurora, Indiana, and began a relentless journey through a handful of colleges, including Ole Miss, Southern Mississippi University, the University of Cincinnati, and finally Toledo University in Ohio, where he attended on a golf scholarship.

Carroll met a young woman at Toledo University, married her in 1967, and dropped out of college a year later to pursue a career as a golf instructor. He and his wife, Corky, landed in Nashville, Tennessee, where he traded his golf clubs for a suit and tie. He apprenticed at a real estate company, learning the ins and outs of leasing and managing office space. Three years later, he persuaded his family doctor and a leading real estate company in Nashville to each loan him $25,000. In 1972, he founded Carroll and Associates, through which he first leased and managed properties. Carroll later expanded into the construction of offices and commercial and residential properties. Sensing in 1985 that the real estate market was softening, he sold 90 percent of his holdings and headed north to Florence, Kentucky.[1] Carroll, always looking for his next opportunity, somehow realized that the undeveloped property near I-75 in Boone County, along with a regional airport poised for explosive growth, would be his gold mine. He found 30+ acres between present-day Curtis Avenue and the express-way, owned by Baron Clift, and convinced the old farmer to sell. Turfway Ridge Park, a multi-building, state-of-the-art office complex, sits on that property today.

However, while first negotiating farmer Clift's land, Carroll noticed the vast, undeveloped property on the outskirts of Latonia Race Track on the other side of the Interstate. He went to the county courthouse to inquire how much land the racetrack owned and was astounded to find out that 363 acres were involved. He moved quickly. He discovered that Stan Phillips was Delaware North's man in charge of the property, and he set up a meeting to discuss the sale of Latonia Race Track. While the racetrack surely piqued his interest, the development of the outlying property was really what Carroll was after. Every Friday afternoon at three-o-clock, Carroll called Stan Phillips at Delaware North, asking to purchase Latonia. Every Friday, he was told no. This continued for three months before Delaware North's executives agreed to meet. Through tough negotiations, Carroll got the asking price of $18 million down to $13.5 million. And, when he offered a forfeitable 90-day down payment of $250,000 in cash, Jeremy Jacobs, the head of Delaware North, accepted. Now all Carroll needed was the financing.

Thinking he would utilize lending institutions he and his Nashville associates had used in the past, Carroll contacted Citibank of New York and Solomon Brothers, only to learn that neither bank nor any other banking business was interested in investing in a racetrack. He then contacted several private investors from as far away as Switzerland and Saudi Arabia, only to receive more negative responses. Finally, Carroll called upon a prominent Central Kentucky businessman who had previously participated in a Nashville land development package with Carroll and his associates. That is where James "Jim" Thornton comes into the picture.

Jim Thornton was born in Lebanon, Kentucky, but his family soon moved to a Louisville suburb. After graduation, he joined Gilbert Dance and Alfred Mallory to form Dixie Dance gas stations. That experience led Thornton to open a gas station of his own and, in 1955, further encouraged a joint venture with Ashland Oil that expanded into 150 Payless gas stations by 1966. Thornton sold his Payless interests to Ashland Oil but remained an Ashland board member until 1971. He founded Thornton Oil, which blossomed to 40 units within two years. In 2020, Thornton's was acquired by BP.[2] At the time of this publication in 2023, there were more than 200 "Thornton's" gas station/convenience stores across Florida, Indiana, Illinois, Kentucky, Ohio, and Tennessee.[3]

Carroll and Thornton discussed the possibilities at Latonia and pitched the investment opportunity to Kelly Downs, the head of real estate development at Citizens Fidelity Bank in Louisville. With Thornton's "Kentucky clout," Downs was far more positive than if Carroll had brought the idea to the bank himself. Selling the concept as strictly a real estate deal with the racetrack as a "throw-in," Carroll and Thornton ended up with a 50/50 arrangement when they purchased the Latonia Race Track property in 1986, all 363 acres. With only 129 acres needed for racing, the plan was to immediately develop the rest of the land while investing heavily in track improvements. In the end, a $9 million loan was split between a consortium of banks, including Citizen's Fidelity, Huntington Banks of Northern Kentucky, and Cincinnati's Fifth/Third. One million was paid in cash, and Delaware North remained with a piece of the pie after agreeing to carry a $3.5 million note secured by a parcel of land adjacent to the barns. They also insisted they continue the operation of the track concessions business.[4] While the racetrack was in new hands, the Mafia still had their fingers in the till.

The scheduled changeover of the business was to be immediately after the 1986 Spring Meet, allowing Jerry Carroll and Jim Thornton time to plan for the Fall 1986 season. That troubled Thornton, however, realizing the duo would have no significant income for five months. In addition, it soon became apparent that the two men disagreed heavily on many proposed plans for the facility. Carroll, for instance, wanted to invest in track renovations and upgrades to attract more patrons. In contrast, Thornton wanted to wait until the Fall Meet and its revenue before spending any money. Their personalities clashed as well. Carroll was the free-wheeling risk-taker who saw immediate improvements necessary for his long-term goals. At the same time, Thornton, 15 years Carroll's senior, was the conservative type who saw money-spending before income as an unnecessary extravagance. With the 50/50 partnership, everything became a stalemate. In addition, Carroll was determined to be directly involved in the day-to-day operations of the racetrack, while Thornton insisted they hire a professional trackman. Thornton won out in that particular fight, and Richard Cummings, a turf manager from Garden State Park in New Jersey, became the senior vice president and director of racing operations at Turfway Park.

Finally, Carroll wanted a new image for the racetrack, including a new name. Suddenly, the Latonia Race Track "name" was gone, but not the track's long and storied history. As for the new name, Carroll borrowed it from the street sign on which the property sat. That is how "Good ol' Latonia" became Turfway Park.

In the first weeks of new ownership, Carroll immediately moved to secure the track's showcase race and win back its sponsor. He flew to Chicago and began a series of meetings with Barry Berish and other Jim Beam officials. In these, Carroll spoke of a far-reaching plan to enhance the overall quality of the horses, to upgrade and modernize the facilities, especially the long-overdue backside. He also announced plans to develop the surrounding property commercially and use those profits to offset expenses until the track could pay its own way. Carroll promised to hire an aggressive management team and elevate the standards of racing at Turfway, with particular attention to stakes racing. He would also enhance the Jim Beam Stakes to a level far beyond what it was currently. Berish and the other Beam executives were highly impressed with Carroll's vision. They signed on for another three-year deal.

Opening Day Program at Turfway Park

Courtesy: Jim Claypool Collection

While Jerry Carroll and Jim Thornton were listed as co-owners in the racetrack's daily program, Carroll had non-mistakenly taken the lead role. He was always the spokesperson for Turfway and always the one to take the blame should there be a problem. Speaking to a group of dignitaries on opening day, Carroll promised more upgrades to the facility. Still, under his breath, he knew that more improvements relied on the amount of income the track was producing and how much of those profits Jim Thornton was willing to spend. Carroll and Thornton's struggles continued for the better part of two years, with each man, at various times, gaining the upper hand. It was a frustrating period in which Carroll's patience and resolve were tested repeatedly. Without immediate additional funding, he had to sit back and wait for the opportunity to divorce himself from these problems. Given those strained conditions, the smoothness of Turfway's grand opening, with only a few glitches here and there, was remarkable. Perhaps just as impressive was the new track's immediate public acceptance. Turfway Park ran its first race, a $4,000 maiden claiming event, on Wednesday evening, September 3, 1986. The feature that night, the Inaugural Handicap, a one-mile test for three-year-olds and up for a purse of $15,000, was won by *Big Pistol*, the favorite, owned by W.C. Partee and trained by Lynn Whiting, with jockey Larry Melancon in the rider's irons.

Opening Day at Turfway Park

Cincinnati Enquirer racing columnist Jack Murray described the track's opening: "Turfway opens to applause. Big crowd, big handle, few problems at the racetrack." Despite oppressive heat inside the glass-enclosed grandstands, Turfway was described in Murray's article as "...opening under new owner-ship, with a bright paint job and modern tote board." The color scheme of the old track was often described as "mud brown," while the new owners chose a green, white, and light gray interior... a much-improved atmosphere.[5] A crowd of 6,027 attended the gala event, wagered $727,932 on ten races, and atten-dance and mutuel handle was up almost 40 percent over the previous year's opening day statistics. During their tenure, Sportservice had failed miserably in upgrading the facilities or improving the quality of racing. One long-time patron remarked, "Jerry Carroll and Jim Thornton put as much money into the racetrack in one month as Sportservice did in the five years they owned it."[6]

One highlight of the Fall 1986 Meet, though utterly oblivious to fans and veteran horsemen at the time, occurred on September 14. An insignifi-cant maiden race (horses who had never won a race) found an unknown horse named *Alysheba* crossing the finish line ahead of the rest of the field. True, the famed Thoroughbred won his first race at little Turfway Park. *Alysheba* became the world's richest racehorse, winning the Kentucky Derby and Horse of the Year honors in 1987. Hall of Fame trainer Woody Stevens (from Powell County, Kentucky) remarked in a barb aimed at his rival in the East, Jack Van Berg, that *Alysheba*, the Van Berg stable's top horse, was nothing more than "that pony from Latonie," a jab that now, given the high quality of racing at Turfway Park Racing and Gaming, is quite archaic and out of place.

But by 1987, there were ominous signs that Turfway's owners, Jerry Carroll and Jim Thornton, were in a frayed and unraveling partnership. On March 13, 1987, *The Kentucky Post* reported on its front page that the two were fighting over control of Turfway, followed by an article the next day stating that the Florence, Kentucky, racetrack might be up for sale. Carroll was quick with his damage control, however. A few weeks later, Carroll announced in the *Kentucky Post* sports section that the rift between him and Thornton had been resolved and that a new $600,000 barn was to be constructed, greatly modernizing and expanding the racetrack's stabling capabilities. The bickering between the two owners remained under wraps for the time being.

The "new and improved" 1987 Jim Beam Stakes offered a prize of $500,000, one of the highest for any Derby prep in America. The Beam was run on a Saturday in previous years, but Carroll scheduled the event on a Sunday. Grandstand admission was raised to eight dollars. There was also a sold-out VIP tent with food and drinks, costing $75 per person. The massive structure drew probably the most impressive collection of horsemen, politicians, and celebrities ever assembled in Northern Kentucky. Jerry Carroll and Jim Thornton were prominent businessmen who invited many of their friends. The Governor of Kentucky, Martha Layne Collins, attended and handed out the trophy to the Beam winner. Also prominent were sports greats Stan Musial (legendary St. Louis Cardinal baseball player), Dan Issel (University of Kentucky basketball stand-out), and Ken Anderson (Cincinnati Bengals quarterback).

While Carroll and his new management team expected a crowd of 18,000 to 20,000, they were marginally disappointed. However, less than 24 hours after the event had ended, Northern Kentucky was blanketed with heavy snowfall, and they exhaled a sigh of relief over what could have been a weather nightmare for the track's debut event. While attendance was only 13,239, Turfway Park set two betting records in 1987. Fans wagered $2,200,086 on the 12-race card, boosting the three-day weekend event to a record $4,027,190. They also bet $1,060,280 on Saturday, producing the first million-dollar day ever recorded on the day before the Beam. The 1987 Beam was broadcast on ESPN and five simulcast outlets, indicating the growing interest in the race nationally and a foreshadowing of the vital part simulcasting would play in Beam's growth.

Regarding the race itself, it was a return engagement for the winning jockey in the 1984 Beam. Pat Day was America's reigning top rider in 1987, taking the title four-of-five straight years. His mount was a three-year-old colt named *J.T.'s Pet*, who along the homestretch, passed a horse named *Faster Than Sound* (which he was not) and won by nearly two lengths. Three of the other finishers in the 1987 Beam had local ties and thereby helped pique interest in the race. Tenth-place finisher, *David L's Rib*, was owned by horseman-restauranteur Bill Melton (the ever-popular Walt's Hitching Post restaurant in Fort Wright). Eleventh-place finisher, *Wayne's Crane,* was owned by a partnership of local business people, including Wayne Carlisle of Carlisle Construction. And *Bengal Fire*, the last-place finisher, had jockey-great Steve Cauthen's assistance in getting the horse ready for the Beam.

Before the Fall 1987 Meet began, Jerry Carroll had enough of Thornton and his conservative ideas. He organized a plan to buy Thornton out. The two men engaged in a bidding war at a private meeting at Thornton's farm outside Lexington. Don Ball, a prominent Lexington real estate broker and horseman, assisted Thornton financially. In addition, he engaged a team of nearly 20 lawyers and accountants. Carroll had contracted with Charlie Deters, a well-known Northern Kentucky attorney, and financially by John R. Lindahl, Sr., a Nashville business tycoon who owned horses, and Lindahl's accountant and friend, James

Lattimore, Jr., chairman of Lattimore, Black, Morgan, and Cain, one of the largest CPA and investment firms in Nashville. It had been agreed that the bidding would be in increments of $100,000, with a twenty-minute break between offers. Carroll was in trouble when Thornton's bid reached $17 million and subsequently climbed to $17.6 million. That was $600,000 over the limit predetermined by his associates in Nashville. While trying to phone John Lindahl for approval to raise the limits, he had to track the man down at a popular Nashville restaurant and nearly ran out of time. At the negotiations and per Carroll's instructions, Charlie Deters sounded off with a bid of $18 million. After a long closed-door conversation, Thornton's entourage emerged with a counteroffer of $18.1 million. With

Courtesy: Kenton County Public Library

James Lattimore

no hesitation whatsoever, Deters barked out "18.2," to which Thornton accepted. On August 4, 1987, the local press reported that Jerry Carroll had bought the track, and two Nashville businessmen had joined him as minority partners.

Soon after taking control of the track, Jerry Carroll implemented a model for its future success. Though he had struggled with Richard Cummings in the previous months, he kept him on, giving him the role of vice-president, and kept Richard Eng as director of public relations to keep some sense of continuity. He also hired Mark Simendinger as chief financial officer. Carroll assumed the role of president.

As planning for the 1988 Beam began, Carroll was ready to spend more money to attract more fans. He paid comedian Jerry Lewis $30,000 to do a short comedy routine at the traditional Call to Post Luncheon, paid $20,000 to hold the Spiral Ball, and also picked up many miscellaneous expenses associated with the Spiral Festival. New construction also took place over the next two years, including general offices, a valet entrance, and elevators against the paddock side of the grandstands. The 1988 Jim Beam Spiral Stakes was moved back to Saturday and was run on April 2. The race was changed to a distance of 1-1/8 miles and elevated to a Grade II Stakes, with a guaranteed purse of $500,000, thus continuing the effort to establish it as a nationally significant Derby prep. Two horses were rumored as favorites, *Brian's Time* and *Dynaformer*, but a 21-1 longshot named *Kingpost*, trained by Dianne Carpenter stood in the winner's circle. The winning jockey, Eugene Sipus, scored the biggest win in his riding career in this race. Unfortunately, none of the horses in the 1988 Beam became factors in the Blue Grass Stakes or Kentucky Derby.

Pik-Three and Inter-track Wagering

On September 9, 1987, Turfway Park introduced Pik-Three wagering to Kentucky. This shortened version of the Pik-Six attracted more bettors and offered better hope for winning all or part of a large betting pool. For optimists and those stout of heart, there was still the Pik-Six wager which, on March 23, 1988, rewarded bettors at Turfway Park with a record payout for Kentucky, $1,474,380, shared by 50 winners. Carroll's innovation plans continued when, on September 8, 1988, Turfway Park introduced Inter-track Wagering (ITW). Turfway's races were sent via cable to Ellis Park in Henderson, Kentucky. Putting it nicely, even a man as farsighted as Carroll could not have imagined the actual scope and impact ITW's rapid development would soon have in Kentucky and nationwide.

Courtesy: Kenton County Public Library

View of Turfway Park grandstands with the new exterior elevator addition

Pik-six wagering proved successful – yet devastatingly damaging – to the career of one lucky patron. On January 25, 1989, three Turfway Park bettors picked the winning horses of six races in a row, an unbelievable feat. After taxes, the trio who had pooled their bet split $201,909.20.[7] Rumors immediately circulated throughout the grandstands that a well-known celebrity held the winning ticket. The rumors quickly proved to be true. That wagerer was, unfortunately, Cincinnati Reds Manager Pete Rose. He immediately denied being the winner, but later confessed after his long-time bookie, Ron Peters, the man who would eventually testify against "The Hit King," revealed the truth.[8] Rose would soon be investigated for both tax evasion and for betting on baseball and other sports, as well as on his own team. He was subsequently banned for life from the sport he so much loved. Unknown to many, his long and painful demise began at Turfway Park.[9]

In 2016, after finally being permitted to be inducted into the Cincinnati Reds Hall of Fame, discussion began concerning the pose in which Rose might be depicted in a statue to be erected at Great American Ballpark. Maybe on first base during the several-minute-long standing ovation after hit number 4,192 (becoming the all-time leader in hits). Maybe in his familiar low batting crouch. "I

View of the new General Offices and valet entrance

sure as Hell don't want it to be standing at Turfway in the $2 window," Rose joked at the Hall of Fame press conference. "I can say that now. There's no one looking over my shoulder."[10]

Pete Rose, speaking at his
Cincinnati Reds Hall of Fame induction

Optimism was particularly high for the 1989 edition of the Jim Beam Spiral Stakes long before it ran on Saturday, April 1, because of the increased quality of the entire field. The outstanding favorite was *Mercedes Won*, trained by Arnold Fink and ridden by Jamie Bruin, Turfway's leading jockey in the 1988 Winter/Spring Meet. *Mercedes Won*'s regular jockey was Earlie Fires, but he was sitting out a suspension for careless riding. Mike Battaglia, the morning-line odds maker, and Jack Murray, veteran local sports writer, both agreed that another Thoroughbred, *Western Playboy*, ridden by one of the best judges of pace in the business, Pat Day, not only had a better chance... but would easily find victory if *Mercedes Won* got burned out on the front end by the other speed horses in the race.

It was a case, as so often happens in horse racing, of the locals knowing what they were talking about. *Mercedes Won* dueled first with pacesetter *Halrose* and later with *Clever Trevor*, and by the stretch, gave up the lead to *Western Playboy,* who won by nearly two lengths, with *Feather Ridge* closing to beat the favorite by a neck for the place spot. The crowd was now being let into the grandstands for $6 each and fell about 1,200 below the previous year. On-track handle was down approximately $375,000, but the total handle, thanks to simulcasting (ITW), was a record $6,025,226, an eye-opening increase of 118 percent!

Hopes ran high for *Western Playboy*, who had never won a stakes race before the Beam. He shipped to Keeneland, where he roared to victory in the Blue Grass, becoming the first Beam winner to "spiral" to Keeneland and win its great spring race. However, he could not fulfill John Battaglia's dream of winning both Derby preps and going on to win the Run for the Roses due to a hind leg injury.

Summer Squall

1990 was the year that heralded a fantastic run for horses that captured the Jim Beam Spiral Stakes at Turfway Park. Carroll boldly implemented a plan aimed at improving the entire package of facilities at Turfway. He elevated purses, thereby improving the overall quality of the racing stock, and used the substantial guaranteed monies of the Beam to attract horses that were still developing. These horses needed a race like the Beam to season and condition them further for the ultimate prize... the Kentucky Derby. Kentucky-born trainer, Woody Stevens, dubbed "the master of the Belmont" for his dominance there, brought *Yonder*, a colt that seemed very promising. Trainer Rusty Arnold entered *Bright Again*, and a third horse, *Tight Spot*, trained by Ron McAnally, a world-class trainer born in Latonia, Kentucky and therefore returning home, were other favorites. But Carroll's diligence and hard work, teamed with Turfway's promotional team of vice president Richard Cummings and racing secretary Gary Wilfert, brought one more top entry to the Beam that year. New York trainer Neil Howard shipped in *Summer Squall*, a small and wiry colt owned by Dogwood Stables of Aiken, South Carolina. Champion rider Pat Day drew that mount. In addition, Steve Ford, son of the former President Gerald Ford, was named Associate Vice President of Turfway Park.

Steve Ford, Associate VP at Turfway Park

In 1990, the Beam was beginning to resemble a miniature Kentucky Derby, displaying a bit of the mayhem, money, and madness that the famed classic in Louisville always seems to produce. For the most part, the mayhem started with young fans willing to brave the shortage of parking spaces that left vehicles covered with mud on grassy hillsides and having paid $4 to get into the grandstands. The rest of the crowd assembled in overflowing numbers on the track's apron or were jammed tightly against each other on the lowest floor of the building. Some were standing in long lines to place a bet; many were drinking, most were socializing and, in general, there was a carefree party atmosphere where everyone seemed to be having fun. In the VIP tent, set up next to the grandstands, about 2,000 gathered to eat prime rib, partake of the open bar, watch races on closed-circuit television, talk and parade their fashionable attire, and gawk and gaze at others in the crowd with particular attention paid to an array of celebrities and politicians that included the likes of singer Lee Greenwood, Kentucky Governor Wallace Wilkinson, and horseman and State Lieutenant Governor Brereton Jones.

The race proved an easy win for jockey Pat Day, his fourth Beam victory in five tries. At 4-5 odds, *Summer Squall* grabbed the lead at the stretch and won by two and a half lengths. There was a brief moment of concern immediately following the race when *Summer Squall* was kicked by the pony horse leading him into the winner's circle. Though he suffered a small cut requiring two stitches, this did not derail him from entering his next event.

Summer Squall shipped to Keeneland, where he soundly won the Blue Grass Stakes, then entered the Kentucky Derby as the second straight Jim Beam Champion to "spiral up" through the Kentucky prep races. Pat Day returned as the colt's rider. Two days before the Derby, Pat Day passed Don Brumfield as Churchill Downs' all-time leading jockey, and it seemed that Day, at the top of his game and aboard the top-rated horse, was finally destined to ride his first Kentucky Derby winner. It was not to be. *Summer Squall* led the field into the top of the stretch after breaking from far out in post fourteen. He was passed by *Unbridled*,

Courtesy: Blood-Horse Magazine

Summer Squall

and, courtesy of a remote camera, Carl Nafzger, that horse's trainer, cheered and hugged the colt's 92-year-old owner, Frances Genter, in a scene likely never to be forgotten in either Derby history or television coverage of the event. This shocking turnabout (*Summer Squall* had just bested *Unbridled* in the Blue Grass by 3-3/4 lengths and now had lost to him by 3-1/2) left trainer Howard puzzled and spoiling for a rematch. It came two weeks later in the 115th running of the Preakness, and this time *Summer Squall* prevailed by 2-1/4 lengths, becoming the first Jim Beam winner to win that, or any other, Triple Crown classic.

Hansel

The following year, it appeared John Battaglia's dream was finally coming true. The tenth running of the Jim Beam Spiral Stakes, on March 30, 1991, drew a field of 11 horses, one fewer than the year before, and Louisiana Derby winner, *Richman*, was favored. Pat Day was *Richman*'s regular rider, but he was drawn to another horse he had previously ridden named *Hansel*. He was dreadfully torn as to which horse to ride. He chose *Richman*, and *Hansel*'s owner, Joe Allbritton, and trainer Frank Brothers brought Jerry Bailey to ride their horse. Day rode a great race, keeping *Richman* in the hunt the whole way. Bailey also kept *Hansel* in contention, staying either third or fourth the entire race, waiting for Day to take the lead. When he did, Bailey pushed *Hansel* to *Richman*'s side, and once the two horses were side-by-side, *Hansel* pulled ahead to win by 2-1/2 lengths.

Hansel went on to win the Blue Grass Stakes at Keeneland and then ran an inexplicably dull race in the Derby, where he finished tenth. *Hansel* shipped to run in the Preakness, blowing away the other entries to win by seven lengths. Three weeks later, he avenged his defeat in the Kentucky Derby by holding off Derby Champion *Strike the Gold* to take the 123rd running of the Belmont Stakes. In doing so, *Hansel* became the first Jim Beam winner to claim two parts of the American Triple Crown. His two wins in the Thoroughbred classics and his narrow victory over *Strike the Gold* led *Hansel* to be selected as the Eclipse Winner in his age group in 1993. He was the first Beam Champion to garner this prestigious award.

Courtesy: Blood-Horse Magazine

Hansel

While 1992 was an exciting season for Turfway Park, one jewel of the Triple Crown remained unclaimed: a Kentucky Derby victory. In 1992, five horses had legitimate chances to win with the eleventh running of the Jim Beam Stakes. The race was billed as the most competitive field ever assembled for a Beam, and it would be difficult to argue this point. One favorite was D.

This page, top: VIP tent at the 1991 Spiral Stakes; Above: Jerry Carroll, former President Gerald Ford, and Steve Ford; At right: Jerry Bailey with Gerald Ford after the 10th running of the Jim Beam Spiral Stakes.

Opposite page, top: *Lil E. Tee* winning the Spiral Stakes at Turfway Park before becoming the Beam's first Kentucky Derby winner; Bottom left: *Lil E. Tee* with jockey Pat Day in the winner's circle; Bottom right: Jerry Carroll, Turfway owner, Brerton Jones, Kentucky Govenor, and former President Gerald Ford, among others, presenting the winning trophy.

All images on this spread courtesy: Kenton County Public Library

Wayne Lucas' *Big Sur*. Another choice was *Snappy Landing*, a horse from the New York circuit. A West Coast entry was *Treekster*, while two other favorites were *Vying Victor* and *Lil E. Tee*, another Whiting-Partee-Day combination.

On a cool but sunny day, a record crowd of 17,852 came to the eleventh Jim Beam Spiral Stakes. The early pacesetter was *Waki Warrior*, ridden by veteran Kentucky reinsman Larry Melancon. At the top of the stretch, *Waki Warrior* had bested almost every contender except for the skillfully ridden *Lil E. Tee*. *Waki Warrior* faded as the field headed for home, and *Saint Ballado* was also kept from

making a move for a win. *Lil E. Tee* found room along the rail and held off, by a length, the fast-closing *Vying Victor*. For the team of Whiting-Partee-Day, this was their third victory in as many attempts, giving Pat Day his fifth Beam triumph.

Lil E. Tee's owners chose to skip the Blue Grass Stakes and instead traveled to Arkansas, where *Lil E. Tee* was bested by the speedster *Pine Bluff*. After that stakes race, both horses headed for Louisville. Eighteen horses went to the post for the 118th running of the Kentucky Derby in 1992. The overwhelming favorite was the French champion, *Arazi*. *Lil E. Tee*, with Pat Day aboard and Day's record at the Derby at 0 for 9, was given little chance and sent off at odds of 16-1. Day broke his horse in front from post ten, settled in, and was squeezed back by a rush of horses. As the field entered the far turn, Day was positioned in the middle of the field, and *Arazi* blew past him on his way to an apparently easy win. Day repositioned, however, and followed *Arazi* down the home stretch. That is when *Arazi* faltered and began to fade, but Day's horse was in high gear, holding off another challenger, *Casual Lies*, for the Kentucky Derby victory.

The Jim Beam had just produced its first Kentucky Derby winner, although John Battaglia's Spiral had taken a detour through Arkansas to get there. Turfway's officials were exuberant. Mary Troilo, wife of successful jockey Billy Troilo, recalls, "We watched the race from the barn area. When I saw those silks, I stood there with tears running down my face. Lynn Whiting and Pat Day were friends, so it made it even more special."[11] Mary was initially hired at Turfway Park as an overnight data entry clerk. It turned into a 35-year career. She became Director of Admissions, oversaw parking, ran the gift shop, and more. She became the first licensed female racing official in Kentucky and was the National Director of Simulcasting. Gary Wilfert, the track's general manager and director of racing, had promised that if Beam winner *Lil E. Tee* won the Derby, he would dance on the roof of the barn that housed him. Accompanied by his daughters, Wilfert, true to his word, donned a custom-made set of silks in the orange colors of W. Cal Partee and climbed up to a wooden platform constructed atop trainer Lynn Whiting's barn. As the strains of his daughter's chosen song, Paula Abdul's *Vibeology* drifted across the stabling area at Churchill, Wilfert danced and gave a convincing demonstration of why he was better suited to manage and direct a racetrack than to dance.

It did not take long for Jerry Carroll and Barry Berish at Jim Beam to make a move to capitalize on *Lil E. Tee's* success. When the following Stakes schedule was announced, it was revealed that Turfway Park and Beam Brands had raised the purse to $600,000, making it the richest Triple Crown prep race in the nation. Billed as "a sure-fire barometer for future successes in the Kentucky Derby," the 1993 Beam attracted a field of nine, headed by the highly regarded *Prairie Bayou*. With two impressive wins at Aqueduct as credentials, *Prairie Bayou* was installed as the 6-5 favorite and lived up to all expectations. Ridden by Chris McCarron and trained by Thomas Bohannan, *Prairie Bayou* was patiently ridden off the pace until the stretch, opened a 1-1/2 length lead on long shot *Proudest Romeo*, who finished second and, under good urging, won by about one length. A new record crowd of 19,327 bet $2,711,625, only the third highest ever, but due to simulcasting, set the betting record for the total handle at $8,362,979, a clear indication that the Beam was sparking interest at betting sites nationwide.

Prairie Bayou went on to win the Bluegrass Stakes in Lexington, and was a slight 4-1 betting favorite in the Kentucky Derby, with Mike Smith replacing McCarron as the rider. *Prairie Bayou* made a robust late surge in the event, but before he did, a long shot named *Sea Hero* pushed through to the lead on the rail and had enough left to hold off the late charge of the former Beam winner.

Prairie Bayou shipped to Pimlico and became the fourth straight Jim Beam victor to capture a classic when he won the Preakness. He was pulled up and did not finish in the Belmont three weeks later. Even so, *Prairie Bayou* was named Cham-

Groom James Brewer giving
Prairie Bayou a well-deserved brushing

pion three-year-old in America in 1993 and became the second Beam winner, along with *Hansel* in 1991, to win this coveted title.

Evidence that the Jim Beam Spiral Stakes had captured the attention of the racing world nationwide came the following season when conservative Keeneland added Toyota as a corporate sponsor, raising the purse of the Blue Grass to $750,000. Wealthy Santa Anita, concerned about losing West Coast standouts *Larry the Legend* and *Lake George* to the Beam, moved its purse to $700,000 and, in 1996, set it at $1,000,000. While Jerry Carroll and Barry Burish were convinced of the Beam's importance as a Derby prep, the purse for Turfway's premiere race stayed at $600,000 and remained there for several years.

The thirteenth Beam, run on April 2, 1994, drew a field of horses with good but not yet outstanding credentials. The race favorite was Southwest Stakes winner *Southern Rhythm*. The one that would win the race was trainer Hugh Robertson's *Polar Expedition*, who came to the Beam with a reputation as a front-runner who had run against and been beaten by several of the best-bred horses in the world, including *Southern Rhythm*, who had bested him in the Southwest at Oaklawn. With jockey Curt Bourque aboard, *Polar Expedition* broke first, was never headed, and having established a two-length lead by the three-quarter pole, held on to win by a neck over third-choice *Powis Castle*, with *Southern Rhythm* putting in a mild late run to finish fourth. D. Wayne Lucas' *Chimes Band* finished third.

Polar Expedition ended the astonishing four-year run of Beam winners, posting wins in at least one of the races that comprise America's Triple Crown of Racing. After the Beam victory, owner Jim Cody and trainer Robertson decided to leave Kentucky. *Polar Expedition* ran in the Illinois Derby, where the sloppy track surface provided a last-place finish. After a short break, the gelding shipped to Maryland to compete in the Preakness. He never fired and finished in tenth place.

Kentucky Cup Day of Champions

Jerry Carroll launched the Kentucky Cup Day of Champions in September 1994. The event included three graded stakes races and events for juvenile and juvenile fillies. The purses of the six races on the card totaled $1,000,000, including $175,000 offered from the Kentucky Thoroughbred Development Fund and $100,000 from the Breeder's Cup Special Stakes Fund. The $400,000 Kentucky Cup Classic race was the fourth-richest race in Kentucky and the richest race for older horses. The Cup consisted of two races – the $50,000 Kentucky Cup Starter Stakes and the $400,000 Kentucky Cup Classic – plus four ex-

Courtesy: Kenton County Public Library

Polar Expedition, with jockey Curt Bourque aboard

isting races, three of which were renamed: the $100,000 Kentucky Cup Juvenile (formerly the Alysheba), the Kentucky Cup Juvenile Fillies (formerly the Clipsetta), the $150,000 Kentucky Cup Spring (formerly the Summer Squall), and the $200,000 Turfway Budweiser Breeder's Cup, which retained its name. Top-rated horses shipped in from across the country, and the festival was a huge hit for over a decade. It was suspended in 2008 but was resurrected briefly in 2011. It was again discontinued and re-established in later years.

Trifecta and Superfecta Wagering

Jerry Carroll spent the following off-season introducing more innovations and technology upgrades. When he brought ITW (Inter-track wagering) into play in 1988, many turf traditionalists believed live horse racing and this new technology were incompatible. They advanced their argument with predictions that many smaller tracks would be forced to close. Carroll and others of like mind countered that applying modern technology to horse racing was a supplement to live racing, not its rival. Live racing must continually institute innovative and new ideas to survive and thrive, especially those increasing track revenues from betting. In line with that model, at the same time ITW debuted, Turfway Park introduced trifecta wagering, a successful betting gimmick that requires picking the exact finish of three horses in a single race – a betting innovation that has helped raise live racing wagering pools and channels critical new monies into live-racing purse development. Trifecta wagering is just another Carroll idea that is now implemented nationwide. He followed that move with Superfecta wagering in 1996, a betting option requiring the exact finish of four horses in a single race.

The "Racebook"

Carroll's most significant introduction at Turfway Park might be considered his overhaul of the first floor of the grandstands building in 1995. With the foresight that ITW would be a huge success, he transformed most of the main level into "The Racebook," a 200-screen, 12-hour-a-day, single-level betting parlor with special seating and dining facilities. Once again, Carroll was right. In doing so, Turfway Park set the pace for off-track and on-track simulcast racing in Kentucky. In 1995 alone, Turfway's take from simulcast racing was $161.4 million. In a single decade, the daily wagering average grew from just under $561,000 in 1985 to $2,287,733 in 1995.

But the whole story behind Carroll's introduction of simulcast racing is even more intriguing. Kentucky, at the time, had four Thoroughbred racetracks. In 1987, when Turfway Park was preparing to introduce inter-track wagering, Churchill Downs' president and CEO Thomas Meeker was negotiating to purchase a trotting track in Louisville called Louisville Downs. Jerry Carroll had approached Meeker about sending Turfway's signal to Churchill Downs, but Meeker believed the increased revenue would be no more than $100,000 a day. Carroll then contacted Bill King, head of Louisville Downs, and struck a deal to send the ITW there. The first night Louisville Downs offered Turfway Park's races via ITW, it did over $400,000 gross and ran out of programs. Later, the trotting facility

Courtesy: Robert Webster

View of the first floor "Racebook"

was purchased by Churchill Downs at a much higher cost because of the success of ITW. Ellis Park, near Henderson, Kentucky, was the first Kentucky track to follow Turfway's lead. ITW saved that racetrack from closing in every sense of the word. The additional revenue immediately helped finance a much-needed upgrade and modernization of track facilities. Keeneland, the track that proudly displays Kentucky's racing heritage in ways that defy commercialization, was the last to introduce ITW. Keeneland is a non-profit charitable enterprise that races a few weeks in the spring and fall and makes millions in its annual horse sales. They established a modest room of chairs and tables and a few television sets for people to place their bets. ITW will likely never be what makes Keeneland exist.

Serena's Song

In 1995, a new wrinkle was added when the field was announced for the fourteenth running of the Jim Beam Stakes. The favorite was a filly. *Serena's Song*, owned by Robert and Beverly Lewis and wearing the white bridle of the racing stable of D. Wayne Lucas, came to the Beam after having swept three graded stakes in California, culminating with a triumph in the Santa Anita Oaks. After training at Churchill, she shipped to Turfway to see if her speed could beat the boys. Her top competition was a late charger named *Tejano Run*, already slated as a Kentucky

119

Derby favorite. Furthermore, Jerry Bailey, one of the turf's best judges of pace and rider of Beam Champion *Hansel* in 1991, had been flown in to ride *Tejano Run*.

The fourteenth Beam was held on April 1, 1995. The mild-weathered day drew a crowd of 19,342. Neither the betting nor the attendance set any records. Still, there was day-long electricity in the air, as many conjectured… if *Serena's Song* won the Beam, would she become the only fourth filly (the first since *Winning Colors* in 1988) to win the Kentucky Derby? But the first question – the Beam – still had to be answered. Jockey Corey Nakatani was aboard *Serena's Song*, who was not a familiar name to most in the crowd, other than veteran trackgoers who knew him as one of the best reinsmen on the West Coast. Jerry Bailey, atop *Tejano Run*, was a more prominent name locally. Since Pat Day was not in the race, many placed wagers on Bailey's colt, causing *Tejano Run* to be a solid 7-2 second choice behind *Serena's Song*, who went off as the race's even-money favorite.

The race was not much of a contest. Nakatani put the brown filly *Serena's Song* in the lead from the very start and never looked back, stretching the lead to four lengths by the head of the homestretch and winning by a convincing 3-1/2 lengths. *Tejano Run* rallied from seventh place in the eight-horse field to finish a clear second. The steadily improving *Serena's Song* went on to the Blue Grass, where she finished third and was beaten only by *Thunder Gulch* in the Derby. After later victories at Pimlico, New York, and Monmouth Park, she shipped back to Turfway Park for its Budweiser Breeder's prep on Kentucky Cup Day, where she finished second. Her remarkable campaign at age three was capped off when she was named filly Eclipse winner, thereby becoming, along with *Hansel* and *Prairie*

Serena's Song

Courtesy: Blood-Horse Magazine

Bayou, the third Beam Champion to take the award in their respective categories. *Serena's Song's* impressive story would later be celebrated at the new Turfway Park Racing and Gaming when one of the restaurants was named Serena's Market.

The fifteenth running of the Jim Beam Stakes at Turfway Park was unique in that the Lukas stable, now with 40 horses permanently stabled on the grounds and competing for the steadily rising purses at Turfway Park, entered two horses in the prestigious contest: *Dr. Caton*, an untested colt thought to be ready to blossom, and *Victory Speech*, the 8-5 favorite. D. Wayne Lukas, who had won five straight Triple Crown races (beginning with *Tabasco Cat*'s victory in the 1994 Preakness), had several promising three-year-olds under his training tutelage. Four of those were slated to run in other Derby preps, including the Santa Anita Derby, the Arkansas Derby, and the Blue Grass, with each of those stakes raising their purses dramatically in the 1990s to compete with the Jim Beam. A Claiborne Farm colt named *Roar* was the second betting choice ahead of *Dr. Caton* and was trained by Claude R. McGaughey III. The headline in *The Enquirer* the next day told the story: "Roar Wins, Fans Roar." Before 19,552 in attendance, jockey Mike Smith urged *Roar* into the lead at the stretch and held on to win the $600,000 Beam. *Roar* broke well from the gate behind long-shot *Ensign Ray*. Another favorite, *Victory Speech*, had trouble and broke slowly. *Roar* stayed close throughout, ran down *Ensign Ray* in the stretch, and won by 1-1/2 lengths, with *Ensign Ray* second and *Victory Speech* third. *Dr. Caton* was never in contention and finished in seventh place.

The fifteenth Beam was considered *Roar*'s acid test, and he passed it with flying colors. With glorious weather and temperatures that soared into the 60s, this Beam was acclaimed by many as the best. The VIP tent held its most impressive list of celebrities to date, ranging from stars of dramatic television such as Harry Hamlin, Linda Evans, and John Forsythe, to singers Kenny Rogers and Wayne Newton, to actor Chuck Norris, to comedians Jerry Van Dyke and Sid Caesar, as well as romantic and personable celebrity, Kato Kaelin (O.J. Simpson's famous houseguest), who mixed with the crowd, signed autographs, and never seemed to forget a name. The overall quality of racing was also of the highest level. A total of $10,155,292 was wagered, and the total purses for the thirteen-race card were $1.1 million, the richest in track history. On an otherwise perfect day of racing, the lone blemish involved parking. As many as 2,000 fans (thus preventing a record crowd) were turned away because there was no room left to park, and some, arriving late, were parked on muddy hillsides returning later to find their vehicles stuck in mud up to their axles. Luckily, these fans seemed to take it all in stride, and much to the track's credit, its hardworking emergency crew did all it could to assist those stranded.

In its 15-year history, the Jim Beam Stakes (Spiral Stakes) had risen in value from $10,000 to $600,000, an astonishing sixty-fold increase. With this kind of money came a parade of horses to Florence, Kentucky that, during the previous five years, had won one-third of the races that constitute Thoroughbred racing's Triple Crown classics. None of this could have been possible without some daring vision and a good measure of faith. It began simply enough when savvy horseman John Battaglia followed his dream and established an early spring event aimed at carrying horses through a series of tests on the Kentucky circuit that would "spiral" into the opportunity to make a run for the glory and roses in the Kentucky Derby. It grew into something unique thanks to David Vance, Victor Zast, Barry Berish, Latonia and Turfway's racing secretaries, and Jerry Carroll, who always grasps opportunity and seizes it. While John Battaglia did not live long enough to see his dream become a reality, the Beam was now Turfway's showcase event, a nationally recognized and legitimate prep for the Derby and the other Triple Crown races, as well as a testing ground for horses whose credentials need the enhancing that a victory in the Beam brought to the winners.

By this time, Jerry Carroll had spent nearly $30 million making Turfway Park a state-of-the-art racing facility, transforming a once run-down racetrack into an industry leader. To finance it all, Carroll drew upon his past skills in real estate, selling off or leasing approximately a third of the original acreage purchased for various purposes: restaurants, hotels, discount department stores, and even a 10-screen discount movie theater. The monies generated financed the demolition of the old barns and new all-weather replacements, the refurbishing of the clubhouse and grandstands, the construction of a new racing barn, track kitchen, and racing office, and a general face-lifting of the whole property, punctuated by a bold green neon sign that spelled out TURFWAY PARK with five racehorses alongside it, lit in timed sequence as if they were racing.

Some remarked that Carroll's spending seemed to be aimed at making Turfway Park a gaming/entertainment center reminiscent of the sort found in Las Vegas. That is precisely what Jerry Carroll intended. In 1996, Carroll secured a $30 million operating agreement with Harrah's Entertainment and Gaming Corporation to convert Turfway Park into an entertainment-casino-horse racing mega-center. Earlier, in 1993, he had launched a one-person crusade to bring legalized casino-style gambling to Kentucky. Following weeks of walking the power-driven hallways of Frankfort, he backed off after learning the "game" of Kentucky politics.

Once again, Jerry Carroll could foresee the future. That fact soon became a reality when casino-style gambling was legalized in nearby Indiana. Adding to casinos in the Hoosier State were several similar establishments in Southwestern Ohio. It devastated Kentucky's horse racing industry. Suddenly, droves of Greater Cincinnati's gambling fanatics made the short trek to full-scale Las Vegas-style gambling boats and stand-alone facilities in Rising

Courtesy: Robert Webster

View of the front of Turfway Park at night, showing the iconic green neon sign

Sun and Lawrenceburg, Indiana, as well as those in and around Cincinnati, Ohio. They chose roulette, blackjack, and traditional slot machines over horse racing. Kentucky would find itself years behind its neighbors, who were collecting tens of millions in tax revenue. A newspaper headline at the time said it best: "Kentucky tracks see business float away: With casinos rollin' on the river, the state's horse racing industry wants to get a handle on slots."[12]

While slot machines jingled just across state lines, the sound in Kentucky was that of distressed horse industry leaders pounding their heads against the wall in frustration with the Commonwealth's politicians. Thomas Meeker, president and CEO of Churchill downs, said, "What we're going through is a mirror image of what's happening in Maryland. We've known for years that this was coming. But the political interests, the legislators said: 'We don't want to make any snap judgments based on projections. We want to see some blood in the water.'"[13] The blood in the water was visible, at least in Jerry Carroll's eyes. The deep-rooted horse industries in Kentucky and Maryland, home of the Kentucky Derby and the Preakness – two flashy jewels in the Triple Crown – were not the only racetracks bleeding profusely at the time. Pari-mutuel wagering was down significantly in every region where slot machine operations or full-scale casinos were nearby.

In 1997, some form of casino gambling was legal in 29 states, meaning Kentucky was in the minority. At that time, four casinos were floating on the Ohio River, which forms Kentucky's northern border and flows past four of its racetracks, including Churchill Downs and Turfway Park. The most recent additions to the riverboat gambling armada were the Grand Victoria in Rising Sun, Indiana, and the Argosy in Lawrenceburg, Indiana. Both are short drives from Turfway Park. About the same time, Ohio racetracks began simulcasting, an industry-wide practice on which Turfway Park, until then, held a regional monopoly. Two tracks, River Downs in Cincinnati and Lebanon Raceway just north of Cincinnati, are also minutes from Turfway. Carroll said in 1997, "We felt the hit right away, and it's killing us. Here I plan to spend $300,000 on advertising, and the riverboats come up with $3 million, and I'm talking about one month! How am I supposed to compete with that?"

The addition of casino-style gambling to racetracks had already proven successful. Before Prairie Meadows racetrack near Des Moines, Iowa, installed slot machines on April 1, 1995, it was $89.3 million in debt. Twenty months later, it threw a "Debt-free Party." It had retired its debt entirely, significantly increased purses – as well as racing attendance and the amount wagered – and its patrons were dropping more than $5 million a day into 1,100 slot machines. In Delaware, where tracks began offering slots in December 1995, guests wagered $2.2 billion in 1996.

While Turfway Park revenues were beginning to fade, the main event went on as scheduled. The 1997 edition of the Jim Beam Spiral Stakes was won by *Concerto*, with Carlos H. Marquez, Jr. aboard. John J. Tammaro III was the trainer, and Kinsman Stable was the proud owner. *Concerto* would race in the Kentucky Derby a few weeks later, finishing in ninth place behind the incredible *Silver Charm*. A sixth-place finish was the best *Concerto* could do in the 1997 Preakness. *Silver Charm* went on to win the Preakness but missed the Triple Crown, as he was defeated in the Belmont Stakes by *Touch Gold*. Once again, attendance was well over 20,000 and, according to a *Cincinnati Enquirer* article, the following was consumed during the day-long event: 5,850 shots of Jim Beam Bourbon, 3,372 glasses of the Golden Beam (the official adult beverage of the Jim Beam – sold in souvenir glasses), 4,080 complete dinners in the VIP tent and dining rooms, 3,236 hot dogs and chili dogs, 2,137 hamburgers, and 5,643 cups of soda.[14]

Just before the 1998 Jim Beam Spiral Stakes, Harrah's operating company announced it wanted out of any partnership with Turfway Park. It was looking for a third party to buy out its right to a one-third interest in the Kentucky racetrack. Harrah's obtained the right to the shares as partial collateral for a $25 million loan to Turfway. The casino giant said Turfway was in default and they were calling in its debt. The fact was, Harrah's had no interest in owning the racetrack in the first place, as evidenced in the 1993 letter outlining the loan agreement. The Florence, Kentucky property was just "thrown in" with the company's purchase of the Downtown Cincinnati casino.[15] Harrah's had no experience operating a racetrack and paid little attention to the property after the purchase. Eventually, a judge ordered the sale of nearly 50 acres of Boone County commercial property to recover at least part of the $25 million loan. The property included the land where a third office building in the Turfway Ridge Office Park was to have been built at Turfway Road east of Interstate 75.[16]

Meanwhile, attendance and wagers and Turfway Park continued to decrease in numbers. Luckily, management still could count on the track's premiere contest – the Spiral Stakes. But the 1998 Jim Beam was nearly a disaster. More than 20,000 fans were expected on March 28; everything looked like the event would mimic recent years and be a huge success. However, high winds with gusts exceeding 60 mph toppled the massive VIP tent. In addition, three power poles were snapped, bringing electric lines to the ground. The race day was postponed. Incredibly, repairs were made during the early-morning hours, and the $600,000 event transpired the following afternoon. More than 25,000 fans attended. Celebrities included Milton Berle, Bo Derek, and John Forsythe. However, high winds returned later in the afternoon, pulling tent stakes out of the ground and toppling over temporary port-a-potties, sending them sliding across the apron toward the winner's circle. By the decision of the local fire Marshall, the VIP was evacuated, and everyone was moved into the grandstands. There, those high-rollers and celebrities resumed their "open-bar" status and, intermixed with the general admission crowd, watched the races from wherever they could find a place to sit or stand. Incredibly, only one person later requested a refund for his $100 VIP ticket.

Event of the Year, with Hall of Fame jockey Russell Baze, stood in the winner's circle at the end of the race. Hall of Fame trainer Jerry Hollendoffer was there as well. *Yukon Pete* and *Yarrow Brae* set a fast pace, but Baze brought his colt from fifth to third at the second turn and blew past the leaders at the beginning of the home stretch. *Event of the Year* raced in the Santa Anita Handicap the following year, finishing second... but beating the great *Silver Charm.*

Immediately after the 1998 Jim Beam Stakes, the famous distillery again threatened to back out from supporting and sponsoring the event. This time, however, they did not change their mind. Sixteen years straight saw the

Jim Beam Spiral Stakes as one of the most significant sporting events in the region. But the stakes have recently suffered from a lack of success in Triple Crown races (Kentucky Derby, Preakness, and Belmont). In 1993, Jim Beam winner *Prairie Bayou* went on to finish second in the Kentucky Derby and win the Preakness, but since then, no Spiral Stakes contender had won a Triple Crown race. That, merged with the public opinion that Turfway Park was starting to look like a wholly neglected facility, caused Jim Beam's management to pull out. Suddenly, Jerry Carroll and his staff were in complete panic regarding the future of the race – and the mere existence of the Northern Kentucky racetrack.

Jerry Carroll's Departure

By 1998, Jerry Carroll realized his dream of making Turfway Park into a multi-faceted entertainment facility was not to happen. Kentucky lawmakers were not going to budge one inch on legalizing full-scale or even slot-machine-only gambling. So many politicians had promised change – if elected – but once the votes were tallied and those new legislators were sitting behind their fancy desks for awhile, their campaign promises somehow changed. Carroll's plans never altered from his original dream. When he and his partners purchased the racetrack in 1986, "New Latonia" quickly became the magnificent Turfway Park. Carroll immediately invested in the racetrack's future, remodeling the clubhouse, opening the Racebook, and launching the Kentucky Cup Day of Champions. Turfway Park was at the peak of its existence. Mutuels had never been higher, purse monies were larger than at all other Midwestern Thoroughbred racetracks, and attendance was off the charts. Everyone in the Greater Cincinnati region, and many throughout the nation, knew about Turfway Park. But for Jerry Carroll, it was time to move on.

Veteran jockey turned Senior State Steward in Kentucky and Clerk of Scales at Turfway Park, Bill Troilo, remarked, "Jerry Carroll had a great vision for the racetrack. He brought Turfway Park into national recognition, but politicians put a hard stop to his vision. Now [2023], Turfway Park is what Jerry Carroll always wanted it to be."[17] Billy's wife, Mary Troilo, another long-time Turfway Park employee, said, "I was very proud of the changes Mr. Carroll made to the facility.

He brought class to the place. He added a Private Club where a tie and jacket were required. It seemed like a 'real' racetrack, something it had not been for a long time. Jerry was a great person, and I really enjoyed working for him. He didn't micro-manage and trusted you to do a great job. And if you did, you were rewarded."[18]

In 1998, Jerry Carroll and investors, including Dick Duchossois of Chamberlain Industries, Richard Farmer of Cintas Corporation, and John Lindahl of State Industries and Outback Steakhouse, purchased land in the middle of nowhere... near Sparta, in Gallatin County, Kentucky. There, they built the Kentucky Speedway, a state-of-the-art automobile racetrack that, over the years, would attract the very best NASCAR drivers, Indy-style racers, pick-up truck competitions, and more. The track opened with great success in 2000, with a seating capacity of over 100,000. The famed NASCAR Cup Series ran from 2011 to 2020. Unfortunately, in 2023, the facility was closed and was being used by the Ford Motor Company as a parking lot for more than 70,000 newly built Super Duty pickup trucks after a global shortage of semiconductor chips necessary to make the vehicles fully operational.

In 1999, Jerry Carroll sold Turfway Park to a group including the non-profit Keeneland Association in Lexington, Kentucky; GTECH Corporation (the Kentucky state lottery operator and a provider of online lottery games); and Harrah's Entertainment (later renamed Caesar's Entertainment, a Memphis-based operator of casinos in the United States and Australia). Like Delaware North, GTECH had the type of reputation often found in mafia-style extortion. A CNN report in 1996 found that "Rare is the company that has faced as many allegations of baldly sleazy conduct as GTECH." Kickback schemes using inflated payments to state-level politicians were apparently commonplace with GTECH. Two company officials, Guy Snowden and David Smith, were found to have "perfected the backroom art of lottery politics, rewarding political friends, annihilating enemies, and crushing the competition. The firm's mob-style tactics rewarded them with a 70 percent market share of state lotteries by 1996.[19] Luckily, in 2005, GTECH sold its Turfway Park interests, leaving Keeneland and Harrah's with 50/50 shares. With a sale price of $37 million for Turfway Park, Carroll nearly tripled his initial investment.

In the short time Jerry Carroll owned Turfway Park, it grew from a second-rate facility to a nationally recognized and respected Thoroughbred racetrack. Like Old Latonia in the late 1800s and early 1900s, New Latonia and Carroll's Turfway Park were the home of innovations. One, on the last day of the Winter Meet in 1969, Latonia became the first track in Kentucky to race at night. Two, when women began breaking into the sport as jockeys in the 1970s, they were welcomed with open arms at Latonia. Three, Carroll introduced numerous innovations in wagering that remain standards nationwide today. But another feature truly set Turfway apart from other tracks; there was a remarkable sense of community. Turfway Park became an "everybody knows your name" kind of place. The art of handicapping was passed down from generation to generation. Those who had placed wagers at Old Latonia in Covington were suddenly bringing their sons and daughters out to New Latonia and Turfway Park in Florence. Folks that worked at New Latonia and Turfway Park were the sons and daughters of those employed at Old Latonia. Everybody had stories and remembrances of the "good old days" at the track. Mary Troilo recalls learning that the track had been sold, "I cried. I knew it would never be the same." Only the future would determine if the great Turfway Park tradition would continue after the Jerry Carroll era.

POST POSITIONS

A "post position" refers to the place within the starting gate from which a horse will start a race. They are randomly picked prior to the day's events. Officials draw the horse's name and then the post position. Some horses do better from certain post positions. "Frontrunners" do best from position one, as they do not have to run as far to get out in front. A "closer" will usually do better from position 6 or higher. Historically, post positions 2 through 10 have produced the most Kentucky Derby winners, and only a few have won from post position 16 and further outside. There is only one post position that has never produced a Derby winner (as of 2022), that being #17.

The colors representing each post position are the same at nearly every Thoroughbred racetrack in the United States. This is so race callers, trainers, owners, and fans can better identify each horse as they round the track.

Chapter Four Endnotes

1. Danielle Sessa, "Kentucky Developer Jerry Carroll Bets on a Motor-Sports Speedway," The Wall Street Journal, October 7, 1998, retrieved on July 10, 2022.

2. "James Thornton," Wikipedia, retrieved on July 10, 2022.

3. "James Thornton, founder and chairman, Thorntons," entrepreneurhof.com, retrieved on July 10, 2022.

4. *The Tradition Continues*, Claypool, pages 221-225.

5. Claypool, page 224.

6. Claypool, page 224.

7. "Rose, Racetrack Chairman won Pik Six at Turfway," *United Press International*, March 25, 1989, retrieved on November 19, 2022.

8. "Oddsmaker testifies about Pete Rose's gambling," *United Press International Archives*, August 30, 1989, retrieved on November 29, 2022.

9. "Pete Rose Chronology," *Associated Press*, July 19, 1990, retrieved on November 19, 2022.

10. "What should Pete Rose's statue look like?" *Cincinnati Enquirer*, January 19, 2016, retrieved on November 29, 2022.

11. Personal interview with Mary Troilo on November 16, 2022.

12. Tom Keyser, "Kentucky tracks see business float away: With casinos rollin' on the river, the state's horse racing industry wants to get a handle on slots," *The Baltimore Sun*, February 3, 1997, retrieved on July 20, 2022.

13. *Ibid.*

14. *Cincinnati Enquirer*, March 22, 1998, page 54.

15. "Harrah's wants out of Turfway," *Cincinnati Post*, March 13, 1998, retrieved on September 12, 2022. "Turfway Park Must Sell Land...," *Cincinnati Enquirer*, June 24, 1998, retrieved on September 12, 2022.

16. Personal interview with Billy Troilo on November 16, 2022.

17. Personal interview with Mary Troilo on November 16, 2022.

18. Peter Elkind and Shaifani Puri, "The number crunchers, you think it's hard to win the lottery? Try competing against the world's leading lottery vendor, GTECH, which almost never loses a contract fight. It plays hard, all right, but does it play fair?" CNN Money, November 11, 1996, retrieved on August 7, 2022.

19. Personal interview with Mary Troilo on November 16, 2022.

Chapter Five

The Bob Elliston Era

In 1999, Turfway Park was under new ownership. Keeneland Race Track, the GTECH Corporation, and Harrah's Casino had taken control of the Northern Kentucky establishment but, after several months, had made no immediate changes in management. A few minor remodeling projects had been completed during the previous two years, but major renovations were still desperately needed. On the plus side, the track was at its peak regarding mutuels, purses, and attendance. More importantly, stakes races at Turfway Park were being recognized by horsemen and racing fans nationwide. And that is where Bob Elliston comes along.

Robert "Bob" Elliston grew up around horses as a boy in Central Kentucky. He learned the "lingo" early, knew some trainers, and eventually became the proud owner of a horse, then another, and another. It is doubtful he ever dreamed of being the head of a racetrack. However, when the 35-year-old president of Firstar (formerly Star Bank) heard that Jerry Carroll had sold Turfway Park to a trio of companies, including Keeneland, he called the Lexington, Kentucky racetrack's president, Bill Greeley – someone he did not know. Mostly, the call was ignored since Greeley explained that the partnership had no plans for immediate changes. However, one month later, his phone call was returned, and Bob Elliston was named president and CEO of Turfway Park. Elliston would later serve as executive chair of the National Thoroughbred Racing Association Board of Directors and treasurer of the Kentucky Equine Education Project (KEEP) Board. He also served with the Thoroughbred Racing Association.

One immediate move by Elliston was registering as a lobbyist for the Kentucky General Assembly before its January 2000 session.   Elliston, like Carroll, was tremendously concerned with various track-related regulatory issues.   He also shared Carroll's passion for expanding legalized gambling in the state. And like Carroll, Elliston took that obsession to state offices dozens of times during his tenure at Turfway Park.

However, Bob Elliston's foremost objective at the time was planning for the 1999 Spiral Stakes. Jim Beam had pulled their corporate sponsorship, but luckily a home furnishing company based in Texas stepped in to back the track's premiere event. With that, Elliston convinced Turfway's new owners to spend some money, and they started early. For the "GalleryFurniture.com Spiral Stakes," Turfway's campaign began on Super Bowl Sunday. The track had never advertised on Super Bowl Sunday before and had never run ads so early for the late March event. More advertising came during the University of Kentucky basketball games. Finally, Turfway teamed with the Kentucky Lottery. For several weeks, ticket machines spewed random coupons for free admission, programs, or parking. The unusual and extreme push in advertising was directly connected to the event's new sponsor. The furniture company's name, logo, and website address appeared on every piece of literature and every billboard. The purse for the event was raised to a whopping $750,000, and attendance was higher than ever.

In the "GalleryFurniture.com Spiral Stakes," the over-hyped Bob Baffert-trained *Straight Man* broke from the rail post, expecting to cruise to the front and never look back. He assumed the lead from the gate under jockey David Flores but began to fade in the third quarter. *K One King* was also thought to be a true contender in the event, and he would have been the first Turfway-stabled Thoroughbred to win the big race. No horse housed at Turfway throughout a winter/spring meet had won the Spiral. *The Groom is Red* was another firm favorite. But the 1999 Spiral was won by *Stephen Got Even*, ridden by Shane Sellers, trained by Nicholas P. Zito, and owned by Stephen Hilbert. Breaking from post eight, the colt circled the field on the far turn and pulled away in the stretch. However, *Stephen Got Even* had a far-from-impressive remainder of the year. He finished in fourteenth place in the Kentucky Derby, then ran fourth in the Preakness Stakes and fifth in the Belmont Stakes, losing both races to that year's Kentucky Derby-winner *Charismatic*. The 1999 event was a success, and Turfway's reputation as a prime Derby-prep race continued.

However, Gallery Furniture owner Jim McIngvale announced in August 1999 that he would not sponsor the popular Spiral Stakes in 2000. "We just didn't sell enough furniture," he told reporters.[1] For some long-time Turfway team members, it was no big loss. "There were signs posted all over the place with Gallery Furniture's logo, but none for Turfway Park. They made us use different paddock vests and saddle towels with large logos – there was hardly room for the horses' names." Another team member stated, "It was like one big circus, and Turfway Park was lost in it all."[2] With McIngvale, it was all about his furniture company and not about the race.

Again, with corporate sponsorship gone, the future of Turfway Park's feature race – and the track itself – was in jeopardy. As a direct result of the furniture company pulling out, the track cut racing dates during their January, February, and March meeting for the first time. While Turfway Park management worked diligently to find a new corporate sponsor for their premiere event, it never happened. The Spiral Stakes at Turfway Park had no corporate backing for the following three years. Incredibly, it still held a purse of $600,000 for 2000 and 2001. In 2002, however, it dropped to $500,000.

Elliston and his team spent more than $100,000 on renovations and upgrades in late 1999. Believing more people might be attracted to horse racing if the facility looked prettier, track officials began mapping out islands of greenspace to be planted in what was asphalt. Workers arranged roses and landscapers mulch, caterers set up grills, and window washers cleaned the glass on the track side of the grandstands. They also proposed to bring horse racing closer to the fans. They did that literally by removing a sand and rock path near the track's rail. For the first time, spectators could walk right up to the rail to watch the races. It is believed that nowhere else in the United States could the fans stand so close to the action at a Thoroughbred racetrack. A new $1 million roof was also installed.[3]

For the 2000 Spiral Stakes, admission to the grandstands was $10.00, with free parking. Tickets to the VIP tent were $150.00 each. Track management aimed to attract new and younger fans to the Spiral in 2000. One new event was a morning breakfast named "Sunrise at the Spiral," where kids could meet jockeys, try on their silks, and take pony rides. A magician plied his trade in the VIP tent. Giveaways included a $6,000 diamond necklace, baseballs autographed by Ken Griffey, Jr., trips to Harrah's in Las Vegas, and a 2000 Chevrolet Blazer. In addition, *Cigar*, the all-time richest Thoroughbred and two-time Horse of the Year winner, was paraded around the grounds for fans to meet.[4] The race was won by *Globalize*, the second Spiral winner for trainer Jerry Hollendorfer. Francisco C. Torres was the rider. Early predictions for the 2000 event saw *Archer City Slew*, winner of the San Vincente Stakes at Santa Anita, as the favorite. However, *Globalize* easily proved to be the better horse. *Globalize* was unable to spiral toward the Kentucky Derby, however. Not long after the victory at Turfway Park, trainer Hollendorfer stated that his horse required four or five stitches for a leg injury and would miss two weeks of training.

September 2000 brought the Kentucky Cup Day of Champions. The *Cincinnati Enquirer* reported that four of the six horses in the $500,000 Kentucky Cup Classic were established winners of Grade I stakes races. Among the favorites were *Sir Bear*, *Golden Missile*, and *Rize* (pronounced Rizzy). At the finish line, however, it was *Captain Steve* nearly one length ahead of *Golden Missile*. In the $150,000 Kentucky Cup Sprint (Grade II), *Caller One*, *Personal First*, and *Millencolin* received the most wagers. *Caller One* beat the rest of the field by nearly five lengths. Day-long music festivities were also a big draw during the event. In fact, country music legend Travis Tritt was the weekend's headliner.

Balto Star

After a ten-year hiatus, the Spiral Festival was back in 2001. The festival started 30 years earlier to highlight the spring racing schedule of what was then called Latonia Race Track. Turfway management canceled the event in 1991, however, believing it had grown unwieldy and required too many people to handle all of the events. By 1999, the festival had stretched nearly two weeks before the main event in March. In 2001, Ted Bushelman, communications director at the Cincinnati-Northern Kentucky International Airport and chairman of the last Spring Festival in 1991, teamed with Turfway president Bob Elliston to revive the event. The new Spring Festival began with a 5K run, followed by a luncheon, a benefit for the Horsemen's Benevolent and Protective Association, and a crawfish boil.

In 2001, only one winner of Turfway's biggest race had won the Kentucky Derby (*Lil E. Tee* in 1992). However, *Balto Star's* performances in early 2001 proved him to be a legitimate contender to become the second. At Turfway Park for the 2001 Spiral Stakes, *Balto Star*, ridden by Mark Guidry and trained by Todd Pletcher, stood proudly in the winner's circle after beating the rest of the field by nearly 13 lengths. After going winless in three starts as a two-year-old, after being gelded and almost offered in a claiming race in December 1999, *Balto Star* suddenly flashed blistering speed in gaining three consecutive wire-to-wire victories, including the Spiral. As for the Kentucky Derby, Turfway's president and CEO, Bob Elliston, was highly emotional about the possibility of a *Balto Star* win, knowing it would be a great selling point for a new corporate sponsor. However, he finished a disappointing fourteenth in the Louisville race. Pletcher would go on to win the Eclipse Award seven times as Trainer of the Year, four of those in consecutive years. His horses *Super Saver* (2010) and *Always Dreaming* (2017) won the Kentucky Derby.

Balto Star was the fourth straight Triple Crown-ready Thoroughbred to emerge from Turfway Park's signature Derby-prep race. As previously noted, *Event of the Year* (which likely would have been the favorite in 1998) and *Globalize* (2000) were Spiral entries at Turfway Park but were injured while working out during Derby week. And *Stephen Got Even*, who won the Galleryfurniture.com Stakes in 1999, went off in the Derby as the solid second choice in betting but finished a miserable fourteenth at the finish line that year.

Under new ownership since March, Turfway Park increased attendance slightly in 2001, but it was still struggling to stay afloat. "We're very encouraged by what we see," said Turfway President and CEO Bob Elliston.[5]

However, a headline in September 2001 summed up well the track's situation: "Turfway Park's Future May Be Bleak." The lengthy, three-quarter page article stated: "Turfway Park opens the 23-day Fall Meet at a crossroads, its livelihood threatened by blistering competition from riverboat casinos, aggressive moves by racetracks in other states, and state taxes much higher than other businesses pay." The amount of money bet at the track dropped by 43 percent since 1996, when the first of three riverboat casinos opened on the Ohio River in southeastern Indiana. Other racetracks, including Churchill Downs, also saw wagering and attendance fall since the casinos opened. Because less money was being spent at the racetrack, Turfway management cut $150,000 from the purses for the Kentucky Cup Day of Champions, one of the track's biggest racing days.

A coalition was formed in September 2001, including Turfway, Keeneland, and Churchill owners, as well as many horse breeders, trainers, and owners, to seek help from Kentucky lawmakers regarding tax relief. Taxes paid in 2000 by the Kentucky racing industry totaled $25.5 million. California, Florida, and Illinois were being assisted with tax breaks to better compete with the growing casino businesses. As a comparison, $614 million was wagered on horse racing in all of Kentucky, while at Indiana's handful of riverboat casinos, a whopping $23 billion was spent.[6]

Turfway management continued to think of new ways to attract more patrons. Special incentives were given to higher-spending customers through targeted marketing, utilizing a "Fast Track" ATM-like rewards card. The track spent more than $2.5 million on improvements for customers, horse owners, and trainers, including renovations and new construction on the track's backside, where the horses are kept and cared for. Special days geared toward families were also scheduled. One remarkable draw was the unforeseen supremacy of female jockeys.

Females Dominate

In a sport still dominated by men, a strange phenomenon occurred for a stretch in the late 1990s and early 2000s. Female jockeys were leading the pack at Turfway Park. Although outnumbered 3-1 by male riders, the girls won nearly 40 percent of the races in the Winter 2000 Meet. Turfway's female riders were photographed for *Sports Illustrated for Women*, featured on ESPN, and interviewed for USA Today. In February 2000, Turfway management capitalized on the success of the girl jockeys by promoting a unique Valentine's Day "Girl's Night Out," featuring free admission for ladies and one race featuring only female riders. It was a huge success. Three local television stations even showed up to cover the event.

The colony of skillful females included Jennifer Bramblett, Rhonda Collins, Patricia Cooksey, and Greta Kuntzweiler. As for the top female rider, Kris Prather was the runaway leader in 2001. The 21-year-old apprentice jockey even topped the nation in February 2001 with 59 victories, nine ahead of veteran Jorge Chavez, who was riding primarily at Florida's Gulfstream Park. In an interview with *USA Today*, Prather credited Hall

Courtesy: www.femalejockeys.com

At right: Jockey Kris Prather.

Turfway Park continues to celebrate the success of female riders. Below: Mike Battaglia is pictured with a female jockey colony circa 2018 . Left to right: Beth Butler, Jodi Fortner, Jennifer Bramlett, P.J. Cooksey, and Kris Prather.

Courtesy: Jim Claypool Collection

of Fame riders Julie Krone and Donna Barton Brothers for her fast and success-ful development.[7] On February 11, Kris Prather set a new track record with six wins on one card.[8] And in March, still leading the nation with overall victories, Prather achieved a new Turfway Park record with 85 wins during one meet.

Lane's End Farm

To protect daily purses and reward horsemen that had remained loy-al, Turfway Park management lowered the Spiral Stakes purse in 2002 to $500,000. Lane's End Farm in Versailles, Kentucky, one of the world's lead-ing Thoroughbred breeding and sales operations, stepped in to sponsor the race from 2002 to 2010.[9] Top-rated Thoroughbreds for the feature race included *Benny the Hawk*, *Gold Dollar*, *Holdthehelm*, *My Man Ryan*, *Perfect Drift*, and *Straight Gin*. At the finish line, it was *Perfect Drift* who crossed a neck in front of *Azillion*, who was closely followed by the favorite, *Request for Pa-role*. Edie Delahoussaye had the mount in the Grade II event. Murray John-son was the trainer, and Stonecrest Farm was the owner. Kentucky Lt. Gov-ernor Steve Henry, U.S. Senator Jim Bunning, and U.S. Representative Ken Lucas, a Boone County native, were among the more than 19,000 who attended.

Since its inaugural run in 1994, the Kentucky Cup Day of Champions welcomed some of the best Thoroughbreds, trainers, and jockeys assembled at any racetrack in the nation. Suspended and reintroduced several times over the track's long history, it was brought back in high fashion in 2002. Bob Elliston's comment to reporters the day before the event proved true, "The nation's eyes will be on Turfway Park."[10] World-renowned trainer Bob Baffert ran five horses that day, and future Triple Crown-winning jockey Victor Espinoza had a mount in the fea-ture race. Other top-rated trainers included D. Wayne Lukas, Shug McGaughey, Kiaran McLaughlin, and Nick Zito. Hall of Fame jockey Pat Day was aboard *Dollar Bill*, and Espinoza, who rode *War Emblem* to victories in the Kentucky Derby and Preakness earlier in the year, rode *Nothing Flat* in the $400,000 feature race. At the finish line, however, it was *Pure Prize* ahead of the field. Trained by Shug McGaughey and ridden by Mike Smith, *Pure Prize* bested *Dollar Bill* by nearly a length. As additional entertainment for the fans, *Crowned King*, who unseated his jockey at the gate, continued riderless within the rest of the pack.

The 2003 $500,000 Grade II Lane's End Spiral Stakes marked a significant Twentieth anniversary. In 1983, a talented gray colt named *Marfa* put Latonia on the map, beating 11 rivals by eight lengths in the first Spiral. The 2003 event's favorites included *Champali*, who had won six of seven starts, including Turfway's WEBN Stakes and the John Battaglia Memorial Stakes. *Lion Tamer* was another graded stakes winner to compete. Other favorites included *Saintly Look* and *Eugene's Third Son*, whose most significant victory was a 1-1/2-mile allowance race but whom Pat Day chose to ride over *Champali*. However, it was the long-shot *New York Hero* standing in the winner's circle at the end of the race. Ridden by Noberto Arroyo, Jr. and trained by Jennifer Pedersen, the horse came from the Paraneck Stable and edged out *Eugene's Third Son*.

On-track wagering during Turfway's entire Spring Meet increased four percent over the 2003 Winter/Spring Meet. Total wagering, including bets on Turfway races at other tracks, jumped twenty percent to $138 million. However, the wagering at Turfway Park and nearby River Downs

"And...they're off!" in the 2003 Lane's End Spiral Stakes at Turfway Park

was dwarfed by the mountains of money bet at nearby Argosy, Grand Victoria, and Belterra riverboat casinos in Indiana. Those three casinos raked in a staggering $9.3 billion, while Turfway's revenue was $351 million.

Overall, 2003 was a challenging year for racing at Turfway Park. Bad weather conditions, always a problem for the all-winter meets, were particularly hard that year, with 15 days of cancellations. However, several records fell despite the difficult conditions. First, Mary Doser became the 14th female jockey in the nation to win 1,000 races. Secondly, Rodney Prescott, a long-time Turfway regular, earned his 1,000[th] career victory. And third, Billy Troilo captured his 2,000[th] career victory during the meet.

While the Latonia Race Track/Turfway Park property hosted many movie production crews over its long history, President Bob Elliston was likely not ready for an announcement one morning in early 2003. Chip Bach, Director of Security, recalled, *"America's Most Wanted* is on-site filming today, I nonchalantly told Bob Elliston." The top-rated weekly television program offered details on unsolved crimes asking for the public's help. Hundreds of crimes had been solved in the show's 30-plus year run. At any rate, film crews arrived at Turfway Park to film a segment very close to the local horsemen.

Husband and wife horse trainers Barbara and Roger Dale Holbrook were married for about 10 years and had recently divorced. A delivery man stopping at the Holbrook house in nearby Dearborn County, Indiana found the body of Barbara, who had been shot to death. The shooting occurred a day before a court hearing on Barbara's request for a protective order against her ex-husband, whom she accused of making threats. Barbara had been suspended earlier in the year by the Kentucky Racing Commission after syringes full of illegal performance-enhancing drugs were found in her stables at Turfway Park. Police said she suspected her ex-husband of planting the drugs. He became the immediate prime suspect when he could not be located for questioning. On the run for nearly six months, Indiana authorities decided to profile the case on television. The show aired on May 17, 2003, and Roger Dale Holbrook was captured within hours.

In the continuing effort to lure younger fans to the racetrack, Turfway Park President Bob Elliston initiated the "Friday Night, Dollar Beer, Dollar Hot Dogs" promotion for the Fall Meet in 2003. Elliston told the *Cincinnati Post* newspaper, "We're going to darn near give away beer." The first Friday night of the meet saw a massive increase in attendance, most of whom were in their 20s and 30s. Management also unveiled an outdoor, beach-themed cantina on the apron not far from the finish line. The beer garden featured a variety of grilled meats, live music, and games.[11] The Friday night beer and hot dogs events continued until the track was temporarily closed in 2010. While the promotion brought in a lot of people, primarily drinkers, there were very few new horseplayers.

At a gambling conference in West Virginia in November 2003, Turfway Park President Bob Elliston once again told his audience that Turfway Park could not survive without some form of casino-style gambling. The Kentucky horse racing industry confronted the General Assembly asking that the controversial issue be placed on the November 2004 ballot as a constitutional amendment, allowing the state's voters to decide. Elliston said, "The resolution would have to pass both houses of the legislature by a 'super majority' – 60 votes in the House and 22 in the Senate. Then it would become a ballot question, asking voters whether they favor amending Kentucky's Constitution to allow expanded gambling at racetracks." Elliston, who served as the industry's spokesperson in Frankfort in 2002 and 2003, said he believed the public supported slots. "Racinos," the marriage of casino gambling and horse racing tracks – was one of gambling's fastest-growing and most controversial businesses at the time. States such as Delaware and West Virginia had approved slots legislation. The result: hefty purse increases and expanded entertainment venues. At West Virginia's Mountaineer, the racetrack was flanked by a sprawling hotel with vistas of the Ohio River and a gourmet restaurant. Elliston was confident that the same could happen at Turfway Park.

Michael Rowland

Like one unfortunate race day in 1915 at the Old Latonia Race Track, a single race during the Winter Meet of 2004 proved equally heart-wrenching at Turfway Park. Sadly, mishaps and thrown jockeys occur from time to time in horse racing and, more often than some might think, they prove deadly. It had been nearly 60 years since a jockey was killed on a Kentucky racetrack (Jorge Alfonso – August 17, 1944 – Dade Park), but 2004 ended that long streak.

Jockey Michael Rowland was on his way to another victory on February 4, 2004. He raced primarily at Thistledown track near Cleveland and, in 2004, was the all-time leading rider there with 29 titles. During their off-season, he ran at Turfway. His wife, Tammy, also trained horses at the Florence facility. Rowland was just two wins shy of the 4,000-career-win milestone on that day. Track officials knew the win would come that night or maybe the next. In fact, a sign had already been made and was ready to be waved when he achieved the feat reached by only a few dozen other riders.

Before the first race on the card, the jockeys likely thought they were invincible. However, statistics show otherwise. There are more than 3,000 registered jockeys in the United States, and according to Jockey's Guild figures, there has been an average of two deaths and 2,500 injuries each year since 1960. Horse racing is a hazardous sport, far more dangerous than football, hockey, motocross, or even auto racing. The riders know the odds but race anyway – simply because of their love and passion for the sport.

In the third race, on his first mount of the night, Rowland rode *Distinctive Blues*, a horse owned (in partnership) and trained by his wife, Tammy. However, *Distinctive Blues* finished ninth, and Rowland had to wait for another try at his 4,000[th] win. In the seventh race on the card, a $17,000 claiming race for 4-year-olds and up, Rowland mounted the more-competitive *World Trade*. Passing the three-furlong pole, Rowland was in the lead, but in an instant, disaster struck. *World Trade* suffered a fractured foreleg and collapsed, throwing Rowland to the track. Two other 1,500-pound Thoroughbreds, *Joanies No Phony* with Jessica Endres aboard, and *Miner Moss* with Mark Johnston in the irons, could not avoid a collision. Mark Johnston suffered a fractured collarbone, and Jessica Endres received cuts and bruises in the three-horse pileup.

Immediately, the other jockeys knew it was catastrophic. Some returned to the jockey's room and waited. Others ran out to the fallen rider. Michael's wife, Tammy, was among the thousands who witnessed the horrific event and stood in near silence with all eyes on the scene. Rowland was conscious, even arguing with the track EMTs that he did not want to be strapped to a backboard. Medics could see in an instant how severe his injuries were, and Florence EMTs were called to the scene. AirCare was then summoned; however, it was decided that

Michael Rowland

he could not be flown due to his specific injuries. He was taken to University Hospital by ambulance. On the way, he lost consciousness and stopped breathing. He was placed on a ventilator and, at the hospital, underwent immediate surgery.

No more races were run that night, and racing was canceled the following night out of concern for Rowland's condition. Fellow rider Bill Troilo told reporters that nearly 40 jockeys, horsemen, and racing officials had gone to the hospital. Bill's mount, *Lite Saver*, was scratched just before the race. "It could have been me," he recalls.[12] Billy's wife, Mary, said, "I remember that spill like it was yesterday. I made the call to one of his close friends in Cleveland. He said, 'How bad is it?' I replied, 'Start driving now, and you need to be here before morning. It was a horrible feeling; so thankful that it wasn't my husband… and immediately feeling guilty for feeling that way with Tammy in so much pain."[13]

Chip Bach was among the many who remained with Michael's wife in the emergency room that night. Doctors eventually came to inform Tammy that her husband had suffered devastating head trauma in the accident and would not recover. It was decided to keep him on life support until the entire family could be at his bedside. Four days later, having never regained consciousness, Michael Rowland was taken off life support and died in the arms of his wife during the early morning hours on February 9, with his 15-year-old daughter, Farren, at his bedside. He is survived by two other daughters, Sara and Randi.

Racing eventually continued at Turfway Park, and in March 2004, Jockey Rafael Bejarano achieved a new track record. After twice tying the Turfway Park record for most wins on one card with six, the 21-year-old Peruvian won seven of Turfway's 12 races on Friday, March

Courtesy: Horseracing News

Rafael Bejarano

12, 2004. Bejarano led all jockeys nationwide at the time with 116 victories, including the $50,000 Tejano Stakes aboard the Bernie Flint-trained *Ask the Lord*.

The threat of rain prompted Turfway officials to pound the track flat before the 2004 running of the Lane's End Spiral Stakes, but the smooth surface did not slow *Sinister G*, who won the $500,000 Derby prep race. Ridden by Paul R. Toscano and trained by John T. Toscano, Jr., *Sinister G* finished the race under gray, but dry skies before a drenching rain began, sending crowds indoors for the remainder of the card. Democrat Nick Clooney and Republican Geoff Davis, who were running against each other for Congress, exchanged pleasantries near the entrance of the VIP tent and were among the nearly 1,000 fans gathered there. *Smarty Jones*, *The Cliff's Edge*, and *Birdstone* were other highly-rated entries.

When Turfway Park officials published the schedule for the 2004 Fall Meet, it was announced that an annual Michael Rowland Award would be presented. Bob Elliston told reporters, "Everybody who knew Mike knew his upbeat attitude. He was at so many tracks in the Midwest that we got together with them on this. We must ensure his legacy continues; his unique attitude is remembered."[14] Jockeys at the five tracks where Rowland competed submitted nominees for the award, with the winner determined from balloting by jockeys from nine midwestern tracks. Nominees for the first annual award were: Luis Antonio Gonzalez (Thistledown), Ivan Gonzalez (Beulah Park), Perry Ouzts (Turfway Park), DeShawn Parker (Mountaineer), and J.J. Sunseri (River Downs). The inaugural award went to Luis Antonio Gonzalez. The award was later discontinued.

When the 2005 Lane's End Spiral Stakes approached, Bob Elliston was interviewed for the *Cincinnati Enquirer*. His statement was extremely simple but profound – and accurate. "Horses can take a lot of different paths to the Kentucky Derby," he said. "So many of them stay in warmer climates like Florida and California, but many have punched their ticket for success right here at Turfway Park." Since 1982, only one horse had entered Turfway's premiere race and gone on to win the Kentucky Derby (*Lil E. Tee* in 1992). Nine horses had finished in the money in the big race, the most recent being *Perfect Drift,* who captured a third-place finish in 2002.

At this point, the Spiral Stakes at Turfway Park had become a springtime tradition. Back in 1971, the first event drew a crowd not much larger than a typical Saturday racing card and featured a far-from-impressive line-up of Thoroughbreds. However, over the next 30 years, the Spiral Stakes at Turfway Park became one of the region's most important sporting events. It had also become largely about pageantry. A reported crowd of more than 22,000 attended the 2005 edition, and patrons arrived to find valet parking and a red-carpet-lined entrance to the enormous VIP tent. There, tickets were $150 each, and food and drinks were aplenty. Nearly 1,000 guests enjoyed a prime-rib buffet and open bar. Ladies arrived with colorful and extravagant hats which rivaled the best headdresses at the Kentucky Derby. Some women showed off their fashionable hair extensions. Men sported bow ties, neatly pressed and starched shirts, and shoes shined to a high gloss on which you could see your reflection. They modeled the snazziest haircuts and, if you looked closely enough, a hairpiece or two. Triple Crown winner Steve Cauthen was in attendance. "I don't know if I've ever seen it so crowded," he said. "It's like a rite of spring, and on a day like today, I'm a fan."[15] Mary Troilo said, "Wow! The stars that came in, the centerpieces that were always handmade, the concert. Everyone wanted to be at the races. The whole community treated the Spiral like it was the Kentucky Derby."[16]

In the grandstands, there was reserved seating on most levels and general admission in the bleachers. Lines at the tellers' windows mimicked those at the most popular rollercoasters at Disney World. Live bands blared music on the second-floor stage and in the VIP tent. Outside amidst the mildly-cold weather conditions, thousands of people gathered in both the paddock and apron, each offering their "tips" on each race to anyone who would listen. Novice bettors chose their favorite Thoroughbred, many simply by the color of their silks. Some chose the horse with the catchiest name, others by the rider's name. Either way, they just **knew** they had the winner.

Back in the VIP tent, it was all about seeing who was in attendance as well as "being seen." Everyone there became high-society celebrities… at least for a few hours. People clustered in groups chatting and laughing, paying little attention to the races and more attention to who else was there. Maker's Mark bourbon flowed heavily, and wax-topping tables were provided for the free Spiral souvenir glasses. Over the years, tables were decorated with everything from hand-fashioned centerpieces to tastefully-arranged flowers. The centerpieces were traditionally auctioned off for charity at the end of the grandiose affair. Later, the beautiful flower arrangements were gathered and taken home by people from each respective table.

Flower Alley won the main event in 2005, the Grade II Lane's End Spiral Stakes. Ridden by Jorge F. Chavez, the win brought trainer Todd Pletcher back into the winner's circle for the second time in five years. It would not be his last visit there. *Flower Alley*, a chestnut horse, has a small white star on his forehead and a small white sock on his back right leg. He is best known as the sire of the 2012 Kentucky Derby and Preakness winner, *I'll Have Another*.

Once again, the Northern Kentucky racetrack attracted Hollywood producers when, in 2005, it was the fictional setting for the PG-rated adventure/comedy *Racing Stripes*. The film tells the story of a young circus zebra accidentally abandoned near a Thoroughbred farm in Kentucky. Taken in by the 13-year-old daughter of the farm owner, he trains and competes as a racehorse. The movie stars Hayden Panettiere and Bruce Greenwood, with voice actors including Snoop Dogg,

Jeff Foxworthy, Whoppi Goldberg, Dustin Hoffman, and Frankie Muniz. However, no filming took place at Turfway Park; the track was mentioned in name only.[17]

Turfway's premiere event was more like the Kentucky Derby than ever in 2006. To many fans in attendance, it was all about the experience rather than the race itself. "You see people from all walks of life here," Bob Elliston stated. "You have folks on the apron in shorts and blue jeans, and on the other end of the spectrum in the Maker's Mark VIP tent, you've got ladies dressed to the nines and men in brightly colored sportscoats. You couple that with lavish food and an open bar – all that together creates the atmosphere making Turfway Park such a fun place to be, even if you've never been to a race."[18]

With A City won the main event in 2006, with Brice Blanc aboard. The trainer was Michael Maker, who learned the business from his father and then went out on his own in 1991. In 1993, he worked as an assistant to famed trainer D. Wayne Lucas before venturing on his own again in 2003. *With a City* would have 13 starts through 2005/2006, with four wins, zero seconds, and two thirds.

In 2006, Turfway Park stepped up financially to assist a struggling charity for disabled jockeys. The Permanently Disabled Jockeys Fund (PDJF) was established by horsemen's associations, riders, and the National Thoroughbred Racing Association to supplement payments, like social security, to disabled riders. Turfway Park President Bob Elliston announced that Turfway Park would donate $10,000 to the fund and that additional payments would be made on an ongoing basis. In 2023, Turfway Park will continue to support this worthy charity.

The 2007 Lane's End Spiral Stakes was billed as "The biggest party of the year in Northern Kentucky" by local sportswriters.[19] In the football field-sized VIP tent, where tickets cost $175, the well-heeled, well-dressed, and well-known mingled with serious racing fans, serious partiers, and those simply wanting to be seen. Favorites included *Forefathers*, *Starbase*, *Sports Town*, and *Bullara*. The only graded-stakes winner in the field of 12 was *Hard Spun*, who crossed the finish line first. Mario G. Pino was in the irons, and J. Larry Jones was the winning trainer. *Hard Spun* placed second in the Kentucky Derby, third in the Preakness, and fourth in the Belmont that year.

The Fall Meet in 2007 included 22 racing days and featured the fifteenth running of the Kentucky Cup Day of Champions. That 12-race card included the Grade II $350,000 Kentucky Cup Classic, a prep for the Breeder's Cup World of Champions.[20] *Hard Spun* returned to Turfway Park for the Classic, achieving a first-place finish, beating the Kentucky Derby winner *Street Sense*, and becoming the first horse in Turfway history to sweep the track's premiere races.

In 2008, the Lane's End was won by *Adriano*, ridden by future Hall of Fame jockey Edgar S. Prado, and trained by H. Graham Motion, who would later find fame for his work with *Better Talk Now* and the 2011 Kentucky Derby winner *Animal Kingdom*. A crowd of more than 20,000 attended the event, even though the temperature at post-time was 35 degrees. Fans in the VIP tent included baseball Hall of Famer Johnny Bench and U.S. Senator Jim Bunning. Turfway's food and beverage department prepared 1,500 pounds of prime rib, 600 pounds of chicken, and 350 pounds of lobster ravioli for the VIP guests.

Turfway Park Spirals Downward

By 2009, the on-track handle at Turfway was down an incredible sixteen percent. Economic conditions were a big part of the double-digit decline, as the unemployment rate in Northern Kentucky hovered around ten percent, nearly twice the year before. Wagering on Turfway races from all sources dropped over six percent to $39,928,281, compared to almost $46 million the year before. To help support the horsemen, Turfway eliminated four stakes and cut the purses of the Kentucky Cup Classic from $350,000 to $200,000. "It's disappointing to cut stakes from your schedule," Elliston told reporters. "But in the current climate, it was necessary to support our horsemen, who are here day in and day out. We appreciate their willingness to work with us as we get through a difficult time."[21]

Good news arrived the same year, however, when the Horseplayers Association of North America introduced a rating system for 65 Thoroughbred racetracks in North America. At that time, Turfway Park was rated as number ten. The track remained in the top 20 throughout the 2010s. Regarding track leaders that year, 18 wins were posted by Billy Hays from 59 starts, the most by any owner. Ken and Sarah Ramsey, Kentucky's perennial leading owners, finished second with 12. The top jockey for the year was Leandro Goncalves, with 33 wins from 157 mounts.[22]

In 2009, jockey Kent J. Desormeaux rode *Hold Me Back* to victory in the Lane's End Spiral Stakes. Kent holds the record for most wins in a single year, with 598 back in 1989. He became a three-time winner of both the Kentucky Derby and the Preakness. Aboard *Real Quiet*, he lost the 1998 Triple Crown by a nose. *Hold Me Back* was trained by William Mott, who is most notable for his work with *Cigar*, whose early career was mediocre at best. Once under Mott's guidance, however, *Cigar* won all ten major races he entered and was named 1995 Champion Older Male and received the Eclipse Award.

In June 2009, it was announced that, once again, a bill to legalize Vegas-style gambling in Kentucky failed. As the *Cincinnati Enquirer* put it, "Monday's demise of a casino gambling bill will have deep ramifications across Greater Cincinnati and Northern Kentucky."[23] The article stated that Northern Kentucky would lose an estimated $100 million in spending on public school construction and higher education projects. More importantly, it was noted that Turfway Park would be forced to close by 2011. Track President Bob Elliston said, "With Ohio considering allowing River Downs in Anderson Township and other racetracks to operate casinos, the Florence Thoroughbred track would be closed by the end of next year. Other racetracks will have a competitive advantage over us. We can probably make it through the rest of this year and 2010, but after December 31, 2010, I don't see a future for Turfway Park."

August 2009 marked the 50th year of Turfway Park, going back to 1959 when New Latonia opened its doors. From August 3 to September 25, historic photos were on display at the Boone County Public Library, including aerial shots of the property when it was nothing but farmland. At the racetrack, commemorative glasses were distributed to patrons during the Fall Meet. Highlights of the small, Northern Kentucky racetrack were featured over several weeks in local newspapers, and "innovations" was the keyword. Turfway Park pioneered the use of several "now-standards" in the industry. "I think that's a source of pride for many people who have worked here," said Elliston. "Turfway Park, a good, blue-collar, hard-working racetrack, doesn't wait for somebody else to become the leader."[24] One would expect these innovations from the top in the industry, like Aqueduct, Belmont, Pimlico, Santa Anita – but they came from tiny Turfway Park. In 1982, Turfway became the first track to offer simulcast racing, broadcasting the Marlboro Cup from Belmont Park in New York. Turfway brought inter-track wagering to fans in 1988 by airing its card to Ellis Park in Henderson, Kentucky. In 1994, then-owner Jerry Carroll opened the Racebook, a state-of-the-art simulcast facility. In 2005, Turfway became the first track in North America to install Polytrack, the all-weather and safer racing surface. Turfway's predecessor, Old Latonia, introduced the $2 bet in 1911, and "New" Latonia brought trifecta and superfecta wagering, which helped make the sport of horse racing affordable and promoted its growth nationwide. Old Latonia also broke new ground with pari-mutuel betting machines and protective gear for jockeys.

In September 2009, track management announced they cut four stakes races from its 22-day fall meet. In addition, the purse for the Sixteenth Kentucky Cup Classic dropped from $350,000 to $200,000. The $500,000 saved was spent on daily purses. "Kentucky has got to step up and do something if we're going to maintain that title of "Horse Capital of the World," said Kentucky Governor Steve Beshear. "I'm very concerned about the future of our tracks in Kentucky, particularly the smaller ones. We don't have a level playing field."[25] Like other governors, however, those were idle words. Beshear, as well as the Genearl assembly, did nothing to help the dire situation.

More and more horsemen were being drawn away from Kentucky to tracks in neighboring states that offered purses fattened by casino-style gaming proceeds. The exodus of horses to Indiana, Pennsylvania, and West Virginia caused a drop in field sizes at Kentucky tracks, which drove away bettors and, ultimately, each track's revenue. Turfway Park saw double-digit declines in handle and average daily purses during its winter/spring meet earlier in the year. Jockey Billy Troilo recalls, "As a rider, I didn't have much interaction with Bob Elliston, but I know he used to get extremely mad when the track was in bad shape and the jockeys refused to ride."[26]

When 2009 ended, figures were again tallied regarding Turfway profitability. Unfortunately, the numbers were comparable to those in recent years. On-track handle was down seventeen percent over the same meet in 2008. All-sources handle, reflecting all wagers made on Turfway races, including bets made at other locations, rose only six-tenths of one percent higher than the same period in the previous year. The Kentucky Horse Racing Commission approved a reduction of 81 live-racing dates at the Florence racetrack. Turfway Park management had asked the Commission to eliminate race dates to continue offering competitive racing experiences for patrons and horsemen on non-stakes days. Cutting the number of live dates helped to ensure larger fields and competitive purses, despite the decrease in the on-track handle.[27]

The 2010 Lane's End Spiral saw *Dean's Kitten* and jockey Cornelio Velasquez standing in the winner's circle. Velasquez was a multiple Breeders' Cup winner and finished second in the 2005 Kentucky Derby. Michael Maker was the trainer; his second Spiral win. The first Spiral win for owners Kenneth and Sarah Ramsey came in 2010. The Ramseys would go on to grab multiple graded stakes races, three Breeder's Cup wins, and several Eclipse Awards for outstanding owner and breeder. Their 1,200-acre farm is located in Nicholasville, Kentucky.

Sarah "Kitten" and Ken Ramsey

Upsetting to the sport of Thoroughbred racing, Sarah "Kitten" Ramsey died in 2022.

In mid-2010, Elliston announced the cancelation of all Wednesday night racing and all but one stakes race from its fall meet. This move, he stated, was necessary to keep Turfway's daily purses at the previous year's already depressed levels. The entire Kentucky Cup Day of Champions, which had produced the winners of seven Breeder's Cup races, was among the latest casualties. The Kentucky Cup had been reduced to three stakes in 2009, the Grade II Classic, Grade III Distaff, and Grade III Sprint. But this was even more devastating to employee morale. Still, Turfway Park team members remained strong and dedicated. Mary Jo Schmiade recalls one winter morning during that time. "In between mutuel department managers, I was asked to fill in. I awoke to several inches of snow and thought for sure we would have to cancel... not having any workers. I started calling tellers, just to see if we would have **anybody** show up. I first called Richard Green, who must have been in his eighties at the time. 'I'm up, warming up the car right now,' was his reply. Then I phoned Ray McPherson, who couldn't have been much younger. 'I just shoveled out the car, I'll be there,' was his answer. Not only did everyone show up, but we had stand-bys who wanted to work. Turfway was that kind of place. You loved it there, and you wanted to be there."[28] Linda Gay, long-time mutuel clerk and, in 2023, Cage Shift Manager at Turfway Park Racing and Gaming, recalls, "One of our regular patrons showed up one morning and asked, 'Where is Linda?' He was told, 'Her car wouldn't start,' and he knew I would miss a day's pay. That man drove from Florence all the way to Hebron to pick me up and take me to work, just so I wouldn't miss out on a day's income. I know it sounds cliché, but we were one big family. We would do anything for one another – employees and patrons alike."[29]

Turfway Park management tried something new to finish out the year. For the first time, they offered a "New Year's Eve Bash." General admission and parking were free, while reservations were available for special seating on the third floor at $100 for a table of six. The Homestretch restaurant on the first floor offered a deluxe buffet for $55 per person. Live music from the band Color Blind, broadcast live on WEBN radio, and a balloon drop at Midnight capped off the affair. It was a huge success and was repeated for several years.

Bob Elliston initiated other promotions and events to attract more people to the Florence, Kentucky racetrack. Incredibly, Turfway Park had become a favorite gathering place for hundreds of young adults due to the Friday night "$1 beer/$1 hotdog" promotions. Free admission, live music, inexpensive brews and food, attracted huge crowds during the live racing meet. However, few new fans were betting on the ponies; they were only there for the party atmosphere and the cheap provisions. The daily handle continued to drop, and purse monies remained stagnant. Still, enough money was made through selling the off-brand beer and dogs to pay most of the track's daily expenses.

Both images courtesy: Dwight "D.A." Brown

Courtesy: Kenton County Public Library

Above: Three wonderful views of Turfway Park in Florence, Kentucky

Chapter Five Endnotes

1. Turfway Park; Key Race Seeks New Sponsor," *Dayton Daily News* (Ohio), August 27, 1999, retrieved on September 22, 2022.

2. Personal interview with two Turfway Park employees who wished to remain anonymous, November 18, 2022.

3. "Turfway Park sprucing up to attract more fans," *Cincinnati Enquirer*, December 2, 1999, retrieved on September 12, 2022.

4. "Turfway adds giveaways, kids' events to gala race," *Cincinnati Enquirer*, March 23, 2000, retrieved on September 12, 2022.

5. "New owners reverse decline at Turfway," *Cincinnati Post*, October 7, 1999, retrieved on September 12, 2022.

6. "Track: Turfway's future may be bleak," *Cincinnati Enquirer*, September 3, 2001, page A1.

7. "Female Jockey Rules at Turfway Park," *USA Today*, February 14, 2001, retrieved on September 12, 2022.

8. "Prather Sets Record," *Cincinnati Post*, February 12, 2001.

9. "Turfway Park," Wikipedia.com, retrieved on September 4, 2022.

10. "Winner of Turfway Park," *Cincinnati Enquirer*, September 14, 2002, retrieved on October 9, 2022.

11. "Turfway going down new track," *Cincinnati Post*, September 12, 2003, retrieved on September 16, 2022.

12. Personal interview with Billy Troilo on November 16, 2022.

13. Personal interview with Mary Troilo on November 16, 2022.

14. "Turfway starts Meet: Adds Rowland Award," *Courier-Journal*, September 8, 2004, retrieved on September 27, 2022.

15. "Lane's End a Kentucky Event," *Cincinnati Enquirer*, March 27, 2005, retrieved on October 10, 2022.

16. Personal interview with Mary Troilo on November 16, 2022.

17. "Turfway Park," Wikipedia.com, retrieved on September 4, 2022.

18. "Day at the Races," *Cincinnati Enquirer*, March 22, 2006, page 78.

19. "Soon… They're Off," *Cincinnati Enquirer*, March 22, 2007, retrieved on October 10, 2022.

20. "Turfway throws up the party tent for Lane's End Stakes," *Cincinnati Enquirer*, March 21, 2008, retrieved on September 13, 2022.

21. "On Track Handel Down 16% at Turfway," *Blood-Horse Magazine*, October 9, 2009, retrieved on August 8, 2022.

22. *Ibid.*

23. "Slots bill dies in Kentucky Senate," *Cincinnati Enquirer*, June 23, 2009, retrieved on September 14, 2022.

24. "Track had been an industry leader," *Cincinnati Enquirer*, September 5, 2009, retrieved on September 14, 2022.

25. "Uncertainty marks Turfway's 50th," *Cincinnati Enquirer*, September 5, 2009, retrieved on September 13, 2022.

26. Personal interview with Billy Troilo on November 16, 2022.

27. "Turfway numbers down at track, up off-site," *Cincinnati Enquirer*, January 6, 2010, retrieved on September 13, 2022.

28. Personal interview with Mary Jo Schmiade on November 20, 2022.

29. Personal interview with Linda Gay on November 20, 2022.

Chapter Six

Animal Kingdom, Historical Racing Machines,
and More Casinos

While Lane's End pulled out from sponsoring Turfway's premiere event in 2011, that year witnessed what was likely the most triumphant race in the Spiral's history. Horse farm giant Vinery Stables picked up the corporate sponsorship in 2011 and 2012, and the race was carded as a Grade III with a purse of $500,000. Jockey Alan Garcia, the leading apprentice rider in Peru in 2003 before coming to the United States, found himself in Turfway Park's winner's circle. H. Graham Motion, born in England, was the trainer. It was Garcia's first graded stakes win.

Decisive Moment took the lead from the gate, with *Positive Response* a neck behind. As they rounded the first turn, *Animal Kingdom* was at the back of the pack. As they headed down the far stretch, *Positive Response*, at 8 to 5, held the lead by a length, with *Son of Posse* (82-1), *Decisive Moment* (6-1), and *Preachtothedevil* (16-1) right behind. In the seventh position was A*nimal Kingdom*, attempting to make a move on the inside. Just before the final turn, *Animal Kingdom*, at 4 to 1, slipped from the inside to the outside of the three leaders, and Garcia proved himself worthy of the mount as he took the lead, entering the home stretch. Through the final furlongs, *Decisive Moment* contended well, giving it all he had. But it was *Animal Kingdom* at the finish to win by two lengths. *Twinspired* rallied for the show position.

Linked with the Spiral win, *Animal Kingdom's* following

Animal Kingdom

success brought even more attention to Turfway Park. At the 2011 Kentucky Derby, *Animal Kingdom* started the day with odds of 30-1. By post time, he was 21-1. He drew post 16 and was ridden by a replacement jockey. John R. Velazquez was initially chosen to ride the early favorite *Uncle Mo*. However, *Uncle Mo* was scratched due to a gastrointestinal illness on the Friday before the race, and Velazquez replaced injured jockey Robby Albarado on *Animal Kingdom*. It was the first time Velazquez rode *Animal Kingdom* and, after 13 tries, it would be his first Kentucky Derby win. In the 2011 Preakness, *Animal Kingdom* closed in from far back in the pack to pass every horse but the winner, *Shackleford*. He finished out of the money in the Belmont due mainly to a bad start on the sloppy track. Still, *Animal Kingdom* was chosen as the American Champion Three-year-old Male in 2011. *Animal Kingdom*, the Spiral's second Kentucky Derby-winning Thoroughbred, is thought to be the most impressive horse to ever race on the Polytrack of Turfway Park.

Bob Elliston was at Churchill Downs for the 2011 Kentucky Derby. Immediately after *Animal Kingdom* crossed the finish line, Elliston began

Courtesy: Augusta Chronicle (Georgia)

Long shot *Animal Kingdom* winning the Kentucky Derby

getting congratulatory phone calls and texts. Elliston believed the three-year-old chestnut colt's win would attract even more top-grade Thoroughbreds to the Florence, Kentucky facility for training. Turfway switched to Polytrack in 2005, and afterward, there was a bias about horses adjusting to dirt for the Derby. Horses had run on Polytrack as two-year-olds and switched to dirt for some Derby prep races, but *Animal Kingdom* became the first to win the Derby on his first start on dirt. "Now that a horse has done it," Elliston said, "the question is if others will follow, especially when next year's Spiral is run."

Historical Racing Machines in Kentucky

In late 2011, there was a hint of optimism at Turfway Park, which came from the far western part of the state. On September 2, Kentucky Downs, a racetrack south of Bowling Green near the Tennessee border, installed historical racing machines (HRMs). The first anywhere in Kentucky, the devices are slot-machine-style wagering machines; they look and perform exactly like a slot machine. However, unlike standard slots (illegal in the state), HRM payouts are based on pari-mutuel-style wagering, which is entirely legal in Kentucky. The machines vary greatly, but all are based on the results of randomized previous horse races. Some devices allow the user to look at the horses' odds and place specific types of wagers. In contrast, most are virtually indistinguishable from standard slot machines, allowing users to push a button every few seconds for each play.

Of course, the installation of HRMs at Kentucky Downs came with tremendous controversy. Several groups believed the devices did not constitute legal pari-mutual wagering under current Kentucky laws. While the odds of winning are entirely different from regular slot machines, the group thought they were too similar to standard slots and

"Bring the Heat" at Louisville's Derby City

157

should not be considered legal in Kentucky. Another faction, led by the Kentucky Center for Economic Policy, believed the machines *were* legal but that the state was grossly short-changed regarding tax revenue. While regular slot machines in other states were taxed at rates averaging 33 to 55 percent, the state realized less than two percent from HRMs. Kentucky's tax rate on the total handle for live horse racing was more than double that of HRMs. In comparison, 70 percent of gross commissions from the Kentucky Lottery went to the state's budget.[1]

Bob Elliston and other officials at Turfway Park tried in vain to convince the owners to jump on the HRM bandwagon. Instead, those 'higher-ups" wanted to wait until outstanding court challenges were resolved. The evidence was already in at this point – HRMs were bringing in billions at other racetracks. By 2020, HRM betting exceeded $2 billion, more than the Kentucky Lottery and horse racing combined. Turfway owners, the "suits-and-ties" at Harrah's, knew this revenue could save the struggling Northern Kentucky track. Still, they were too afraid of an unfavorable court ruling to spend the money to purchase and install the devices.

WinStar Farm

With no immediate plans for HRMs, Turfway Park once again found itself in desperate need of financial assistance. It came in the fall of 2011 in the form of WinStar Farm, a Thoroughbred horse breeding and racing corporation located in Versailles, Kentucky. With their backing, Turfway announced a full slate of events for the Fall Meet in 2011, including 16 dates over four weeks, followed by a break during Churchill Downs' fall meet before racing resumed in December. New was the Maker's Mark Bourbon Dinner on opening night. Turfway also resurrected its Kentucky Cup Day of Champions in September 2011. The Dollar Friday series continued, which included live music, games, giveaways, dollar draft beer, and dollar hot dogs.

The positive outlook represented a marked change from just one year prior when the Northern Kentucky racetrack canceled its three remaining Kentucky Cup races and eliminated the Day of Champions. Many in the industry viewed the cancellations as the last nails in the coffin for the racetrack, but Bob Elliston told reporters, "Maybe we've pried a few of those nails loose."[2] WinStar Farm signed a three-year agreement as the Cup's first corporate sponsor and helped ensure the return of the five races that highlighted the stakes-day card. Dodson H. Skaggs, a trainer for 42 years, got his first graded stakes win with the Grade II WinStar Kentucky Cup with *Future Prospect*. Trainer Michael Maker, who kept a stable of horses at Turfway, collected five wins on the day, including three stakes victories. Maker trained *Hansen*, winner of the juvenile race, for Kendal Hansen, a Northern Kentucky pain specialist. *Hansen* would go on to have a great racing career.

Even with the addition of the new stakes races, the return of the Kentucky Cup, and special events such as the Friday night deals and live concerts, there is no doubt Bob Elliston took over Turfway Park when it was at the beginning of a slow spiral toward its darkest hours. Overall, purse monies dropped considerably during his tenure, attendance was at an all-time low (except for Friday nights), and the quality of the Thoroughbreds racing at Turfway Park plunged. The popularity of the riverboat casinos nearby was wreaking havoc on the track's bottom line. If not for the annual Spiral Stakes, it is doubtful Turfway Park would have survived.

Right after the 2011 Spiral Stakes, Turfway announced it was closing its stable area during the summer months, citing a lack of horses. "We simply do not have enough horses to make it a break-even proposition," said Bob Elliston. In 2006, when the track chose to keep the stables open during the off-season, nearly 700 horses were housed there for year-round training. Since then, the numbers have averaged around 350. "There needs to be at least 500 for it to be a viable business option," Elliston continued. The sharp decline was attributed to the ongoing struggles of Kentucky's racing circuit, where trainers have opted to spend summers at tracks in other states that offer higher purses. Similarly, Churchill Downs closed its trackside training center during the winter months, citing a lack of horses.[3]

Casino gaming in nearby Lawrenceburg, Indiana and Downtown Cincinnati's newly opened Horseshoe Casino had devastated Turfway Park's profitability. Adding to the problem, River Downs racetrack outside Cincinnati had just installed video lottery terminals. In 2012, Turfway Park canceled its premiere fall racing event, the Day of Champions, for the second time. Three more of the track's stakes races lost their graded status with the announcement. In past years, the Kentucky Cup Day of Champions was a launching pad for horses prepping for the Breeder's Cup. However, Turfway canceled the event to bring funding to its regular slate of races. These cancelations left the track with only two graded events in the spring, the Grade III Vinery Spiral Stakes and the Bourbonette Oaks.[4] The devastation witnessed at Turfway Park was not an isolated problem, and the misery was not felt only in Kentucky – the "Thoroughbred Capital of the World." The reverence of Thoroughbred racing across the country was plummeting and was nearly dead. An article in the *San Diego Union-Tribune* dated March 23, 2012, summed it up nicely:

"Away from the picturesque farms dotting the bluegrass country, the mega-dollar yearling sales at Keeneland and the twin spires at Churchill Downs, the tradition-laden sport of horse racing is in danger of vanishing from its old Kentucky home. Venerable tracks offer $1 beer-and-hot dog promotions, live music, and night racing to boost attendance. While tracks in other states have parlayed casino gambling into higher purses, Kentucky lawmakers have resisted allowing such a move. Everyone from breeders to railbirds worries that the home of American horse racing will eventually vanish entirely. Even storied Churchill Downs, home of the Kentucky Derby, has felt the pressure. But at least Churchill has the Derby, a cash cow, to support its racing seasons."

Bob Elliston added, "Times are especially tough at Turfway Park, and the odds look worse now that slot machines won't offer a lifeline. From the backside to the executive offices, there's grim talk that the winter haven for Kentucky horse racing could someday turn into a shopping mall. I hope I don't have to consider that. I'm not that interested in being a shopping mall manager. But we have to look at other options if the track can't make it as a racing or gaming facility."

It's a domino effect: larger purses attrack better-quality Thoroughbreds, as well as more wagering, as everyone from owners to racing fans look to cash in. In Pennsylvania, purses at "racinos" (horse racing with casinos) approached $123.5

million in 2011. Kentucky's overall purses were $89 million for far fewer races. Purses were up sharply at Aqueduct Racetrack, thanks to a new gambling parlor. In January, purses there were about $400,000 per day, compared to $275,000 per day in January 2011. Other New York tracks also witnessed higher purses.

Other sectors of the racing business also took the axe. Kentucky had long been the hub of Thoroughbred breeding. For decades, many horses stayed put to compete in Kentucky, which offered year-round racing during rotating meets at Churchill, Ellis Park, Keeneland, Turfway, and now Kentucky Downs. Kentucky's horse industry generated about $4 billion a year in 2011. It was responsible for tens of thousands of jobs – everything from training horses to caring for their health, cleaning up after them, shipping them, and producing the hay they munch. But the number of live racing days had shrunk tremendously as tracks struggled to offer the purses required to attract more horses. In 1993, Kentucky tracks offered 2,976 races. In 2010, the total shrank to 2,107, a nearly thirty percent drop.[5]

Trainer Dale Romans, a fixture on the Kentucky racing circuit, shifted much of his stable to New York in pursuit of larger purses. Romans, who won the 2011 Preakness with *Shackleford*, stated, "I'm Kentucky through and through – born and raised. It devastated me not to be able to race there full-time. But it was hard to convince clients – and most of my clients were from outside Kentucky – that we should run there instead of New York."[6]

Everyone struggled at Turfway, from Thoroughbred owners to the horsemen to the breeders to the cooks. Tom Scherz, who operated the kitchen on the track's backside, said his business was off at least fifty percent. "We're at rock bottom," he told reporters in 2011. "We'll probably be gone in 24 months."[7]

The Downward Spiral Escalates

The yearly Spiral Stakes once again kept Turfway Park above water, but barely. On a typical Saturday night in 2011, two floors of the six-story clubhouse were empty – closed to patrons. A modest crowd pressed near the rail or clustered around clubhouse monitors to watch horses run. On the backside, paint was peeling or fading on nearly every horse barn. Roads into the facility were dotted with potholes. Painted lines once present to indicate the thousands of parking spots were non-existent. Inside the clubhouse, dozens of garbage cans were scattered about to catch the water seeping through cracks and holes in the structure. On more than one occasion, a waterfall descended from above and cascaded down the front stairs onto the first floor. Plastic bags covered many plumbing fixtures that were out of order. Turfway Park president Bob Elliston estimated that casino gambling would pump $100 million into Turfway Park, allowing it to double purses and completely renovate the facility. But in early 2012, that remained a dream.

A capacity field of 12 three-year-olds was entered in the $500,000 Vinery Spiral Stakes in 2012, with Gulfstream Park allowance winner *Heavy Breathing* as the 3-1 favorite. The co-second choices on the card included *Went the Day Well*, trained by H. Graham Motion and ridden by John Velazquez, the same combination that took *Animal Kingdom* to victory the year before in the Spiral and the Kentucky Derby, and California shipper *Handsome Mike*. At the finish line, *Heavy Breathing* found his way to a disappointing third-place finish, right behind *Holiday Promise*. *Handsome Mike* came in fourth. It was *Went the Day Well* in the winner's circle. In the Kentucky Derby, *Went the Day Well* finished in fourth place, and a fifth-place finish was achieved at the Preakness.

Went the Day Well winning the Spiral Stakes

Following the Spiral Stakes in 2012, more cuts were announced by Turfway Park officials. Non-stakes purses were slashed once again. In contrast, purses at Belmont Park's spring meet rose 44 percent, and those at Saratoga went up 39 percent due exclusively to slot machine wagering. Bob Elliston told reporters, "Quite frankly, this unfortunate cut in purses for the remainder of the meet won't resolve our overpayment entirely, and further reductions in operations and staffing are likely as we move into September and December."[8]

The biggest hit to Turfway Park may have come in October 2012, when the Kentucky Racing Commission granted Churchill Downs' request to take all of Turfway's September racing dates for 2013. Losing the Summer Meet was both savage and traumatic to the Florence, Kentucky, track. Turfway ran only 81 days in 2012 and dropped 45 days in 2013.

Chip Bach recalled his meeting with the Commission when the announcement was made. "They told me, 'You're losing the September dates. It's already done, and there's nothing you can do about it. Just find a way to work around it.'"[9] He added, "It's pure speculation, but when Caesar purchased us and agreed to sustain our losses... I feel that, at the time, they were actually trying to *block* gaming here... to not interfere with their successful Cincinnati casino. What I do know: Caesar's told me in no explicit terms, 'We want you to get as much sympathy from the Commission as you can, but we *don't* want you to win those dates back.' Somehow, they thought more racing dates were bad."

Bach, then Turfway's Director of Operations, said that once it was clear the track would lose the September racing dates, officials had to develop a new business model that made financial sense. Turfway Park was at a competitive disadvantage, as casino revenues allowed racetracks in neighboring states to not only enhance purses but to upgrade their facilities. While interviewed for the *Kentucky Post*, Bob Elliston stated, "We were up against competitive forces that were completely out of our control. We put up a big fight, we really did, but unfortunately, it fell on deaf ears in Frankfort."

Rock Gaming

Things began to look a little brighter when, in April 2012, it was announced that Rock Gaming, the developer of casinos in Cincinnati and Cleveland, Ohio, acquired 40 percent ownership of the struggling Turfway Park from Keeneland, leaving the Lexington, Kentucky track with just 10 percent. Caesar's Entertainment held the other 50 percent. Horse racing fans and Turfway employees all rejoiced that the future of Turfway Park held promise. Caesar's and Rock Gaming had billions of dollars, and much could be spent on the ramshackle facility. Significant renovations were long-overdue, and heavy construction was necessary at many places to keep it from falling in on itself. For example, many patrons were afraid to utilize the metal staircase leading from the grandstands to the paddock because of the heavy rust visible at every joint.

However, when a casino company purchases a racetrack, the question is whether the new owners will relegate horse racing to second-class status – or even abolish it altogether. After all, "gaming" is their primary focus. The ownership change at Turfway Park provided a bit of optimism, since the latest investors had successfully worked to legalize gambling in a state where such efforts had historically failed. Caesar's already owned casinos in Cleveland and Cincinnati, as well as the Thistledown racetrack near Cleveland. Dan Gilbert was an investor in some 40 firms, including Quicken Loans (the most prominent online retail mortgage lender in the United States) and the Cleveland Cavaliers of the National Basketball Association. Rock Gaming was instrumental in the 2009 voter referendum in Ohio that legalized casino gaming.[10] Significant monies were now available to save the troubled Turfway Park. And, if anyone was going to bring legalized gambling to Kentucky, it was them. Plans were immediately drawn to renovate Turfway and pressure state officials even harder to legalize casino-style gaming in Kentucky.

With the new ownership and the fans' belief that things might improve at Turfway Park, on-track handle rose over six percent to $5,647,604, and handle on races simulcast from other tracks rose more than 13 percent to $15,689,677 through the end of the live meet.[11] But in 2012, casino gaming was once again denied by state officials. Immediately, purses at Turfway Park were cut by a staggering 25 percent. "There was no good course," Elliston told the *Daily Racing Form*. "We felt like this was the least intrusive way to go. Against all these other tracks raising purses and everything else going on, we're in a tough spot right now. It's very frustrating, to say the least."[12]

On August 14, a *Courier-Journal* article stated, "The white flag has been raised at Turfway Park. The track can no longer pretend that it can support any semblance of quality racing, except for the Bourbonette Oaks and the Grade III Vinery Racing Spiral Stakes, which produced Kentucky Derby winner *Animal Kingdom* last year. They can't even afford a watered-down version of the Kentucky Cup. At the same time, West Virginia's Mountaineer Park, which has casino gaming, staged a nine-race all-stakes card – a minimum purse of $100,000 – for which 50 of the 91 horses entered could be in some way considered Kentucky horses."

Courtesy: America's Best TRacing

Perry Ouzts

If there was a highlight for Turfway Park in 2012, it came in the face of one of horse racing's most dedicated riders. On September 29, 58-year-old jockey Perry Ouzts mounted *Tanner Me Boy*, trained by Thomas McCann, to a two-length victory. While not a prestigious race by any means, the win gave Ouzts his 6,000th victory, an accomplishment achieved by very few riders. In a post-race interview, Ouzts remarked, "When you're sitting in the gate, you don't think about nothing else but the race and the best way you can get him home. That's how you block out all the fear – everything. It's tunnel vision. You don't think about anything else." Aaron Spurlock, long-time mutuel department manager, said, "Perry Ouzts is the toughest man I know."[13] Perry's career and those of other top riders at Latonia/Turfway Park will be chronicled later in this publication.

Behind the scenes, Bob Elliston had had enough. Maybe he could see into the future and knew what was in store for Turfway Park. Perhaps he was privy to inside information and was all too sure of the new ownership's game plan. He needed a way out. While he had a nice run at Turfway Park and was respected by many in the industry, as a manager he was terrible. It was said, "He was great at managing up, meaning he could suck up and butter up those above him. However, he was horrible at managing down."[14] One manager stated, "He was difficult to work with. In general, it was his way or no way."[15] Elliston was often seen yelling and screaming at employees. He seemed to have little respect for anyone below him. "He was a bully! Elliston was a huge micro-manager. He was constantly in your face," said another.[16] One long-time mutuel room team member may have summed up Elliston's managing style the best. "It got so bad that I literally prayed. 'Lord, I don't want something bad to happen to him... it can be something good. But please, Lord, make him go away.'"[17]

It worked. In 2012, Elliston was named chief operating officer for the Breeder's Cup, based in Lexington, Kentucky and left Turfway Park. The Breeder's Cup, a two-day, $26 million event that year, attracted the best horses, trainers, and owners from across the globe. The high-profile race is recognized as the unofficial end and culmination of the Thoroughbred racing season. Elliston could not have been happier with his new position. Taking over the reins at Turfway Park was Chip Bach.

Daniel "Chip" Bach

Raised in Chicago, Chip moved to Versailles, Kentucky, the heart of horse country, in seventh grade. He was the captain of Woodford County's first varsity soccer team. Bach earned his bachelor's degree in public and police administration from Eastern Kentucky University. He began his professional career in the Information Technology sector overseeing loss prevention, security, and technical training at firms on the East Coast. Having been friends with Bob Elliston at EKU, Chip and his wife Kendra reunited with Bob years later. Kendra worked with Elliston at Firstar Bank, and when Bob was named president of Turfway Park, he needed some people he could trust on his bench of managers. He urged Chip to join his team in July 1999 as training and safety director. When a case of equine herpes was discovered at Turfway Park, it was Chip who devised a special protocol for communications and response to high-risk infectious diseases now standard in the industry. Before becoming general manager, Bach was named director of operations in 2006

Courtesy: Nkytribune.com

Chip Bach, with the Racebook in the background

and assumed oversight of all day-to-day on-track activities, including racing, mutuels, admissions, facility, grounds, customer service, and horsemen relations.[18]

Chip learned how different the racetrack world was from the corporate world during his second weekend as security director. "As security director of a computer company, I was always getting calls in the middle of the night. They were very sensitive about every little detail of the industry. When I started working here, I remember being called into Bob's office early one Monday morning. He asked me, 'Did someone die here this weekend?' I told him I didn't know, but I would ask around. So, I went to the backside gate and asked the night security guard. 'Silly question... did somebody die here last night?' He said, 'Oh, yeah... but the coroner ruled it natural causes, so I didn't want to bother you at home.' I told him, 'From now on, if the coroner is on property, I need to know.' What a difference between the two industries."

"I still remember my first meeting as general manager. One Commissioner told me, 'You're an embarrassment to racing. You're an embarrassment to Kentucky racing.' But he was right. Turfway Park was falling apart. We did not represent the brand well. We did not represent the brand of Kentucky racing well. We were becoming like a single-A ball club instead of a major-league club. For five months of the year, we were a stain on Kentucky racing. I absolutely understood it."

Chip also recalled a somewhat embarrassing incident. "I thought I saw a famous jockey in the paddock one night. He looked very familiar. I couldn't remember his name, but I knew he was a famous rider. As soon as he spoke and I heard that accent, I knew who he was. It turned out to be Davy Jones of the Monkees." Davy had owned many horses over the years and ran a few at Turfway Park.

Chip recalled a few of his favorite races as well. "When *Hard Spun* and *Street Sense* had what was basically a match race during one of our Kentucky Cups – our classic September race. *Street Sense* had just won the Kentucky Derby that year, and *Hard Spun* beat him at Turfway. That was pretty cool! Of course, I remember *Animal Kingdom*, who went on to win the Derby. *Flower Alley* was another great horse. My favorite was *Caller One*, a sprinter. *Caller One* came from Turfway and went on to win the Dubai Golden Shaheen Stakes – twice!"

What a difference in management styles – Chip Bach versus Bob Elliston. Chip seems to have a genuine, personable relationship with the guests who came to Turfway Park (and now who come to Newport Racing and Gaming and Turfway Park Racing and Gaming). Maybe more so on the track side of the business; he does his best to ensure that everyone has a great time. Brooke Hoskinds, a frequent visitor with her mother Renee from around age eight to 16, recalls the night she was invited into the paddock as a pre-teen to announce "riders up" to the colony of jockeys before a race. What a thrill. Chip is often known to allow certain privileges to such loyal patrons. Invitations to the announcer's booth or the winner's circle are also commonplace with Bach. It is thought that very few racetracks in the country allow for such special accommodations. Bach says, "I feel it is the greatest privilege in the world to manage a Kentucky Thoroughbred racetrack, and I understand the huge responsibility to figure out how to restore the profile of the sport in the area."[19]

Long-time team member Dan Coletta summed up well Bach's philosophy on the "entertainment" angle of this business. "He had a poster hanging up for the longest time. It was a play on the famous Maya Angelou quote, and I truly feel that is how he cares for our guests." Dan recalled the poster from memory: "People will soon forget what you said, but they will never forget how you made them feel."

Disappointment in the Air

Disappointment with the transfer of ownership at Turfway Park – by the fans, employees, and horsemen – was realized almost immediately. While extensive plans for upgrades and renovations were discussed, nothing happened for months, and employees felt the track was, in a way, stuck in limbo. Once again, the Kentucky Cup Day of Champions was canceled, and by the end of the year, all-source wagering came in at $20.49 million, a decrease of nearly 25 percent. In addition, on-track betting totaled $1.21 million, down over 26 percent from the year before. Turfway officials said they averaged at least one fewer horse per race during the two-week overlap with Kentucky Downs. Field sizes averaged eight horses per race for the entire meet, down 8.4 percent from 2011.[20] The loss of the racing dates in 2012 and the upcoming 2013 season was also causing significant heartbreak and worry among team members, especially those who had been working at the facility for decades. Billy Troilo retired from riding in 2009 but worked at Turfway as a steward in 2013. "Things were terrible. Employees were being laid off left and right, purses were way down, and the building was literally crumbling apart."[21]

Rock Gaming and Caesar's Entertainment eventually devised an elaborate master plan, but the progress was unbelievably slow. Architects were hired, measurements were taken, plans and schematics were drawn, and executives wearing hard-hats could be seen in the building over a short span during the summer. However, no work was actually performed. The Kentucky Racing Commission continued to pressure the owners to install HRMs, but it never happened. Still, Turfway Park continued with their meet, offering exciting racing nights mixed with various special events.

Individual highlights continued at the track as well. On December 27, 2012, Rodney Prescott achieved his 3,000th career win aboard *Heart of Class* in the ninth race. The two-year-old filly, who faced all males in the race, was trained by Wayne Mogge. Prescott, a Turfway Park regular, went on

Courtesy: Pat Lang

169

to notch his 4,000th win in November 2021 while at Indiana Grand racetrack near Shelbyville, Indiana. He rode *We All See It* to an 11-length victory in that race.

Unusual excitement was witnessed at Turfway during a typical night of racing on March 6, 2013, just as *Joseph the Cat Fish* rounded the turn and headed for home. Track spokesperson Sherry Pinson said, "It was his very first start. The whole way around, he was fighting with the jockey. Suddenly, he threw the rider and jumped the rail." Bob Webster, the winner's circle security guard, followed the loose Thoroughbred, running across the apron and through the paddock tunnel, then across the parking lot, alerting backside officials by radio of the loose horse's path. In the adjacent hotel parking lot, a young couple unloading luggage yelled out, "He went that-a-way," and the security guard's pursuit continued. On horseback, starter Steve Peterman and one of the track's veterinarians caught up with *Joseph the Cat Fish* near the on-ramp for southbound Interstate 75. Neither the horse nor the jockey was injured, but motorists along Turfway and Houston roads no doubt witnessed a very unusual sight that night.

The 2013 main event, the Horseshoe Casino Spiral Stakes (named for Rock Gaming's Horseshoe Casino in Downtown Cincinnati), saw the favorites as *Uncaptured* at 3-1 and *Balance the Books* at 7-1. *Balance the Books* won two graded stakes on grass but had never run on Polytrack. *Uncaptured* swept Churchill Downs' Iroquois and Kentucky Jockey Club races. In the winner's circle, however, was the 15-1 long-shot *Black Onyx*, with Joe Bravo aboard. *Uncaptured* ran second, while *Balance the Books* finished out of the money. *Black Onyx* was trained by Kelly J. Breen and owned by Sam Hetzberg and Sterling Racing. The purse was set at $550,000, and a crowd of over 10,000 flocked to Florence, Kentucky for the event. General admission was $10.00, with grandstand seating options starting at $25.00. By 2022, Bravo had won 22 riding titles at racetracks in New Jersey (13 at Monmouth Park and nine at the Meadowlands).

Turfway Park continued arranging country music acts and other performers to get crowds into the park during their off-season. Jim Claypool, this compi-

Courtesy: USA Today

Courtesy: Daily Racing Form

Top: 15-1 long shot Black Onyx winning the 2013 Spiral Stakes at Turfway Park;

Middle: The winning jockey, Joe Bravo;

Right: Turfway's premiere event is renamed the Horseshoe Casino Spiral Stakes

Courtesy: Blood-Horse Magazine

lation's co-author and a Turfway Park regular, suggested a "Bluegrass Series" to then publicity manager Jack Gordon and he concurred. A Thoroughbred historian, Claypool also authored a popular book about Kentucky Bluegrass music. Incredibly, in August 2013, Dr. Ralph Stanley and the Clinch Mountain Boys appeared at Turfway Park. Ralph Stanley (1927-2016) was a bluegrass music legend, and his appearance at Turfway Park was one of his last performances. Stanley was a three-time Grammy Award winner whose career spanned six decades. The concert, held in the paddock on a beautiful summer night, drew a large crowd and kept Turfway Park in the news, even though the facility continued to tread on thin ice.

In November 2013, Tyler Picklesimer was named director of racing at Turfway Park. Picklesimer had been Turfway's assistant racing secretary since 2002 and replaced long-time secretary Rick Leigh. A 1994 graduate of Northern Kentucky University, Picklesimer was hired by Turfway Park that year as a placing judge. He also served as an alternate association steward, clocker, and paddock judge.

Once again, the subject of casino gambling was featured in both local newspapers. It was stated that Hollywood Casino, just a stone's throw from Turfway Park, generated the most gambling revenue in the entire region. This remained the critical argument for the expansion of gambling in Kentucky – to aid the struggling horse industry, rapidly losing ground to states such as Ohio, Indiana, and West Virginia, which all used gambling revenue to boost horse racing purses. It had been six years since Kentucky's debate over expanded gambling was ignited when Governor Steve Beshear campaigned – and won – on a platform of using gambling revenue to aid the state's ailing horse industry and shore up funding for education and other priorities. Nearly every year since, the General Assembly debated whether to legalize casinos, racetrack slots ("racinos"), or some combination of the two. Each year, they failed to reach a consensus and pass a bill. Meanwhile, Northern Kentucky watched helplessly as the region's gambling market exploded across the Ohio River, where the number of gambling establishments in Ohio and Indiana had doubled since 2007.[22]

Courtesy: www.flicker.com

Dr. Ralph Stanley and the Clinch Mountain Boys

Courtesy: Dwight "D.A." Brown Collection

An exciting shot of "Racing at Turfway Park" rounding the final turn

Courtesy: John Engelhardt

Courtesy: Turfway Park staff

Courtesy: Dwight "D.A." Brown Collection

Courtesy: www.Courier-Journal

Courtesy: www.Courier-Journal

Opposite page, top: Aerial view of the Turfway Park property, circa 2013;

Middle: Morning workouts;

Bottom: Another great shot from Dwight "D.A." Brown;

This page, top: Warming up in the paddock for night racing;

Bottom: One of the many iconic horse heads which decorated the apron and paddock (many of these were retained and now line the main entrance to Turfway Park Racing and Gaming).

Chapter Six Endnotes

1. "What is historical racing, and how do the betting machines work?" *Courier-Journal*, September 30, 2021, retrieved on September 19, 2022.

2. "Turfway Park finding reasons for optimism," *Cincinnati Enquirer*, September 8, 2011, retrieved on September 15, 2022.

3. "Turfway Park to close stables in summer," *Courier-Journal*, March 15, 2011, retrieved on September 15, 2022.

4 ."Turfway Park scratches its premiere event," *The Gleaner* (Henderson, Kentucky), August 9, 2012, retrieved on September 15, 2022.

5. *San Diego Union-Tribune*, March 23, 2012.

6. *Ibid.*

7. *Ibid*

8. "Turfway Park slashing non-stakes purses 25 percent," *Courier-Journal*, March 1, 2012, retrieved on September 15, 2022.

9. Personal interview with Chip Bach on October 15, 2022.

10. Bill Shankin, "Turfway Park Under New Ownership," *Horse Racing Business,* June 11, 2012, retrieved on September 4, 2022.

11. "Turfway handle rises," *Cincinnati Enquirer*, April 5, 2011, retrieved on September 15, 2022.

12. Paulick Report Staff, "Turfway's Elliston: We are doing all we can," *Paulick Report*, March 3, 2012, retrieved on August 7, 2022.

13. Personal interview with Aaron Spurlock, Mutuel Room Manager, on October 28, 2022.

14. Personal interview with a team member who wishes to remain anonymous.

15. Personal interview with Aaron Spurlock, Mutuel Room Manager, on October 28, 2022.

16. Personal interview with a team member who wishes to remain anonymous, December 1, 2022.

17. Personal interview with Linda Gay, long-time mutuel room employee, on October 20, 2022.

18. "Bach Named General Manager at Turfway," *Blood-Horse Magazine*, retrieved on September 12, 2022.

19. Quote taken from Chip Bach's Facebook social media post on November 15, 2022.

20. "Turfway Park wagering drops sharply," *Courier-Journal*, October 2, 2012, retrieved on September 15, 2022.

21. Personal interview with Billy Troilo on November 16, 2022.

22. "As state mulls a bet on casinos, NKY is already the biggest loser," *Cincinnati Enquirer*, November 25, 2013, retrieved on September 15, 2022.

Chapter Seven

Mike Battaglia, Jeff Ruby,
and... "It Was All A Ruse"

After a seven-month hiatus, live racing returned to Turfway Park in late November 2013. With the Kentucky Racing Commission's decision to revoke Turfway's September racing dates, fans had to wait until the weekend after Thanksgiving to pursue their interests. For 50 years, the Northern Kentucky racetrack had conducted a fall meet, but no more. Turfway offered races Thursday through Sunday in December, but cut down days from January through March. While lobbying strongly to keep the warmer-weather dates on its schedule, General Manager Chip Bach said there were advantages to running what amounts to one continuous meet. "We didn't realize how expensive it was to keep the barns open for those three months."[1] Previously, Turfway Park offered live races in September, then had only simulcast wagering in October and November when Keeneland and Churchill Downs had live meets before resuming in December. Starting in 2013, the track had two meets – the Holiday Meet and the Winter Meet – for recordkeeping purposes – but live racing ran continuously from December through March. Many fan favorites returned for the 2013-2014 season, including the Friday Night "Dollar-Beer-Dollar-Hot-Dogs," dollar bets, games, prizes, and live music. The New Year's Eve party that year hosted local music icon and Rock and Roll Hall of Famer Bootsy Collins.

March 22 brought the 2014 edition of the Horseshoe Casino Cincinnati Spiral Stakes to Turfway Park. *Tamarando*, winner of the Grade III El Camino Real Derby at Golden Gate Fields in Northern California, was the early 3-1 favorite. Other contenders to win the premier race included *We Miss Artie* (4-1), owned by Ken and Sarah Ramsey and trained by Todd Pletcher, and *Almost Famous* (6-1), trained by Patrick Byrne and ridden

Roaring from the starting gate in Turfway Park's "Horseshoe Casino Spiral Stakes"

by Calvin Borel. The Ramseys had been Turfway's leading owners several times and won three Eclipse Awards in that category, including in 2013.

The big day was still dubbed "Northern Kentucky's Derby" by local sportswriters. "People come out here yearly," commented Boone County judge-executive Gary W. Moore. "It's a sign of spring; it's a sign that great things are to come, and today was a home run for Turfway Park."[2] There was a festive and celebratory atmosphere from the grandstands to the VIP tent. Crowds gathered along the rail to cheer on the horses, and executives and politicians in the VIP tent put business aside. In the winner's circle after the race, *We Miss Artie* had rallied to win the $550,000 Grade III by a nose. It was the second Spiral win for the Ramseys and another Spiral victory for jockey John R. Velazquez. *We Miss Artie* ran in the Kentucky Derby a few weeks later, finishing tenth. Still, this was another premiere Thoroughbred who competed on the Turfway Park racetrack.

Mike Battaglia

Mike Battaglia, who had set the morning line at Turfway Park, Keeneland, and Churchill Downs for 40 years, turned those duties over to his son, Bret, for the

2014 Spiral. Bret became the third generation of Battaglias affiliated with Turfway Park. Mike would retire from calling races a couple of years later. His 43-year career as a track announcer is likely a record. Mike remained at Turfway Park, however. He became an ambassador for the racetrack, speaking to groups and hosting handicapping seminars and other community events. He continued making the morning line for Churchill Downs and Keeneland, where he did the pre-race analysis and post-stakes interviews for the Lexington track. In 2016, Mike Battaglia became the ex-

Courtesy: www.nkytribune.com

Mike Battaglia at Keeneland

ecutive vice president of Turfway Park. "He'll be our face and voice," Chip Bach said. "It's hard to come by his credibility. He's so identifiable in this industry."

Mike Battaglia began calling races at Turfway Park in 1973 when the track was known as Latonia, and his father, John Battaglia, was the general manager. He first called Thoroughbred events in 1971 at long-gone Miles Park in Louisville's West End, a track managed at the time by his father. Young Mike was a last-minute replacement for legendary announcer Chic Anderson, who left for Rockingham Park in New Hampshire. Mike called his first race at the prestigious Churchill Downs in 1975, when Chic Anderson fainted mid-race. John, Mike, and brother Bruce Battaglia had driven to Churchill early during Derby Week to watch and bet on the races as fans. "Half-way through the first race, the PA system went dead," Mike recalled. "Then I heard a voice over the PA system, and I realized it was CBS's 'Woodie' Broun saying, 'Mike Battaglia report to the announcer's booth.' I go, 'What the heck's going on?' I walk up to the announcer's booth, and it's Heywood Hale Broun, Lynn Stone (Churchill president) with a big cigar, a doctor and a nurse, and Chic still lying on the floor. Lynn looks at me and says, 'You think you can call the next race for me?' Crazy, but that's how I became Churchill's backup announcer."[3]

Team members and fans will long remember one true testament to Mike Battaglia's talent in calling races. It is forever known as the "Fog Call." A heavy fog rolled in during a typical night of races and covered the entire track. No one could see past the homestretch. Mike announced the start of the race, a one-mile run with the starting gate directly in front of the grandstands, in his typical fashion, "Anddddd, they're racing." He kept fans aware of who was in the lead and the order of the rest of the field as they entered the first turn and made their way toward the backstretch. However, it was there that the entire group of horses disappeared into the fog. Rather than offer nothing but silence to the audience, Mike, without skipping a beat and totally ad-lib, rendered a promotional spot that went

Mike Battaglia at Turfway Park

Courtesy: Dwight "D.A." Brown Collection

something like… "Fans, don't forget to stop by the gift shop. You'll find a wide assortment of caps, T-shirts, mugs, and other souvenir items." And after a few more words of wisdom, the horses reappeared in the final turn and headed for home, and Mike's professional call of the race resumed as usual. Billy Troilo, former jockey and long-time Turfway Park Clerk of Scales and Steward, said, "Mike is a great announcer and handicapper. He always tried to carry on the legacy of his dad. Turfway Park was always 'home' to him."[4]

Turfway officials continued to pursue other ways to attract people to the facility during the off-season months. Many events were strictly charitable fundraisers, but they also showed community members who had never been to Turfway Park that the facility existed. If people attended the off-season events, they might come back for live racing. In August 2014, it hosted a Back-to-School event where more than 2,600 children and 1,500 parents and guardians from low-income families received school supplies, hygiene items, and clothing. Within two-and-a-half hours, 16,700 backpacks were given away to kindergarten through eighth-grade children. Free donuts, pizza, hot dogs, hamburgers, and other treats were provided. Face painting and two bounce houses provided the children with day-long fun. Other off-season events presented at Turfway Park included wrestling matches and Mixed Martial Arts (MMA) fighting. MMA nights brought in huge crowds and were repeated for several years.

In September, racing of a different sort was witnessed at Turfway Park when the second Polytrack Puppy Party was hosted. Benefitting the Stray Animal Adoption Program (SAAP) and the Boone County Animal Shelter, more than a dozen dogs competed for trophies and prizes. Mary Troilo, Turfway department manager, National Director of Simulcasting, and the driving force behind the event, said, "Where better to hold the races than a real racetrack? These races are a lot of fun for everybody, and they're a great way to raise money to help stray and abandoned animals."[5] The popular event continued at Turfway for many years.

The Kentucky Racing Commission continued to give Turfway's fall racing dates to Churchill Downs going forward. The Commission believed that providing the dates to Churchill would allow the Louisville track to offer bigger purses and keep more quality horses in Kentucky. At the same time, Turfway, with its synthetic surface, could focus on winter racing. Turfway Park management initially protested the change but then seized it as an opportunity to revamp its entire racing schedule. Turfway also cut some dates from December, January, and February. Fewer races would mean the track could offer larger purses on the nights it remained open. Many felt this was a last-stitch effort to stay afloat.

It Was All a Ruse

Ownership of Turfway Park changed slightly in 2015 when a bankrupt Caesar's Entertainment sold off its interests to Rock Ohio Ventures, making Rock Ohio the majority owner of the track. However, the biggest news in 2015 was the Kentucky Racing Commission's decision to allow HRMs at Turfway Park. If track owner Detroit-based Rock Gaming pursued the project, 250 machines could be installed. "It would be the largest upgrade to the facility in more than a decade," said General Manager Chip Bach. "It's another opportunity to improve our racing product." However, Rock Gaming did nothing to initiate the plan.

The 2015 Spiral Stakes was won by *Dubai Sky*, ridden by Jose Lezcano, and trained by William I. Mott. In 2015, Lezcano had an impressive past. In 2008, he finished first with his only Breeder's Cup mount, *Maram*, and tied a Monmouth Park record on June 22, 2008, riding six winners on one card.[6] He is still going strong in 2023, especially on the turf, where he is deadly. *Dubai Sky* broke tenth but soon stalked the pace under Lezcano, who also captured the $150,000 Bourbonette Oaks aboard *Don't Leave Me*. He was four-wide most of the way, taking the lead in the upper stretch after moving to the rail. He won by nearly three lengths.

In March 2016, Turfway Park continued their charitable giving. It hosted an autograph signing event to benefit the Permanently Disabled Jockeys Fund (PDJF). The event featured 19 former jockeys who rode at Turfway Park, including Hall of Fame rider Chris McCarron, Derby winner Mike Manganello, and Patti "P J" Cooksey, one of the only female riders in history to win more than 2,000 races. For a donation to the fund, patrons received a poster featuring a photo of the former jockeys and a picture of Turfway's current jockey colony. Guests could have the poster signed or bring an item of their choice to be signed for a donation. Other jockeys featured at the event included Mike Bryan, Gene Chalk, Tony D'Amico, Carl Faulconer, Darlene Green, Ronnie Herbstreit, Bob Jackson, R. A. "Cowboy" Jones, Jim McKnight, Johnny Oldham, Suzie Picou-Oldham, Otto Thorwarth, Bill Troilo, Kaoru Tshuchiya, Melinda Vest, and Dana Zook. The night was highly successful, and long lines gathered at the signing tables.

The 2016 edition of the $500,000 Horseshoe Casino Spiral Stakes saw jockey Brain Hernandez, Jr. and *Oscar Nominated* standing in the winner's circle. Hernandez won 243 races in 2004 and received the Eclipse Award for Outstanding Apprentice Jockey. Also, Kenneth and Sarah Ramsey returned as winning owners. It was their third Spiral Stakes victory. Running in the middle of the track, *Oscar Nominated* came off the far turn and fended off several rivals to squeeze out a win.

Meanwhile, Horseshoe Casino in Downtown Cincinnati had a name change in 2017. As a result, the 2017 premiere race at Turfway Park became the $500,000 Grade II JACK Casino Spiral Stakes. *Kitten's Cat* was the 4-1 favorite. Trained by Joe Sharp and owned by Ken and Sarah Ramsey, the Thoroughbred drew the 8th post in the 12-horse field. *Parlor*, trained by Eddie Kenneally, was the 5-1 second choice. At the finish line, however, trainer Michael J. Maker was back. Owner Kendall E. Hansen joined him with his entry, *Fast and Accurate*. Tyler Gaffalione, the Eclipse Award Champion Apprentice Jockey winner in 2015, had the mount. Gaffalione would go on to win the 2019 Preakness and returned as a Turfway Park Spiral winner that same year. *Fast and Accurate* ran in the Kentucky Derby in 2017 but finished a depressing seventeenth.

On August 30, 2017, newspaper headlines read: "Turfway Park Announces Changes." General Manager Chip Bach announced that the track would open its 59th season with upgrades to its most important day of racing and modifications to its stakes schedule. One significant change was another resurrection of the Kentucky Cup Classic, to be run on the Spiral Stakes undercard. Last run in 2011 as a Grade II race, the Kentucky Cup Classic Trophy had gone to such standouts as duel Classic winners *Tabasco Cat*, *Silver Charm*, and *Thunder Gulch*, Dubai World Cup winner *Roses in May*, and Grade I winners *Perfect Drift* and *Hard Spun*.

Also significant, unfortunately, was the reduction in the purse for the Spiral Stakes, from $500,000 to $200,000. The Spiral Stakes continued its role as a Kentucky Derby prep race, offering 34 points – 20 to the winner. Turfway's Bourbonette Oaks offered 34 points toward the Kentucky Oaks (Grade I). In addition, the Wintergreen Stakes for older fillies and mares took a new name and gained new visibility, as well as a $25,000 purse increase. The new name, the Latonia Stakes, recalled the track's original name and its long-enduring heritage from the late 1800s. Like the Kentucky Cup Classic, this race was moved to the Spiral Stakes undercard.

General Manager Chip Bach stated, "Reviving the Kentucky Cup Classic and celebrating our history with the Latonia Stakes will make Spiral Stakes day more exciting for fans. Adding stakes for older horses rounds out the card and gives trainers wider opportunities and greater incentive to ship here. Three-year-olds looking to enhance their chances at making the Kentucky Derby or Oaks field will have that opportunity in the Spiral or Bourbonette. Focusing on higher-caliber races across the entire card will also make the day more attractive to bettors."

The enhanced 2018 Spiral featured five stakes, with the balance of the card reserved for maiden special weight and allowance races:

$200,000 Spiral Stakes (G3) for three-year-olds, nine furlongs
$100,000 Bourbonette Oaks (G3) for three-year-old fillies, 8 furlongs
$100,000 Kentucky Cup Classic (BT) for 4-year-olds and up, 9 furlongs
$75,000 Latonia Stakes (BT) for older fillies and mares, 8.5 furlongs
$75,000 Rushaway (listed) for 3-year-olds, 8.5 furlongs

The Ruse

In February 2018, the *Cincinnati Enquirer* featured a lengthy article about Turfway Park, and fans and team members were finally excited about the facility's future. Rock Gaming had taken over in 2012 and had made several promises, but nothing had materialized. In early 2018, however, it was announced that significant renovations would finally begin at the struggling Florence, Kentucky racetrack. The owners had allocated $500,000 for architectural drawings and engineering plans to overhaul its five-story enclosed grandstand. Chip Bach presented the strategies to the Kentucky Horse Racing Commission and noted that the upgrades were long overdue. The makeover was to include a revamped entrance, modern restrooms, and other accommodations. Most importantly, the entire second floor would be dedicated to historical racing machines (HRMs). In Kentucky, Churchill Downs in Louisville and Keeneland racetrack in Lexington had already installed HRMs, and those devices would bring a more profitable draw, allowing Turfway to remain open. Rumors had circulated for several years that Turfway Park was drowning, and many saw this news as the Godsend the track needed.

In reality, however, Turfway Park owners had no intention of remodeling. Unbeknownst to Chip Bach and the rest of the management team, the announcement was nothing more than a ruse to appease the Kentucky Horse Racing

Commission. The Commission had threatened to remove all of Turfway's racing dates if the track did not install the HRMs – and install them immediately. Large plywood walls were erected on the grandstand's main level, giving the appearance that major remodeling was happening behind. However, the area was used as storage. Reinforcing the rotting steel beams in a section of the front of the building also made it appear that the owners had begun extensive reconstruction. Weeks went by, then months, with no work ever taking place. Fans were excited that work had finally started on repairing and upgrading the dilapidated facility, but the track employees knew otherwise. Mutuel Department Manager Aaron Spurlock stated, "I felt like a ham, to be honest, due to all the smoke blown our way."[7]

General Manager Chip Bach recalls, "During those years, there were several times I was called upon. I was asked what we were going to do to improve the facility. I would go with my creative drawings… my concept drawings, and all this stuff, and I was fairly confident that these guys (the casino owners) would do what they said they would do. In hindsight, I think that at some point, they were going to make the upgrades. However, when there were whispers that we might be looked at… that we might be for sale… that all went away."[8]

"At any rate," Bach said, "I went to at least three Commission meetings with different renderings. At the third one, Doc Richardson, one of the Commissioners, said, 'Chip, we love you, but please don't bring any more renderings to these meetings.'" At the very last meeting, Chip was once again asked to present a plan to the Commission by the casino heads. "I just couldn't do it," Bach stated. "Back when I had some faith that renovations were going to happen, I was happy to do it. I was sincere in my belief that it was going to happen. But when the last meeting came up, I said, 'I just can't do it.'"[9]

There were several highlights during this period, however. On Saturday, March 3, 2018, the ageless Perry Ouzts hustled *Need the Wall* out of the gate in the third race at Turfway Park for his 50,000[th] pari-mutuel mount. Sixty-three years old at the time, he ranked ninth by the number of wins in the history of North American racing with 6,881. He also accumulated 6,509 second-place finishes and 6,181 thirds, raking in more than $44 million since he first mounted up in 1973.[10] "It would have been much more dramatic had I won," Ouzts said, bringing the three-year-old filly from last place along the rail for a second-place finish. "I want to keep going until I pass Russell Baze" (for the number of career mounts), referencing the all-time leader both in mounts (53,578) and wins (12,842). One of the oldest jockeys still active, Ouzts gallops and breezes horses three or four times a week in the afternoons, only to ride six to eight mounts each race day.

Jeff Ruby

Certainly, the brightest highlight in 2018 was the appearance of a new corporate sponsor for Turfway Park's Spiral Stakes. Jeff Ruby, a long-time horse racing fan and local celebrity, signed a multi-year deal with the racetrack. Ruby owns a string of high-end restaurants, including The Precinct and Carlo and Johnny, in Cincinnati, and his Jeff Ruby's Steakhouses, with locations in Cincinnati, Columbus, Louisville, and Nashville. Because of his "steak" houses, the spelling of Turfway's premiere event appropriately became the Jeff Ruby Steaks. His sponsorship continued through the publication of this book in 2023.

When asked how Ruby came to be the new sponsor, Chip Bach told this story. "I was tasked to find a new corporate sponsor and, for some reason, I had Jeff's number. During one of my son's soccer games, I texted him. 'How would you like to sponsor our Derby prep?' He wrote me back, 'How about the Jeff Ruby *Steaks*?' I replied, 'I love it!'"

"So, he called me and wanted to talk more about it. 'I don't want to insult horse racing,' Ruby said, thinking his play on "steaks" rather than "stakes" might offend someone. "There's a lot of tradition... but let me think about it."

"A week later," Bach continued, "I'm at another soccer game, and I get a text that says, 'Call me now.' I reply, 'Can I call you at halftime?' Ruby texts back, 'No, call me now.' So, I call him, and he says, 'I was talking to Chris Collingsworth (retired Cincinnati Bengal great), and he says this is a [expletive] home run! The Jeff Ruby Steaks s-t-e-a-k-s is a [expletive] home run!' So I say, 'Great, but when I said it was a good idea, you didn't listen.' And he said, 'Well, Chip, you got to understand, Chris Collingsworth is a very smart guy.' And that's how it all started." The first Jeff Ruby Steaks was run in March 2018, and Turfway Park's premiere race gained the national attention it deserved.

Ruby's philosophy was first planted in his mother and stepfather's restaurants on the Jersey shore. After graduating from Cornell University, Ruby worked at the Holiday Inn in Downton Cincinnati, later becoming the Regional Director of all seven Holiday Inns in Cincinnati. Financially backed by Reds legends Johnny Bench and Pete Rose, Ruby opened the Precinct in 1981, followed by The Waterfront in 1986, and his other high-quality establishments.

Courtesy: Paulickreport.com

Above: Jeff Ruby; Below: First program cover

Ruby has become great for Turfway and horse racing in general. He gives heartily to the Permanently Disabled Jockey's Fund (PDJF). "You see many of his pants on jockeys, and that's because of the tremendous amount he gives to the Fund," Bach stated.

Blended Citizen and jockey Kyle Frey shot up the rail to win the 2018 $200,000 Grade III Jeff Ruby Steaks. With a span of just one neck, *Blended Citizen* bested *Pony Up* to give owners Greg Hall and Sayjay Racing 20 points on the road to Kentucky Derby. Doug F. O'Neill was the trainer. O'Neill had trained the 2012 Kentucky Derby and Preakness winner, *I'll Have Another*, and the 2016 Kentucky Derby winner, *Nyquist*.

Blended Citizen enjoyed a long career, finishing ninth in the Belmont in 2018, and even returned to Turfway Park in 2020 to run fourth in the Kentucky Cup Classic.

Before the 2019 Jeff Ruby Steaks, another type of excitement beheld the fans and team members on February 16. Bob Webster, then-security-guard and author of this book recalls, "I was standing in the winner's circle, as I was the guard posted there for many years. Chip, his parents, and a few other dignitaries were also taking in one of the early races on the card. The field of horses had just left the gate. Suddenly, over my radio came a voice, 'I think the clubhouse is on fire.' Chip looked at me the same instant I looked at him. He asked, 'Did he just say what I think he said?' I turned my back to the small crowd so as not to cause panic and returned the radio call. I ascertained **who** made the comment and asked anyone to confirm the report. Then came the bone-chilling reality. Guards on the backside, who had a far better view of the roof of the main building, came on the radio once again, 'Those are definitely flames coming out of the roof of the grandstands.'"

"I turned to Chip and quietly informed him of what I had learned. 'It's confirmed. There's a fire on the roof.' Knowing there would be no time to get another guard to the winner's circle to perform my duties before the current race had ended, I added, 'Do you have this?' 'Yes. Go!' was his quick reply. 'I'm on it,' I said as I bolted from the winner's circle and announced on the radio that we had

a confirmed fire on the roof. Two other guards met me on the fifth floor, and we made our way to the press box and judge's level of the structure. Climbing through a small hatch and making our way onto the roof, we could see flames shooting into

Fire on the roof at Turfway Park

Courtesy:Turfway Park videographers

the sky in the distance. Luckily, we were able to extinguish the fire shortly before fire crews arrived. Meanwhile, other security guards and team members successfully evacuated the entire building. It was a busy Friday night, so a quick and safe evacuation was a tribute to the security staff. No one was severely injured. The cause was a faulty gas-fed heating unit, one of about a dozen on the roof.

The 2019 running of the Jeff Ruby Steaks saw a familiar jockey in the winner's circle. Tyler Gaffalione, with trainer Michael Maker, stood proudly with *Somelikeithotbrown*. It was the fifth Spiral victory for Maker, and he would have another before this compilation was completed. *Somelikeithotbrown* had won the John Battaglia Memorial at Turfway Park a month earlier. He finished fourth in Lexington at the Blue Grass Stakes but skipped the Kentucky Derby. *Somelikeithotbrown* continued with an impressive career and is still racing in 2023.

Hard Rock Entertainment

Things still looked bleak for Turfway Park, even after the recent purchase by JACK Entertainment. None of the promised remodeling projects had taken place, and fans and team members alike were not impressed by the new corporate giant. While ownership changes came to Turfway Park again in April 2019, they would prove insignificant as time progressed. It was announced on April 8 that "Hard Rock Entertainment purchases Turfway Park."[11] However, it was soon revealed that the Turfway Park property was part of a "joint venture" in the buy. Hard Rock's purchase of JACK Casino in Downtown Cincinnati was the more significant part of the acquisition. Turfway Park was, apparently, just thrown into the deal for good measure. JACK Casino was renamed Hard Rock Cincinnati, and all rebranding dollars, remodeling, and upgrades were focused on the already-profitable Cincinnati casino.

Like with JACK Entertainment, Turfway Park was seen as the "stepchild," the "thorn on the rose," and the "eyesore" by Hard Rock. This was evidenced in the initial press releases, as Hard Rock chairman and CEO Jim Allen never mentioned the racetrack at all. "We look forward to introducing our unique brand of casino entertainment to Cincinnati. On behalf of the 40,000 Hard Rock team members worldwide, I am pleased to welcome the more than 1,000 JACK Cincinnati employees into the Hard Rock family."[12] He never once mentioned Florence, Kentucky, nor any plans for the ill-fated racetrack. The new $780 million investment gave ownership to both Hard Rock and the VICI corporation, a New York-based real estate investment trust with golf courses, restaurants, hotels, and casinos included in their vast portfolio.

In the following months, what was expected by Turfway Park team members came to fruition, that being nothing. Hard Rock management quickly announced "renovations and remodeling" to employees of the aging facility, but team members had seen and heard that before. The new owner's focus was all on the casino... and rightfully so. After all, that was where the money was. The popular attraction, right in the heart of Downtown Cincinnati, was bringing in millions, while Turfway Park was losing millions and about to cave in on itself.

In mid-2019, Hard Rock announced they would soon install hundreds of historical racing machines (HRMs) on the property to appease the Kentucky Racing Commission... and the highly-skeptical team members. At the time, Turfway Park was the only racetrack in Kentucky that had not yet installed the extremely profitable gaming devices, but nothing happened. The Commission came down hard, threatening to revoke already-scheduled racing dates from Turfway's calendar if the devices were not soon in place. Hard Rock management stalled and stalled... each month with empty promises.

With the earlier purchase of Turfway by JACK Casino and suddenly Hard Rock, most employees and horsemen alike had little hope for renovations. They worried more about the track's mere survival. Most in the business knew neither Jack nor Hard Rock owned racetracks at the time. They seemed to have no connection to the horse racing industry whatsoever. Why would they buy Turfway? In the end, the team members – as well as Turfway management – were right. While fans and employees waited and waited, no renovations or upgrades to the dilapidated grandstands ever came. The facility was literally falling apart.

While the love for Turfway Park ran deep with many fans and nearly every long-term employee, those visiting the place in 2019 had no difficulty seeing the ramshackle and worn-out conditions of the whole structure. On rainy days, as many as 15 garbage cans were scattered around on every floor of the main grandstands… to catch the rainwater pouring down from above. The outside stairwell, allowing racing fans access to the paddock and apron, was so rusty that most lacked the bravery to step foot upon them. Standing along the viewing platforms protruding from the front had been forbidden for years. The paint on the outside had faded so badly that the raw sheet metal was visible nearly everywhere. As for the interior wall colors, they could not be matched by even the most talented Sherwin and William experts. The restrooms were atrocious. While the cleaning crew did their best, some felt it might be more hygienic to urinate outside than to use the filthy and ill-smelling bathrooms… and many did!

The End Seems Near

The most devastating news eventually came in September 2019, when Churchill Downs announced they were asking the Kentucky Racing Commission to revoke *all* of Turfway's racing dates and award them to the already profitable Louisville racetrack. Absolutely Heartbreaking! And if that was not enough punishment, Churchill announced plans to build a "New Latonia" racetrack somewhere in Northern Kentucky! "Where would it be built," everyone asked. "Why would they do that?" There were few kind words expressed by the horsemen, patrons, and the loyal staff of Turfway Park... and just as much disbelief by those in the business nationwide. Rumors and speculation circled the racetrack and backside for weeks. Employees and fans alike pondered where the new track would be constructed. Rural Kenton County was one thought, somewhere in the Independence area – or maybe southern Campbell County near the AA Highway. At any rate, the loyal staff, many who had been there for decades, was devastated.

JACK Entertainment had taken over Turfway Park in 2015 and, with Churchill's announcement, a JACK representative said, "We will not go down without a fight. We are shocked and thoroughly disappointed by Churchill's recent attack on Turfway Park, which has been a significant part of the Northern Kentucky community for over 60 years. JACK Entertainment and Hard Rock International will jointly defend the longstanding racing dates that have regularly been awarded to Turfway Park and contest the inappropriate actions of Churchill Downs."[13]

Phase One of Churchill's New Latonia facility was a $150 million project that would include a historical racing machine facility, a clubhouse, a one-mile synthetic main racetrack, an inner dirt track, and stabling facilities. Phase Two would add a hotel, with an additional investment of up to $50 million.

"Our willingness to make a sizable investment in the neglected Northern Kentucky market is our latest effort to improve Kentucky's valuable horse racing and agricultural industries," Churchill Downs president Kevin Flanery said in a news release. "Just as Derby City Gaming's historical racing machines have supercharged purses at Churchill Downs Racetrack, we plan to do the same for Northern Kentucky's racing fans at New Latonia. We aim to deliver an ultra-competitive racing product with more entries and higher-quality horses that appeal to bettors and horseplayers nationwide."[14]

All blame went to the former owners, who refused to spend the money to place historical racing machines at Turfway Park. Other tracks in Kentucky had installed such devices and were already reaping significant revenue increases. But at Turfway Park, it seemed JACK would not spend the money for long-overdue renovations to make the new machines an option. "We heard lots of things... saw lots of drawings," said Florence Mayor Diane Whalen. "We've been through years of empty promises," added Gary W. Moore, Boone County judge-executive.[15] Kentucky State majority leader Damon Thayer, once Turfway Park's director of communications, had called the track "the weak link" in Kentucky's racing circuit, complaining about its failure to install the historical racing machines that have sparked a dramatic surge in race purses at the state's other tracks. Mark Simendinger, formerly the track's president, said Turfway Park was "being held hostage by the casino in Cincinnati (JACK), implying that the former racetrack owner had conflicting interests regarding Turfway Park

Courtesy: Robert Webster

Courtesy: Robert Webster

A vacated Turfway Park --

Top: The Paddock, where over the years thousands of fine Thoroughbreds roamed;

Bottom: The main grandstands, viewed from the aisle just below the third floor level

While a group of photos without any people might seem boring or unmeaningful to some, the pictures on this and the following spread mean a lot to those employees and patrons of the Old Turfway Park. These are included here so those long-time team members and guests can reminisce and dream about the "good ol' days" at Turfway Park.

Opposite page: Top row, left to right: First floor view standing in front of the maintence/security departments; First floor smoking section looking toward the mutuel windows from in front of the Homestretch restaurant;

Second row, left to right: Homestretch restaurant; First floor non-smolking carroll section;

Third row, left to right: First floor concession area;   First floor, non-smoking area;

Bottom photo: First floor program booth.

This page: Top photo: Second floor "dark-side" -- parking lot side; Bottom photo: Second floor track side.

All images on this page courtesy: Robert Webster

195

All images on this page courtesy: Robert Webster

This page, top photo: Third floor view from in front of the Party Deck;

Bottom: Second floor view, looking from in front of the concession area;

Opposite page, top left: Fifth floor hallway;

Top right: View of the Paddock;

Bottom two images: The last known photos taken before the demolition of Turfway Park.

and their popular casino in Downtown Cincinnati. "JACK Casino continually misled racing fans, horsemen, regulators, and legislators," Thayer said.[16]

But in October 2019, Churchill Downs revealed their actual plan. The rumors were over. It was true; they were going to build a multi-million-dollar gaming and racing facility "somewhere" in Northern Kentucky. However, it was going to be built on the grounds of old Turfway Park in Florence, Kentucky![17]

Chapter Seven Endnotes

1. "Turfway Park on track to host live racing once again," *Cincinnati Enquirer*, November 30, 2013, retrieved on September 30, 2022.
2. "Spiral shines at Turfway Park," *Cincinnati Enquirer*, March 24, 2014, retrieved on September 30, 2022.
3. "After 43 Years, Battaglia Calls it Quits," *Thoroughbred Daily News*, March 4, 2016, retrieved on June 30, 2022.
4. Personal interview with Billy Troilo on November 16, 2022.
5. "Wiener dog racing comes to Turfway," *Cincinnati Enquirer*, September 19, 2013, retrieved on September 14, 2022.
6. Jose Lezcano, Wikipedia.com, retrieved on August 31, 2022.
7. Personal interview with Aaron Spurlock, Mutuel Room Manager, on October 28, 2022.
8. Personal interview with Chip Bach on October 18, 2022.
9. *Ibid.*
10. "Jockey Perry Ouzts, 63, rides his 50,000 race, hustling his mount to second place at Turfway Park," *nkytribune*, March 4, 2018, retrieved on September 30, 2022.
11. "Hard Rock Entertainment Purchases Turfway Park," Blood-Horse Magazine, April 8, 2019, retrieved on September 3, 2022.
12. *Ibid.*
13. "Turfway Park is shocked by move: Churchill Downs out to overtake 2020 race dates," *Courier-Journal*, September 7, 2019, retrieved on September 30, 2022.
14. *Ibid.*
15. "New Day for Turfway," *Cincinnati Enquirer*, January 25, 2020, retrieved on September 18, 2022.
16. Tim Sullivan, "Churchill Downs is set to buy Turfway Park after tense dispute," *Courier-Journal*, October 3, 2019, retrieved on July 17, 2022.
17. *Ibid.*

Chapter Eight

Churchill Downs to the Rescue

It is quite possible that Churchill Downs' executives pulled a fast one on JACK/Hard Rock International. With their announced plan to build a "New Latonia" racetrack somewhere in Northern Kentucky, the casinos saw their ownership of Turfway Park as a massive money pit about to become a vacant ghost town. They knew the dilapidated structure could not be renovated without spending tens of millions of dollars, money they were absolutely unwilling to allocate toward their recent acquisition. They knew Northern Kentucky could not support two Thoroughbred tracks, and that the Kentucky Racing Commission would not likely approve a second track anyway. When Churchill management offered to purchase the property, JACK/Hard Rock never hesitated before saying yes. After all, they wanted nothing to do with the racetrack in the first place. Unbeknownst to the casino giants, however, Churchill's plan from the very beginning was to acquire Turfway Park. Their announcement to build something new elsewhere in the region was simply an attempt to lower Turfway's value for a quick sale.

In October 2019, employees at the destitute Turfway Park were called to the fifth-floor Racing Club. Unaware of the pending announcement, they anxiously waited, and rumors again circulated. "Amazon had purchased the property for a massive warehouse," they thought. "The nearby airport had bought the land for a runway expansion." The most prevalent – "The business would cease to exist, and a new racetrack would be built elsewhere in the upper three counties of the state." After takeovers had failed twice in recent years and many empty promises had come along, team members were far from eager to hear the news. That morning, executives from Churchill Downs Incorporated announced that, through its wholly-owned subsidiary NKYRG, LLC, it had signed a definitive agreement to acquire Turfway Park from JACK Entertainment and Hard Rock International for a total consideration of $46 million in cash.[1] The financial closing would be contingent upon approval by the Kentucky Racing Commission, but their decision was expected to be quick and positive.

The announcement was first-class all the way. Churchill Downs even had representatives from their human resources department make the journey from Louisville, to answer questions from team members about the overall transition, what health benefits would be available, PTO, existing seniority, etc. To say the mood in the room changed from fear and depression to cheer and optimism is an extreme understatement. The feeling amongst those on hand could better be defined as euphoric. Most employees knew that the various companies who had taken control of Turfway Park over the past few years had no experience running a Thoroughbred racetrack. JACK's purchase of the trendy and already financially successful Downtown Cincinnati casino simply included Turfway Park. In contrast, Turfway employees knew Churchill's impressive background. They knew the company had tremendous success operating a racetrack, and they knew there would likely be millions upon millions of dollars available for the future success of their beloved workplace.

According to their website, in 2023, Churchill Downs, Incorporated owned more than a dozen entities across the country, including Churchill Downs racetrack and two Derby City Gaming venues in Louisville; Oak Grove, a racing, gaming, and hotel property on the Tennessee border below Hopkinsville, Kentucky; Twinspires, an on-line wagering corporation; UnitedTote gaming services; Calder Casino in Miami Gardens, Florida; the Fair Grounds, a racecourse and slots facility in New Orleans, Louisiana; Harlow's Casino Resort and Spa in Greenville, Mississippi; Lady Luck Casino in Farmington, Pennsylvania; Miami Valley Gaming in Lebanon, Ohio; Ocean Downs Casino in Berlin, Maryland; Oxford Casino Hotel and Event Center in Oxford, Maine; Presque Isle Downs Casino in Erie, Pennsylvania; Rivers Casino in Des Plaines, Illinois; Riverwalk Casino/Hotel in Vicksburg, Mississippi; and Queen of Terre Haute Casino Resort in Terre Haute, Indiana.

As the meeting continued, it was stated that racing dates for the 2019-2020 Winter Meet would remain as scheduled; those already approved by the Commission for JACK. The more important news: Churchill Downs announced it would not pursue the construction of a "New" Latonia Race Track elsewhere in Northern Kentucky. Furthermore, they did not propose any remodeling of the current facility. Instead, they told team members that demolition of the grandstands would begin immediately after the following season, making room for "Turfway Park Racing and Gaming," a $200 million state-of-the-art live and historical Thoroughbred racing facility, right on the original Turfway Park property.[2]

When then-President of Churchill Downs Race Track, Kevin Flanery, spoke to the large group of employees, news media, and a handful of long-time bettors, he said, "We are thrilled to welcome Turfway Park to the Churchill Downs family. Our team is poised to restore Turfway to its former glory, anchored by Northern Kentucky's first historical racing machine facility. The result will be a first-class racing product, fueled by increased purses, that keeps high-quality horses in Kentucky year-round and appeals to horseplayers nationwide." This was the extreme opposite style of promotion from those made by the big casino owners a few years earlier. Those CEOs never even mentioned Turfway Park when announcing they had purchased the Downtown Cincinnati property.

The New Turfway Park would support up to 400 full- and part-time positions and create an estimated 800 construction jobs. The project would include a historical racing machine facility featuring up to 1,500 machines, a state-of-the-art clubhouse, food and beverage venues, and a new inner dirt track to complement the existing one-mile synthetic track.[3]

While the Winter/Spring Meet continued as usual, all attention was placed on the future. Artist's renderings of the proposed facility were hung on a wall on the first floor of the grandstands adjacent to the concession stand, along with historic photographs of the original building's construction in 1959. For months, fans stood in awe of what was to come and, at the same time, reminisced about what was about to fade away into history. By early 2020, staff began the arduous task of packing and labeling boxes, removing photographs and artwork from all five floors of the grandstands, and filling a dozen large storage containers lining the west-side parking lot. In the closing days of the meet – the final days of a tired old Turfway Park, many patrons took what they could of the broken-down place as souvenirs. Small signs designating "The Racebook," decorative mirrors, and even a few pieces of valuable memorabilia hanging in the general offices

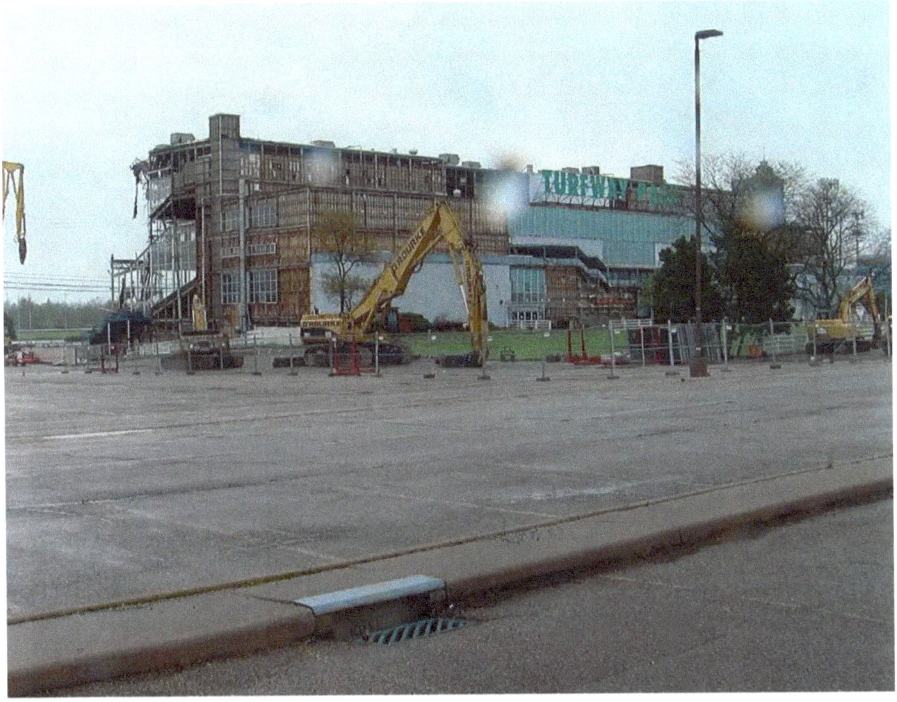

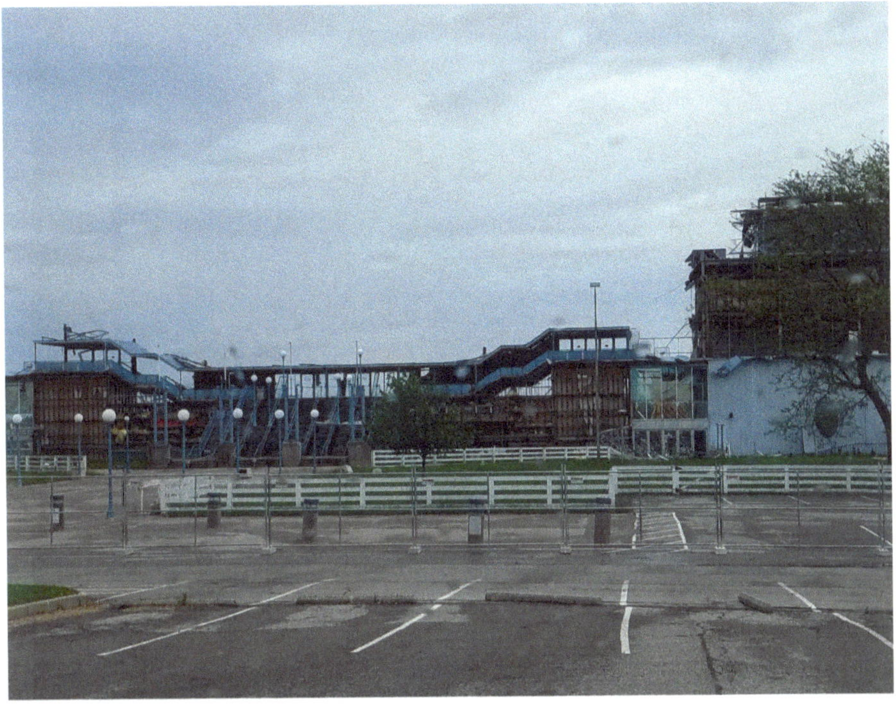

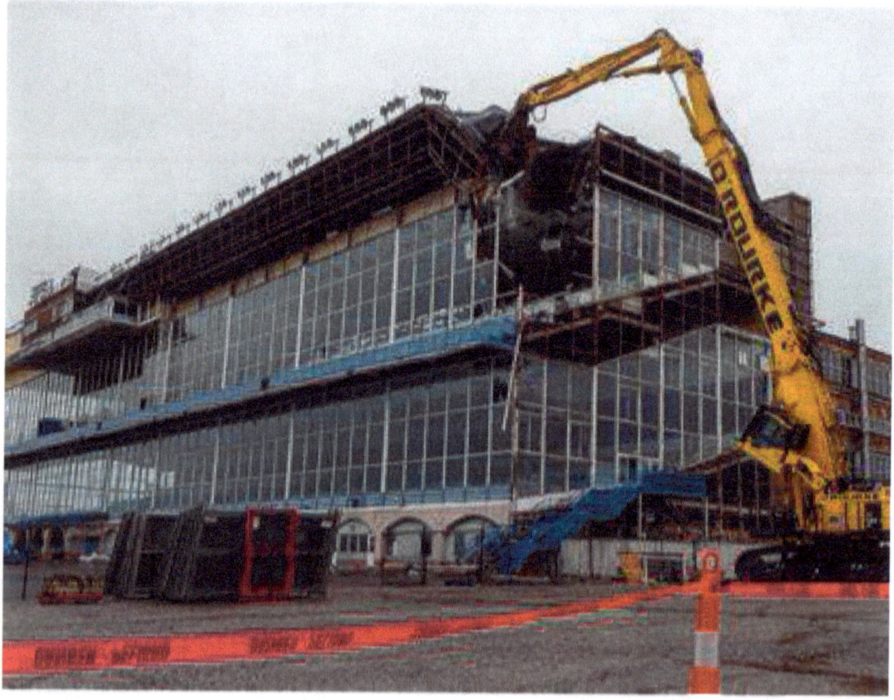

All images on this spread courtesy: Robert Webster

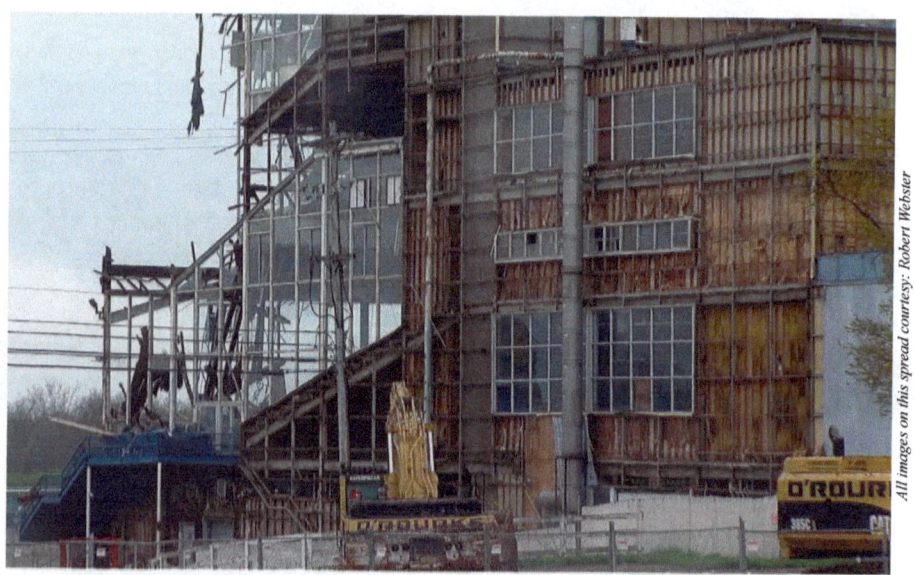

had suddenly gone missing. A few employees also grabbed what they could. The hundreds of blue seats that once held tens-of-thousands of horse racing fans over the years, were carefully removed by the demolition crew and sold. The hand-painted ceramic jockeys in the paddock and the concrete-molded horse heads lining the apron and paddock had to be removed or guarded by security.

Covid-19

Then, with only a couple of weeks left on the racing card, the Covid 19 (Coronavirus) epidemic hit. This was devastating to team members, especially those life-long employees of the company. Some racing dates were canceled out of fear of spreading the sickness. Bill Troilo, Clerk of Scales and Senior State Steward, said, "I didn't think we would survive."[4] General Manager Chip Bach recalled early meetings with Churchill Downs' management regarding the situation, "The conversation was basically that they thought this [epidemic] might last a couple of weeks," he stated. "Churchill's priority was to protect the team members, and I was extremely impressed by that. Of course, as a publicly held company, they wanted to make the correct fiduciary decisions, but at the same time, their first priority was to protect the employees. I couldn't help but think... if this were JACK, they would have used this as an expense-reduction exercise, and they would have clobbered the workers until whatever time they were needed again. Churchill was totally the opposite. I immediately said to myself, 'Thanks for keeping me... and this is the company I want to work for.' Indeed, it was Churchill to the rescue in more ways than one."[5]

As the day of the 2020 Jeff Ruby Steaks, approached, worry became prevalent that it, too, might be canceled. While the day went off as scheduled, it cannot be said that the event went off as anticipated. Due to the forecast of cold weather, management knew that spectators would have been forced to seek indoor refuge. The VIP tent was ready to seat 1,000, and fans in the clubhouse would be shoulder-to-shoulder. Bach realized that the possibility of spreading the virus was high, with people being in such close proximity to each other. At the last minute, he had no choice but to rule the enormously popular event "closed to the public."

The $250,000 Grade III Jeff Ruby Steaks in 2020 was the last big event at "Old Turfway Park" – a name reminiscent of how the original Latonia Race Track became known as "Old Latonia." To an utterly non-existent audience, *Field Pass*, trained by Michael Maker and ridden by Irad Ortiz, Jr., sped by the projected leader *Invader* in the final furlong to an eerily silent victory. It was the sixth Spiral win for Maker. Ortiz had won the 2016 Breeder's Cup and would go on to win the 2022 Belmont Stakes. He won the Eclipse Award for Outstanding Jockey in 2018 and 2019. *Field Pass* continues an impressive career at the time of this compilation, with several graded stakes wins, including Keeneland's Transylvania Stakes and the Ontario Derby in 2020, the Baltimore-Washington International at Pimlico in 2021, and the Texas Turf Classic in 2022.

Immediately after the big event, and with only a few days left in the 2022 meet, Kentucky Governor Andy Beshear signed his "Healthy at Home" executive orders. Suddenly, the general public was no longer permitted in the facility. However, the track's backside remained open for training because it fell under the "life-sustaining business" category. It provided "food, shelter, and other necessities of life for animals." Only a handful of employees were allowed to remain on the property. There, they carefully continued removing any viable items and packing them up for the move.

Demolition of the massive, aged structure began almost immediately after the final weekend of racing. Laural Bishop, Union Steward and a mutuel clerk with the company for more than 40 years, organized a "Thursday Lunch Outing" in the parking lot closest to Turfway Road. She recalled, "A group of clerks and other friends would bring lunch and gather for a couple of hours. Yes, wine was often involved. It was a great way to keep in touch. On the first day of the tear-down, we had a pop-up tent (it was raining). Because of Covid, Chip sent security by to tell us to take it down and space ourselves out. From then on, we all wore masks and kept our distance. Several tears were wept that first day as she [the building] went down." This heartfelt ritual continued for many weeks as the still-grieving team members watched sorrowfully at the loss of their place of employment. Many knew there were good things to come, but the sight of the cranes with their wrecking balls and bulldozers pushing debris aside was nearly too much for them to handle.

Meanwhile, the Covid virus also wreaked havoc on the demolition. Workers became scarce, as so many were down with the bug. The enormous expansion of nearby manufacturing and shipping companies added to the problem. Construction projects in the surrounding community were booming at the time, with the $1.5 billion Amazon complex and other equally-impressive developments. The county's population, about 132,000, had doubled since 1980. For several months, it seemed that the building stood half-demolished. What an eerie sight to stand in the jockey's parking lot and look *into* the building, into the fifth-floor restrooms, and behind the third-floor concession stand. When the Covid-19 virus subsided somewhat, everything was a "go" again, and within weeks, the property was leveled to the ground and enormous amounts of debris had been removed.

Tapeta Track

It did not take long for Turfway Park team members to realize that Churchill Downs' promises would be fulfilled. Of course, they promised the old structure would be demolished – and it was. Also guaranteed were higher purses. Incredibly, they rose significantly immediately after Churchill signed the check to purchase Turfway. Another early assurance was a new track. In March 2020, before demolition was complete, workers began replacing the existing Polytrack with a $5.6 million Tapeta synthetic track, one of the world's leading surfaces for racing and training. Tapeta comprises a carefully selected mixture of silica sand, wax, and fibers that have been extensively researched to simulate the root structure of turf.[6] It had been tested in all climates at training and racetracks worldwide. For Turfway Park, it will permit continued racing in extreme weather conditions and allow for the track's ongoing successful record regarding breakdowns and jockey injuries.

Newport Racing and Gaming

Churchill Downs management knew there would be no revenue from Turfway Park Racing and Gaming until after its completion, and that property was not scheduled to open until late 2022. Therefore, they made other plans. In May 2020, the Kentucky Horse Racing Commission approved a plan for Churchill to lease space in the Newport Shopping Center at Monmouth Street and Carothers Avenue. Churchill's board approved up to $38.4 million in spending at Newport on the same day as the commission's decision. Remodeling of the 47,000-square-foot venue began immediately.

Newport Racing and Gaming was to employ approximately 70 full-time people. Billed as an "extension" of the upcoming re-opening of Turfway Park, Churchill revealed they had been looking for a second location for a casino gaming facility in Northern Kentucky for months. Newport City Manager Tom Fromme said, "This is a tremendous announcement for the city of Newport. We are grateful that Churchill Downs, one of the most revered names in the horse racing and gaming industries, will develop an attraction that will create jobs and bring visitors and excitement to the city. There's no other way to put it... this is big!" Newport Mayor Jerry Peluso added, "Along with the world-class indoor-outdoor music venue now under construction, one of the region's top attractions with the Newport Aquarium, theaters, and many other entertainment options, it just makes sense that the Churchill group is bringing gaming back to Newport. Their investment will create jobs and help the city financially."[7]

The preliminary concept for the facility called for a large gaming floor with 500 historical racing machines (HRMs). It would have a horse racing simulcast area with a VIP room and bar. Churchill CEO Bill Carstanjen said the Newport facility would "...immediately generate larger purses for live racing at Kentucky racetracks, attract better horses, spur interest in pari-mutuel wagering in Kentucky, and increase the value of horses as they transition into breeding.[8]

However, the Kentucky Supreme Court upended the entire state's $2 billion racing industry in September 2020. In a surprise 7-0 ruling, the high court defined "pari-mutuel wagering" more narrowly than the Kentucky Horse Racing Commission and the state's racetracks preferred. The court found that the gaming devices reviewed in the case, made by Exacta and currently used at three of the

All images on this spread courtesy: Robert Webster

state's gaming venues, did not constitute pari-mutuel wagering. Slot machines and other forms of casino gambling were constitutionally barred in Kentucky. Still, racetracks had installed thousands of devices that look and feel like slot machines over the previous decade. Historical horse racing machines are based on the premise that players are betting on previously run horse races invisible to them. While the court ruling's long-term impact was not clear, Churchill Downs moved forward with their plan, based on the fact that *its* gaming systems, in use at Derby City in Louisville, Oak Grove in Southern Kentucky, and the planned venue in Newport, are made by a different vendor and were not examined as part of the court case.[9] Eventually, Kentucky lawmakers passed a bill to legalize the devices, which Governor Andy Beshear, a Democrat, signed. The bill changed the definition of pari-mutuel wagering in Kentucky to include those specific types of machines.

In October 2020, gambling returned to Newport, Kentucky, where it had once thrived. More than 50 *illegal* casinos were scattered across the city from the 1930s through the 1950s but, now, Newport Racing and Gaming opened as a legal entity due to recent changes in the law. When it opened, however, the Covid-19 Virus was still strong in the region. From day one and for many months afterward, plastic dividers separated the gaming machines, dozens of hand-sanitizer stations were scattered about the place, and any guest could press a game's service button to have the device wiped down and sanitized. Many compliments were bestowed by guests regarding the cleanliness of the gaming floor and restrooms – especially from people who often frequented other area casinos.

Michael Taylor

Michael Taylor was named president of both Turfway Park and Newport Racing and Gaming in 2020. Working with Chip Bach, who remained general manager, Taylor became responsible for successfully leading the overall direction, administration, and coordination of all activities. He brought 20 years of gaming leadership experience in regulatory and corporate roles. Taylor, whose calm demeanor projects both confidence and professionalism, led various operational teams, including gaming, racing, food and beverage, and security, and had already served on the opening teams for three gaming properties. With a background in law enforcement, Taylor started his gaming career as Surveillance Supervisor for the Seneca Gaming Authority in Niagara Falls, New York. He was later named General Manager of Empire City Casino in Yonkers, New York, and served as Vice President of Operations and Vice President of Hospitality. Bill Mudd, the new President and Chief Operating Officer for Churchill Downs, Incorporated, later said,

"Michael's leadership style focuses on the importance of mentoring team members and growing talent from within, so we look forward to witnessing hundreds of new jobs develop into rewarding careers."[10]

"I am incredibly excited to join the team in Northern Kentucky as we continue preparations leading up to Turfway's grand opening," Taylor said. "I also look forward to develop-

Courtesy: Churchill Downs

Michael Taylor

ing strong relationships with the community and growing our team to continue building on the legacy of Turfway Park and our success in Newport."[11]

In a later interview, Taylor stated, "Horse racing's well-documented multi-billion-dollar impact notwithstanding, there is little doubt that the Turfway Park/Newport Racing and Gaming combo will be a boom to the local economy and regional tourism market. Besides high-tech improvements for the horse racing enthusiasts and bettors at both locations, Turfway Park will host weddings, parties, group outings, and more. With CVG [Cincinnati/Northern Kentucky International Airport] right in the backyard," he continued, "we will host trade shows, VIP events, and more, at the scenic and iconic Turfway Park, with exhilarating live racing as the backdrop. I can't imagine another entertainment venue matching that type of excitement."[12]

Back at the Turfway Park property, the Kentucky Horse Racing Commission granted dates for the Holiday/Winter Meet for 2020/2021. Of course, there was yet to be a new facility. Still, Thoroughbred racing continued. Covid-19 regulations remained, meaning no spectators were permitted on the property. It was an extraordinary sight with only the horses, jockeys, trainers, and owners at the track. No cheering from the apron or paddock, no loudspeakers blaring the announcer's voice as he called the races. But even with no spectators, the purchase by Churchill Downs brought still higher purses at Turfway Park. In addition, better-quality horses, jockeys, and trainers were commonplace. Daily purses before the acquisition ranged around $95,000, but topped $179,000 afterward – due to Churchill's involvement and nothing else.

On Friday, March 19, 2021, Churchill Downs hosted a groundbreaking ceremony at the Florence, Kentucky, property for the $145 million renovation project: Turfway Park Racing and Gaming. At the private event, management announced they would replace the rusty grandstands, build a new, state-of-the-art clubhouse facility, install 1,500 historical racing machines, and build a new one-mile synthetic track – all part of the company's plan to revitalize Thoroughbred racing in the region. The venue was projected to be open by late summer 2022. While not open to the public due to Covid-19 restrictions, the entire cere-

Courtesy: WCPO Cincinnati

Groundbreaking ceremony for the New Turfway Park Racing and Gaming

mony was streamed live on Facebook, a social media platform. Guest speakers included Kentucky Governor Andy Beshear, Boone County state Senator John Schickel, Kenton County State Representative Adam Koenig, City of Florence Mayor Diane Whalen, Churchill Downs CEO Bill Carstanjen, and Turfway Park General Manager Chip Bach. Bach said, "The new facility will greatly benefit the community. Not only will we have a robust gaming operation here, but our horse racing has been in the area in one form or another since 1883, and it's been tremendous. We'll continue to expand upon our ability to provide top-level entertainment to this area, satisfy the community with more entertainment options, and hopefully draw more people to the area." Bill Carstanjen, CEO of Churchill Downs, reminded the public, "This project will revitalize the Kentucky winter Thoroughbred racing circuit as well as fuel the health of the Commonwealth's entire signature horse industry. There are many people who are a part of this community and a part of this state who are the unsung heroes in making this project happen." Kentucky Speaker of the House, David W. Osborne, added, "The impact of this project on the Northern Kentucky economy cannot be understated. Additionally, the overall impact on Kentucky's horse industry and, consequently, our entire economy is dramatic. Turfway Park's return to racing prominence secures and enhances Kentucky's year-round racing circuit and will result in the return of horses and the investments of owners, breeders, and trainers from around the country."[13] According to Governor Andy Beshear, horse racing in Kentucky brings $3.4 billion in yearly revenue, a significant portion of Kentucky's $8.9 billion in tourism dollars. City of Florence Mayor Whalen said, "We have seen so much growth and development recently. There is much positive energy in our community. This [Turfway Park] was a diamond in the rough, and we are very appreciative of Churchill Downs for polishing that diamond for Florence and Boone County."

New Latonia and Turfway Park have always played an essential role in the Northern Kentucky community. Numerous charities have been assisted over the years, and that standard of excellence will undoubtedly continue into the future. Some street names adjacent to the park have even been given names familiar to horse racing fans. They stand as evidence of the importance Turfway

Park plays in the city and in the region. One can find Pat Day Drive, named for the Hall of Fame jockey, and Hansel Avenue, named for one of the many successful horses that ran at Turfway Park. Also present are Beam Avenue, named after the Jim Beam Stakes; Spiral Drive, named for the 40-year history of Turfway's premiere race; and Thoroughbred Avenue, named for the extraordinary breed of horses that have made Kentucky the Thoroughbred Capital of the World.

The 2021 running of the Jeff Ruby Steaks was won by *Like the King*, with Drayden Van Dyke in the irons. Wesley Ward was the trainer, giving him his first Spiral victory. Van Dyke won the 2014 Eclipse Award for Outstanding Apprentice Jockey and was victorious in numerous stakes events ranging from Grade I to Grade III races. *Like the King* went on to the Kentucky Derby that year, finishing a disappointing eleventh place. He had several finishes in the money through 2022, but the Jeff Ruby Steaks was his only graded stakes win.[14]

Soon after the Jeff Ruby Steaks was run, it was announced in *Blood-Horse* magazine that Churchill Downs was investing even more money in the Florence, Kentucky property. "We have decided to invest an additional $26 million to improve the dormitories for the track workers and build five addition-al barns for the horses. We are also replacing or improving some of the basic infrastructures to improve the overall facility," said Bill Carstanjen, CEO of Churchill Downs, Inc. "The positive impact of historical racing machines on the Kentucky Thoroughbred racing circuit is undeniable, and this additional infra-structure is warranted to support the growing operations at Turfway Park." Again, what a difference between the recent casino ownerships and Churchill Downs.

In November 2021, Newport Racing and Gaming opened a new 14,000-square-foot section after Ace Hardware moved to a larger facility nearby. The new area includes a climate-controlled smoking/gaming area, a new bar, and a stage for live entertainment. The Newport Racing and Gaming team moved 150 existing historical racing machines to the new expansion area to make everyone comfortable. Before the expansion, more than 500 machines were on the main gaming floor, making it somewhat difficult for guests to walk through the prop-

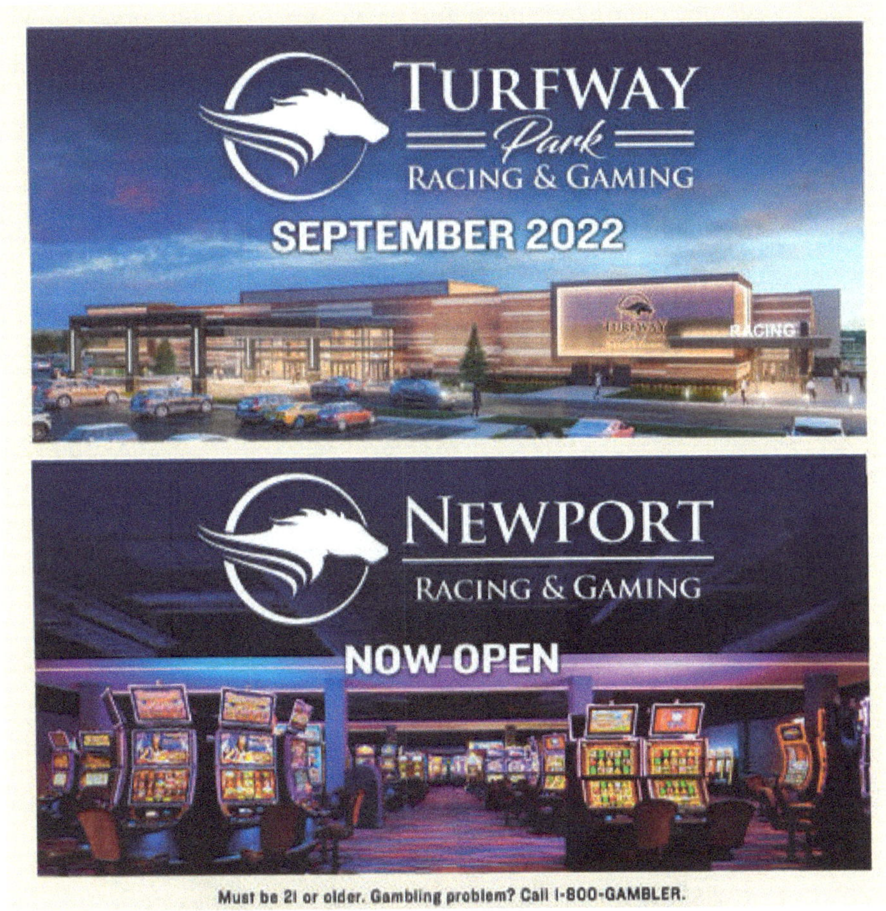
TURFWAY
Park
RACING & GAMING
SEPTEMBER 2022
RACING
NEWPORT
RACING & GAMING
NOW OPEN
Must be 21 or older. Gambling problem? Call 1-800-GAMBLER.

TURFWAY
Park
RACING & GAMING
A NEW WINNING LEGACY BEGINS
GRAND OPENING SEPTEMBER 1

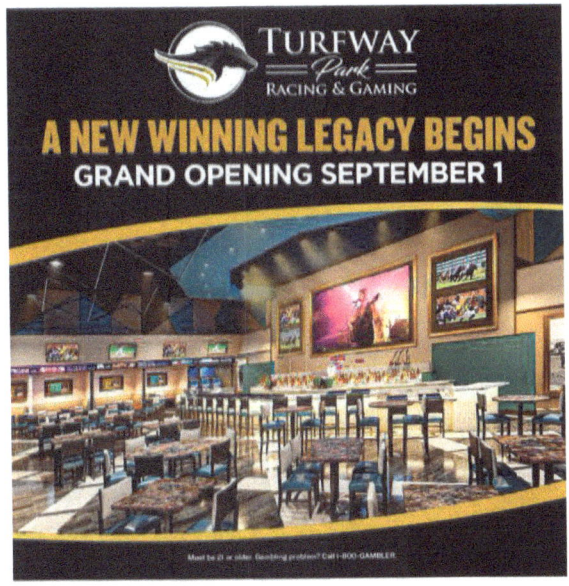

erty. The addition came a little more than a year after the facility opened. Since then, the nearly $40 million project has created more than 70 permanent jobs.

In the spring of 2022, live racing still could not be viewed in person at Turfway Park. Everyday races went off in silence, yet winners and losers still found their way into the record books. It remained a most-unusual setup; live racing was conducted every Wednesday, Thursday, Friday, and Saturday – with no fans whatsoever. "I'm not aware of anyone else in the country doing this," said Chip Bach, General Manager, who had been running the show since 2012 and working there since 1999. "It's an intimate way to race, but somewhat depressing since fans can't enjoy it."[15] For the time being, wagering was done off-track, online, and at Turfway's "sister" facility, Newport Racing and Gaming.

The 2022 Jeff Ruby Steaks

The 2022 edition of the Jeff Ruby Steaks featured an astounding $600,000 purse to the winner and served as a 120-point qualifying race for the prestigious Kentucky Derby. It is remarkable how the purchase of Turfway Park by Churchill Downs increased the purse of the premiere race from $250,000 to $600,000 in such a short time. The new track surface made a difference as well. While called the "Jeff Ruby Steaks," Ruby was no longer under contract at the time. Bach explained, "Actually, the contract ran out a couple of years prior. But due to Covid and the construction going on, I told him, 'Why don't we just keep your name on the race? There's no value in asking you for money for it, because we don't have any fans here. We're not going to do a tent, either.'" Jeff Ruby was quick to agree to those terms.

The 2022 Jeff Ruby Steaks, the last major event at "Old Turfway Park," witnessed jockey Brian Hernandez, Jr. back in the winner's circle. Hernandez had won the 2016 Spiral aboard *Oscar Nominated*. This time, trainer Kenneth G. McPeek and Magdalena Racing brought *Tiz the Bomb* to the event. *Tiz the Bomb* had won the John Battaglia Memorial at Turfway Park one month earlier. While there were no fans to experience the race, the 2022 Spiral would prove to be one of the most historic of any event ever held at Latonia/Turfway Park. *Tiz the Bomb* found himself in sixth place entering the first turn, with *Tawny Port* a neck ahead. *Rich Strike* was dead last as the field of 12 entered the backstretch. *Tiz the Bomb* made his move along the outside just before the far turn and never looked back, winning by nearly three lengths. *Tawny Port*, with Manuel Franco in the irons, finished second. *Rich Strike*, ridden by Sonny Leon, remarkably moved from last place to third. It is what happened a few weeks later that made the race historic.

For the first time in Spiral history – or Turfway Park history, three Thoroughbreds who raced on the "minor-league" track in Florence, Kentucky, made it to the big time – the Run for the Roses – the Kentucky Derby – all on the same day! Turfway had hosted an impressive list of horses who achieved greatness over the years. Some were stabled at and trained at Turfway, choosing to work out on the consistently fast and safe Polytrack and now Tapeta track. Some were entered in a single Turfway race before moving on to more significant competitions. A selected list of world-class Thoroughbreds with a history at Turfway Park (Old Latonia and New Latonia) includes *Leonatus* (1883), *Zev* (1923), *Inca Roca* (1976), *Marfa* (1983), *Summer Squall* (1990), *Hansel* (1991), *Lil E. Tee* (1992), *Prairie Bayou* (1993), *Polar Expedition* (1994), *Perfect Drift* (2002), *Flower Alley* (2005), *Hard Spun* (2007), and *Animal Kingdom* (2011), and the list will continue to grow with Churchill Down's purchase of the facility in 2019.

Rich Strike

Another horse was added to the Turfway legacy in 2022. *Rich Strike*, a chestnut colt with a white blaze and two white socks on his hind legs, made his three-year-old debut in the Leonatus Stakes at Turfway Park on January 22, 2022. As had become his pattern as a two-year-old, he was well back in the early running, then made a late run to finish third. He turned in a similar performance on March 5 in the John Battaglia Memorial Stakes at Turfway, finishing fourth. For his third start of the year, *Rich Strike* entered the Jeff Ruby Steaks on April 2. He was near the back of the field for most of the race but found an inside path in the stretch and as previously noted, closed well to finish third behind *Tiz the Bomb* and *Tawny Port*.

The third-place finish in Turfway's Jeff Ruby Steaks gave *Rich Strike* 20 points on the road to the Kentucky Derby to sneak in as an "also eligible" entry. It was not until *Ethereal Road* was scratched from the Derby at the last minute that Turfway's colt was placed in the 20-horse field. In fact, the call from Barbara Borden, chief steward, came to trainer Eric Reed just 30 seconds before the deadline.[16] The field for the 2022 Derby was considered by many to be the deepest in recent memory. There were at least six highly regarded entries but no clear standout. *Rich Strike* was completely overlooked at odds of 80-1. He broke well from the outside post position and settled into the back of the pack, where he was in eighteenth place after the first half-mile. *Summer is Tomorrow* and *Crown Pride* battled up front. *Rich Strike* made his move on the final turn while weaving through traffic, shifting out four horses wide of the rail and then back toward

the fence. In the stretch, he was checked briefly by a tiring horse, but again found racing room and launched a sustained drive to the inside of *Epicenter*. Jockey Sonny Leon brought *Rich Strike* clear of all others in the final furlong to win by three-quarters of a length.

Courtesy: www.en.liderendeportes.com

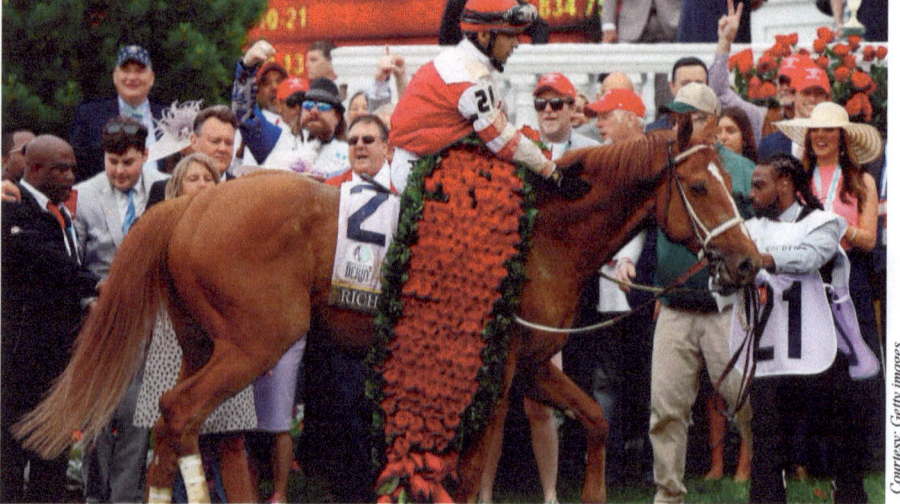

Courtesy: Getty images

Top: Sonny Leon; Bottom: Sonny Leon aboard Rich Strike, winner of the 2022 Kentucky Derby

Rich Strike was the second-biggest longshot to ever win the Kentucky Derby after *Donerail* (92-1 odds) in 1913. The 2022 Derby was the first graded stakes win for Leon, who rode six horses to victory at Cincinnati's Belterra Park the day before the Kentucky Derby. He is a frequent competitor at Turfway Park and lives in Florence, Kentucky. At the time of this publication in early 2023, Leon has racked up over 830 career wins in the United States.[17] *Rich Strike* skipped the Preakness and finished sixth in the Belmont Stakes.

Turfway Park was undoubtedly well represented in the 2022 Kentucky Derby, with *Tiz the Bomb* finishing ninth, *Tawny Port*, another frequent Turfway entry finishing seventh, and *Rich Strike* as the victor. Chip Bach said the new Tapeta track would entice even more high-quality Thoroughbreds and more premiere stakes races, including a revamped Latonia Derby. In a June 2022 interview, Bach reminded readers, "The Latonia Derby used to be the biggest race in the nation. It was bigger than the Kentucky Derby. Now that Churchill Downs owns us," Bach continued, "they have invested a lot of money to bring that race back to its original luster." Purses at Turfway Park skyrocketed again. During its 2021-2022 season that concluded April 2, Turfway paid $17,711,412 in purses, up 79 percent compared to the $9,896,500 paid out during racing at the 2019-2020 meet.[18] And for Bach's overall impression of the new owners, "It's been three years now, and they've done every single thing they said they would."[19]

Construction Continues

During the summer, Sam Knef from Louisville's *Spectrum News* said, "Kentucky horse racing hype is at its peak around Kentucky Derby time, but many people in Northern Kentucky wonder when they will be able to play games and watch races at the region's newest state-of-the-art facility."[20] The last steel beam had been lifted to the top of a skeleton structure in September 2021. In early 2022, there were walls, a roof, and a sharper view of what the facility would look like when completed. While future patrons were unaware of what was happening inside, those who stopped by the property knew the wait would not be long.

Meanwhile, Newport Racing and Gaming had been open for two years and had become quite successful. On the gaming end, nearly 600 historical racing machines (HRMs) were in use between the main gaming floor and the very-popular smoking area. The restaurant/sports bar served everything from delicious cheeseburgers and wraps to freshly-made salads and pizzas. The simulcast viewing area, one of the largest in the region, provided bettors with more than a dozen large-screen televisions to watch races from around the world. The facility was extremely popular from day one but was still billed as the "sister facility" to the upcoming Turfway Park Racing and Gaming.

Opening Day at Turfway Park Racing and Gaming

On August 31, 2022, Turfway Park Racing and Gaming held its "Soft Opening" for friends, family, and a large contingent of VIP guests. It was a huge success. Guests were given a tour of the property and a bag packed with promotional souvenirs, and most were in awe of the features and overall ambiance. Most impressive to many was the massive Event Center. Of course, there were a few minor glitches to work out (a broken fire sprinkler head cascaded thousands of gallons of water onto a few HRMs the night before the event and had to be replaced).

Turfway Park Racing and Gaming provides nearly 1,500 HRMs on one of the largest gaming floors in the region. Included is a "Smoking Patio," but the name is misleading. It is fully enclosed within a separate wing. Two restaurants are available: "Churchill Bourbon and Brew," a sports-bar-style eatery, serves everything from cheeseburgers and hot dogs to gourmet entrées. Behind the bar is a stage for live music, and more than a dozen wide-screen televisions on the outer walls display various sporting competitions. The room's best feature might be the 300" television directly behind the bar. "Serena's Pizzeria" is named after *Serena's Song*, one of Turfway's most successful Thoroughbreds. There, guests can enjoy a variety of pizzas, Italian sandwiches, and more. The Event Center is the most grandiose of the facility's magnificent features. With a seating capacity of 1,250, the room will be available for spectators during live racing and can be reserved for special events such as wedding receptions and corporate parties.

Courtesy: Turfway Park Racing and Gaming

Courtesy: Robert Webster

While the main gaming floor is only open to those 21 and older, a separate entrance is available for the racing end of the business. Therefore, just like at "Old Turfway," guests of all ages can come and watch the races. The entire apron and paddock, where the fine Thoroughbreds warm up and are saddled before each race, have also been completely revamped. The cracked and crumbling asphalt has been replaced by yards and yards of concrete. Benches have also been placed there for the comfort of those watching the races from outdoors. And, like before, patrons can get "right up close" to the action by standing up at the rail. Turfway Park Racing and Gaming offers free admission, free parking, one of the largest simulcast venues in Kentucky, and larger purses than ever.

The Holiday/Winter Meet of 2022-2023

November 30, 2022, saw the opening day of the 63rd year of racing at Old Latonia/New Latonia/Turfway Park/Turfway Park Racing and Gaming. Fans flocked to the new facility, not unlike a young child running down the stairs on Christmas morning. The new Event Center was packed with people placing their wagers live and in person once again. Mutuel clerks had their hands full as steady lines formed at the dozen or so teller's windows. Fans enjoyed the nearly three-story-high windows overlooking the racetrack and several 255" monitors in the room. Thoroughbred owners experienced a luxurious private suite, which directly overlooks the finish line and the winner's circle. Riders, too, arrived at a fully-remodeled jockey's quarters and paddock, although construction workers still had a few finishing touches to attend to. On the backside, five new barns had been constructed, allowing housing for more than 1,100 Thoroughbreds. A new 121-room dormitory was also built, providing accommodations for those whom the owners pay to feed and take care of their prized racing stock. The new dorms replace what can only be defined as "primitive" housing – 10-foot by 10-foot concrete-block cells with no running water. A total of $31 million had been spent just on the racetrack's backside during the new construction and renovations.[21]

"We have 72 racing dates scheduled for this year," Bach said of the upcoming Holiday/Winter Meet of 2022-2023.[22] The first season began on a nostalgic note. "Dollar Beer and Dollar Hot Dogs" returned, along with a concert by fan-favorites, the Naked Karate Girls on Friday night. Though the first night of racing was a Wednesday evening, the place was packed, no doubt a sign of the future success of the new facility. The season's stakes races were also announced, and what an impressive list it was:

STAKE	AGE	DISTANCE	PURSE	DATE
Holiday Inaugural	Fillies 3 and up	6 furlongs	$125,000	12/3/2022
My Charmer	Fillies 3 and up	1 1/16 mile	$125,000	12/10/2022
Prairie Bayou	3 and up	1 1/8 mile	$125,000	12/17/2022
Gowell Stakes	2-year-old fillies	6 furlongs	$125,000	12/31/2022
Holiday Cheer	4-year-olds and up	6 furlongs	$125,000	1/1/2023
Turfway Prevue	3-year-olds	6.5 furlongs	$125,000	1/7/2023
Likely Exchange	4-year-olds and up	1 mile	$125,000	1/14/2023
Leonatus Stakes	3-year-olds	1 mile	$125,000	1/21/2023
Wishing Well	4-year-olds and up	6.5 furlongs	$125,000	1/28/2023
The Forego	4-year-olds and up	6.5 furlongs	$125,000	2/4/2023
The Valdale	3-year-old fillies	6.5 furlongs	$125,000	2/11/2023
Dust Commander	4-year-olds and up	1 1/16 mile	$125,000	2/18/2023
Wintergreen Stakes	4-year-olds and up	1 mile	$125,000	2/25/2023
Cincinnati Trophy	3-year-old fillies	1 mile	$150,000	3/4/2023
Battaglia Memorial	3-year-olds	1 1/16 mile	$150,000	3/4/2023
The Big Daddy	4-year-olds and up	6 furlongs	$125,000	3/11/2023
Queen Stakes	4-year-olds and up	6 furlongs	$125,000	3/18/2023
Kentucky Cup	4-year-olds and up	1 1/8 mile	$300,000	3/25/2023
Jeff Ruby Steaks	3-year-olds	1 1/8 mile	$700,000	3/25/2023
Rushaway	3-year-olds	1 1/16 mile	$250,000	3/25/2023
Bourbonette Oaks	3-year-old fillies	1 1/16 mile	$300,000	3/25/2023
Animal Kingdom	3-year-olds	6 furlongs	$250,000	3/25/2023
Latonia Stakes	4-year-olds and up	1 1/16 mile	$250,000	3/25/2023
Serena's Song	3-year-old fillies	6 furlongs	$125,000	4/1/2023

The first race on the card at "New" Turfway Park was a $5,000 claiming event for three-year-old geldings with a purse of $15,000. The first horse to cross the finish line was *Good One*, ridden by Gerardo Corrales and trained by Genaro Garcia. Tragically, the opening night celebrations were marred by an unfortunate

Opening day program for Turfway Park Racing and Gaming

spill in the first race. German Terraza's mount, *Anytimeallthetime* went down in the final turn after suffering a fatal heart attack. Terraza was not injured in the mishap.

Opening weekend at the races proved there were still a few things to iron out at the New Turfway Park. With the advertised "Nostalgia Night" festivities, scores of racing fans were disappointed in the whole set-up. Due to the Naked Karate Girls concert, the Event Center provided few tables and chairs for those simply coming to watch and bet on the races. "Either have a concert on non-racing nights or don't have one at all," was heard throughout the evening. "I've come out here every year for a long time," said another. "I'm no high-roller, but I always had a place to sit." The concert, itself, drew a huge crowd of course, as that band is a local favorite. However, most racing fans could have done without.

The following Saturday, December 3, 2022, racing was conducted during the afternoon, and crowds were much larger than on a typical Saturday night. While windy, the day was unseasonably warm, and spectators thoroughly enjoyed the revamped paddock and apron. In the daylight, they could easily see the major renovations on the far side of the track, those being the barns and dormitories. The highlight of the day was the first stakes race to be held at New Turfway. The Holiday Inaugural Stakes, for fillies and mares – three-year-olds and up, was won by *Ready to Venture*, with Gerardo Corrales in the irons. Michael Stidham was the trainer. *Last Leaf* and *Beat the System* took the place and show spots.

On the gaming side of things, jackpots and giveaways were and continue to be commonplace. On nearly a daily basis, guests are photographed holding large checks indicating their incredible winnings. The amount is handwritten; five, ten, $20,000 or more, written with a black marker on a dry-erase board, and then cleaned and readied for the next big winner. In addition, between November 28 and December 31, tickets from thousands of wagerers were collected and placed in a hopper for a drawing to win a 2023 Alfa Romeo SUV or $40,000 cash. Planned for 2023 are more vehicle giveaways, helping to lure even more fans to the gaming side of the business.

All images on this spread courtesy: Robert Webster

This page, top two photos: Racing fans are gathered on the newly remodeled apron and paddock; Middle: "Hot walkers" warm up their horses for the next race; Bottom: "And they're off" in one of the opening weekend's races.

Opposite page, top: View of the paddock from atop the stairs leading to the main building; Middle, left: The new tote board; Middle. right: View across the lake showing some of the newly constructed barns; Bottom: photo of the new dormitories located on the backside.

Management had anticipated that the brand-new Event Center would host big-name entertainment, and they wasted little time booking a nationally-known celebrity. On December 10, 2022, with live racing rescheduled to another night, Turfway Park Racing and Gaming hosted Sara Evans as a stop on her "Go Tell it on the Mountain" Christmas tour. To a sold-out audience (with ticket prices ranging from $49 to a $215 VIP Package), Evans performed a long list of Christmas favorites, and the show was a huge success. Besides major events scheduled for the Event Center, the stage in the Bourbon and Brew restaurant hosts musical acts nearly every Friday and Saturday night. Well-known local bands have included Buzz Bin, the Danny Frazier Band, the Kevin McCoy Band, the Michelle Robinson Band, and The Whammies.

New Year's Eve at Turfway Park

New Year's Eve at Turfway Park Racing and Gaming in 2022 was an epic celebration. The enormous crowd (many unfortunately had to be turned away due to room capacity restrictions) was well-behaved, and enjoyed excellent food, music, and souvenir party favors while "watching the ball drop" on the massive monitors throughout the Event Center. There is little doubt that this venue will become a favorite for other special events in the future.

At the end of the 2022 Holiday Meet, jockey Gerardo Corrales, trainer Paulo Lobo, and Larry Best's OXO Equine won their respective titles. The trio was hoping to continue their momentum at the Winter/Spring Meet, scheduled through April 1, 2023. Corrales tabbed 30 wins from 104 mounts, a stout 29 percent win clip. His meet was highlighted by a victory in the $125,000 Prairie Bayou Stakes aboard Lobo-trained *In Love*. The 26-year-old rider also won the $125,000 Holiday Inaugural Stakes aboard *Ready to Venture*.

While the first Meet at the new Turfway Park was exciting and profitable, everyone from upper management to the incredible housekeeping crew soon had their attention focussed on planning for the Spring Meet and the running of the 2023 Spiral Steaks. While no contract had been signed, all involved believed wholeheartedly that Jeff Ruby would again sponsor Turfway's premiere event. On March 2, 2023, it became official. Jeff Ruby Culinary Entertainment agreed to a five-year extension to their partnership regarding the $700,000 Jeff Ruby Steaks (Grade III). Since 2018, Jeff Ruby has been the presenting sponsor, and in 2022, the race produced the winner of the 148th Kentucky Derby, Rich Strike. "Turfway Park recognizes our responsibility to provide best-in-class Thoroughbred racing that will complement the Jeff Ruby brand," Turfway Park President Michael Taylor said. "Mr. Ruby has always been an advocate of supporting important causes for our industry, especially the Permanently Disabled Jockey Fund (PDJF). We are grateful for his continued partnership in what has become Northern Kentucky's premiere Spring sporting event." Ruby added, "This race has a long and storied history in Northern Kentucky. We're thrilled to be a part of it and continue our partnership with Turfway Park and Churchill Downs." Turfway Park General Manager Chip Bach added, "We're so happy to extend our partnership with Jeff Ruby and his team for the next five years to support our Jeff Ruby Steaks. To have the ability to continue to associate our premiere race with Ruby is a dream come true."

Courtesy: Robert Webster

A field of Thoroughbreds round the first turn at the new Turfway Park Racing and Gaming

Chapter Eight Endnotes

1. "Churchill Downs set to buy Turfway Park after tense dispute," *Courier-Journal*, October 3, 2019, retrieved on November 22, 2022.

2. "Churchill Downs Incorporated Buys Turfway Park," paulickreport.com, retrieved on June 21, 2022.

3. "Churchill Downs is buying Turfway Park. What that means for Northern Kentucky and racing," *Cincinnati Enquirer*, October 3, 2019, retrieved on July 15, 2022.

4. Personal interview with Billy Troilo on November 16, 2022.

5. Personal interview with Chip Bach on October 18, 2022.

6. Tapetafootings.com, retrieved on October 23, 2022.

7. "Churchill Downs to build $38.4 million gaming facility in Newport," WLWT News, May 4, 2020, retrieved on July 18, 2022.

8. *Ibid.*

9. Chris Otts, "Despite court ruling, Churchill Downs to open Kentucky's Sixth Vegas-style Gaming Venue," WDRB News (Louisville, Kentucky), October 1, 2020, retrieved on July 18, 2022.

10. Churchill Downs website, retrieved on November 17, 2022.

11. Churchill Downs website, retrieved on October 26, 2022.

12. "Turfway Park Seeks a Return to Glory, Future Success with Renovated Facility, Newport Gaming," *Northern Kentucky Business Journal*, May/June 2022, pages 24-25.

13. Information contained at the company's website, Turfwaypark.com/racing, retrieved on November 14, 2022.

14. Like the King, *Horse Racing Nation*, retrieved on August 31, 2022.

15. "Live racing but no fans at Turfway Park as it gears up for a September 1st opening," *Northern Kentucky Tribune*, March 4, 2022.

16. "Rich Strike," Wikipedia.com, retrieved on September 5, 2022.

17. *Ibid.*

18. "Reopening of Turfway Park Grandstand on Schedule," *Blood-Horse Magazine*, retrieved on July 29, 2022.

19. Personal interview with Chip Bach on October 18, 2022.

20. "New Turfway Park set to bring racing and gaming to Northern Kentucky," Sepctrumnews1.com/ Louisville, May 7, 2022, retrieved on July 18, 2022.

21. Information contained at the company's website, Turfwaypark.com/racing, retrieved on November 14, 2022.

22. "Reopening of Turfway Park Grandstand on Schedule," *Blood-Horse Magazine*, retrieved on July 29, 2022

23. Press Release sent on Wednesday, December 14, 2022, from Churchill Downs.

Chapter Nine

The 2023 Spiral, Sports Betting, and The Future of Turfway Park

At "Old" Turfway Park, advertising was completely ignored, even after its purchase by Caesar's and Hard Rock. Lack of adequate funding was the cause suggested by the new owners. However, it was no surprise to employees and management that the two casino giants paid little attention to their newly-acquired Northern Kentucky racetrack. Business went on as usual but, as was mentioned previously, the promised remodeling and upgrades never transpired.

While everything was about to change, there was still much to learn after Churchill's October 2019 acquisition and the opening of Turfway Park Racing and Gaming and Newport Racing and Gaming. For example, television and radio commercials became commonplace, but these spots were created by the same team who devised special incentives and promotions for the HRM gaming floor. Commercials were all about gaming and nothing else. "Sign up as a new Player's Club member and receive up to $1,000 in free play" and "Enter a drawing to win a 2023 Jeep Grand Cherokee" were phrases heard hundreds of times over the airwaves and printed on tens of thousands of postcard mailers. However, no television commercial or print ad featured a race, mentioned a racetrack, or even included a picture of a horse! While they say "Turfway Park Racing and Gaming," the sport of horse racing was never mentioned (except for one short and ill-fated promotion for a 2023 Kentucky Derby Watch Party). Therefore, most regional residents had no idea that live and simulcast Thoroughbred racing was back at Turfway Park and that the new track, paddock, apron, barns, and tote board were among the finest features of the new venue.

With the incredible aesthetics of the new facility, linked with the prime location just seconds away from I-75 and I-275, just a minimal amount of strategically-targeted advertising could place Turfway Park onto the list of top ten Thoroughbred racetracks in America; an achievement enjoyed 120 years ago at Old Latonia. But management, at least the current top officials at Turfway Park/ Churchill Downs, seem to only have their eyes on the gaming side of the business. Given the insight of those at Churchill Downs and its incredible history, hopefully that will change in the near future.

Year-round Training

Just before the 2023 Jeff Ruby Spiral Steaks, it was announced that Turfway Park's barn area and racetrack would remain open for year-round training. This was both encouraging and satisfying news for the industry, because local trainers could stay on property and not have to move their operations to other states. Turfway constructed a new dormitory for backstretch workers and five new barns in 2022. The track can now stable approximately 1,000 horses. Local trainers who stated they would keep their stock on-site during the first offseason included Steve Asmussen, Brad Cox, Jeff Greenhill, Michael Maker, Will Walden, and Ethan West.

The new Turfway Park Racing and Gaming had been open for a few months by March 2023, but the real anticipation was with the upcoming Jeff Ruby Spiral Steaks. Everything had been cleaned and polished, tables were placed and set up beautifully in the Event Center, and top-notch Thoroughbreds and jockeys had made their way to Northern Kentucky. While planning meetings took place months in advance, some of the new management team failed to heed the advice of those who had been through the event for decades. While the Spiral was successful overall; in retrospect, the number of food and beverage stands, mutuel tellers, automatic betting machines, and overall staff should have been nearly double what was initially approved. However, with prevailing "let's get it right" philosophy, management will surely address these issues when the 2024 Spiral is run.

2023 Jeff Ruby Steaks

The week preceding the Spiral, talk amongst the experts was that *Two Phil's* would emerge the winner. Owned by Patricia Hope and Phillip Sagan, the three-year-old colt had an impressive fall on all dirt tracks. Trainer Larry Rivelli said his horse was ready to go. *Two Phil's* won the Street Sense Stakes at Churchill Downs, had a runner-up finish to *Instant Coffee* in the Fair Ground's LeCompte Stakes, and a third-place finish to *Angel of Empire* and *Sun Thunder* in the Risen Star at Fair Grounds. Later, *Two Phil's* ran second to *Mage* at the 2023 Kentucky Derby in May.

Other top-rated entries in the 2023 Spiral included Todd Pletcher's *Major Dude*, Wesley Ward's *Event Detail*, Michael Maker's *Maker's Candy*, Antonio Sano's *Congruent*, and Kenneth McPeek's *Escapologist*. The Jeff Ruby Steaks program also included the 41st running of the $300,000 Bourbonette Oaks, the 23rd running of the $300,000 TwinSpires Kentucky Cup Classic, the 37th running of the $250,000 Animal Kingdom Stakes, the 41st running of the $250,000 Latonia stakes, and the 36th running of the $250,000 Rushaway.

Compared to previous Spirals at "Old" Turfway Park, the 2023 event lived up to the hype, but what could only be characterized as adequately. With limited advertising, the crowd was only about half what had been experienced in years past, just before Covid. Rather than the usual VIP "tent," the new Event Center became host to the upper echelon of arrivals. Tickets there went for a minimum of $300 a seat, and guests enjoyed an incredible feast provided by Jeff Ruby Culinary Entertainment. A live band performed on a stage at the west end of the room, and over a dozen mutuel tellers and automatic betting machines were available to handle the crowd. Outside, a tent was erected to house the general admission patrons, but it was a far distance from the paddock, apron, and finish line. A gravel pathway was laid, but it was hardly accessible by handicapped patrons. In addition, a small temporary grandstand-style seating structure allowed spectators a nice view of the homestretch, but not the finish line. Therefore, hardly anyone took advantage.

Compliments were aplenty in the Event Center, however, mainly by those guests who had been in the VIP "tents" of previous seasons. A lack of seating near the rail and a muddy portion of the apron prevented the outside patrons from fully enjoying themselves. In the preliminary events on the card, *Eye Witness* won the Animal Kingdom Stakes, *Rarified Flair* was victorious in the Rushaway, *Idiomatic* finished first in the Latonia Stakes, *Wolfie's Dynaghost* won the TwinSpires Kentucky Cup Classic, and *Botanical* was the winner of the Bourbonette Oaks.

Courtesy: Robert Webster

Dr. James Claypool, racetrack historian and this book's co-author, presents the trophy to the owners and entourage of Eye Witness, winner of the Animal Kingdom Stakes.

In the 52nd running of the Jeff Ruby Spiral Steaks, *Funtastic Again*, (5-1), broke well from the gate and led the field as they entered the first turn. Following closely were *Major Dude* (8-5), two longshots, *Bluebirds Over* (31-1) and *Baby Billy* (43-1), and *Congruent* (6-1). At the half-mile mark, *Funtastic Again* remained in front, with *Wadsworth* (5-1), *Bluebirds Over*, *Two Phil's* (5-2), and *Major Dude* all within two lengths of the leader. *Funtastic Again* pulled away a bit in the final turn, followed by *Wadsworth*, *Major Dude*, and *Two Phil's*. But at that moment, jockey Jareth Loveberry, in the irons on *Two Phil's*, made his move. Sliding to the outside, Loveberry poured it on as the field entered the homestretch. In the final furlong, *Two Phil's*, the son of *Hard Spun*, pulled away to finish five lengths ahead of the second-place finisher, *Major Dude*, and seven lengths ahead of the show horse, *Funtastic Again*.

All images on this page courtesy: Robert Webster

2023 Jeff Ruby Steaks Day

Above: Jeff Ruby stands proudly in the Paddock. He and his company has sponsored the event since 2018;

Above, right: *Two Phil's*, with jockey Jareth Loveberry, at the wire;

Right: GM Chip Bach ready to present the traditional blanket of flowers;

Below: Winner'c Circle group photo, including Turfway Park President Michael Taylor (to Ruby's left).

Top, left: guests watch Spiral Day races from Bourbon and Brew restaurant; Top right and bottom left: scenes from the Event Center VIP experience; Bottom, right: a crowded day near the Paddock.

The leaders for the 2023 Winter/Spring Meet were apprentice jockey Walter Rodriguez with 48 wins in 250 starts, and trainer Wesley Ward, with 22 wins in over 50 starts Ward was also tied with Three Diamonds Farm (Kirk Wycoff) in the "top owners" category. "We're so thankful for all of our owners, trainers, jockeys, and horseplayers for their continued support of our racing season," Turfway Park General Manager Chip Bach said. "Thanks to Churchill Downs Incorporated's continued investments in Turfway Park's facility and racing product, we can confidently look forward to a thriving future of horse racing in Florence."[1]

Turfway Park's memorable 48-day Winter/Spring Meet – the first at the new facility – concluded with a massive 62% gain in all-source handle and a 43% increase in purse money awarded. In total, more than $145 million was wagered at the Winter/Spring Meet, nearly $56 million more than in 2022. Along with the sizable handle increase, the participants who raced at Turfway Park were rewarded with more than $19 million in prize money, an increase of nearly $6 million. "The racing season at Turfway Park was a huge success across the board," Turfway Park President Michael Taylor said. "Our team delivered a competitive racing product while welcoming back fans to our newly remodeled facility."[2] Credit for the success of the first season can be attributed to one thing, and one thing only: Turfway's purchase by Churchill Downs. Just the Churchill name being associated with the Northern Kentucky property brings better horses, owners, and trainers to the facility.

Sports Betting

Though it faced long odds on the last day of the 2023 session, House Bill 551, a bill to legalize, regulate, and tax sports betting in Kentucky, passed through the Senate. The vote was 25-12 on the bill, which is estimated to generate up to $23 million yearly for the state. Governor Andy Beshear, who had previously stated that he supported the idea of sports betting, signed the Bill into law on March 30, 2023. Scheduled to take effect in September, Kentucky would become the 38th state to legalize sports betting.[3] The Kentucky Racing Commission, tasked with regulating the new industry, spent a great deal of time considering license applications and laying down the foundations for the launch. Under the Bill, the Kentucky Speedway near Warsaw and the state's horse racing tracks must pay a fee to operate as sports betting facilities, with bets only allowed there and on licensed websites and phone apps. Beshear said wagering licenses for racetracks come with an initial fee of $500,000 and a $50,000 renewal fee. Operators such as FanDuel and DraftKings, who would handle the online betting, have an initial fee of $50,000 and a $10,000 renewal charge.[4] Lawmakers revealed their hope to have everything in place before the upcoming fall football season.

"When you look back at this, the odds were against us, but we were determined to get sports betting passed in Kentucky, and we got it done," Governor Beshear stated. "Bringing sports wagering to the state," he continued, "not only gives Kentuckians a much-anticipated new form of entertainment but also brings money to the state to support pensions, freeing up money that can be used to build a better Kentucky through the funding of education, economic development, and disaster recovery."

The new law will allow Kentuckians aged 18 and over to place their wagers at brick-and-mortar retail locations starting September 7, 2023, the first day of the NFL regular season.[5] Online wagering was scheduled to begin before October 1st. At Turfway Park Racing and Gaming and Newport Racing and Gaming, plans were unveiled to have sports betting machines in place by October 1, 2023. Devices would be placed in the Bourbon and Brew restaurant and other locations throughout Turfway Park's gaming floor. More than a dozen machines would also be strategically placed within the Newport property.

Popular Entertainers

While plans were being made for the upcoming Winter Meet and the 2024 Spiral on the track side of things, event planners continued to work diligently to book top-quality acts at Turfway Park Racing and Gaming. The 2023 season included such nationally renowned musicians as Jefferson Starship, Joan Jett and the Blackhearts, Martina McBride, Night Ranger, and Tanya Tucker. In addition, Theresa Caputo, the "Long Island Medium," performed her psychic talents to a sold-out audience. The Event Center has become and will continue to be a hot-spot venue in the region.

Looking Toward the Future

To no surprise, the gaming side of the business at both Turfway Park Racing and Gaming and Newport Racing and Gaming was booming from day one. Oversized checks with the guests' names and the amount of their winnings are seen on social media pages daily. Compliments regarding the cleanliness of the restrooms and gaming floor are heard often. However, racing clearly took a back seat. Incredibly, most management members who came from Old Turfway knew this would be the case. Those people clearly understand that the majority of the company's revenue comes from the gaming floor. Conversely, it must be recognized that Thoroughbred horse racing is the primary reason the property existed in the first place. With just a little advertising and a tiny bit of targeted promotions, Turfway Park could quickly move into the upper echelon of all North American Thoroughbred racetracks. Should that happen, the increase in revenue from the racing side of the business would undoubtedly grab the attention of the higher-ups.

One of the most encouraging signs for the future is that, even without much promoting, the success of the racing side of the business also grew – the number of races on the card, the purse size, and the quality of the jockeys and horses – all are well above the average across the country. This is solely attributed to the fact that Churchill now owns the place. Meanwhile, negative comments from the racetrack "regulars" are frequent and sometimes brutal. "There is nowhere for us to sit and watch the races," said many. "The windows in that room (the Event Center) only show your reflection if you're more than 10 feet away from them," said dozens. "I can't believe there are no grandstands," said literally hundreds! At nearby Belterra and Miami Valley, situated on the outskirts of Cincinnati (both offer gaming and a racetrack), seating for racing fans is aplenty. Grandstand-style seating with a capacity of well over 500 is available at Belterra, along with a far wider variety of dining options. At Miami Valley, the main viewing area is similar to Turfway, but they have dozens of tables and chairs outside on the track's apron. Of course, Miami Valley is open during warmer months, so outdoor seating for patrons can be quite comfortable. Outdoor seating at Turfway Park can only be enjoyed a few weekends a year. Better indoor seating options at Turfway Park are a must, and the importance of live Thoroughbred horse racing has to be enhanced.

The first logical solution to upgrading the importance of live racing at Turfway is to recognize that the business' racing half can become a corollary to the gaming half of the property. Gimmicks and schemes targeting the gaming guests are published every month at both properties: Military Monday and Sunday Salute for Veterans, Golden Gamers for those over 50, Bring a Friend, Birthday Blast, and more than a dozen other continuing promotions. Cars and trucks have been given away on the gaming floor, as well as cash prizes of $50,000 or more.

However, a widely-publicized promotion has never been directed solely at racing fans. Those guests would be equally excited if given the same chances for extra cash or racing perks. They could spin a wheel to win a free bet on the next race or reach into a barrel and grab a pre-printed mutuel ticket for the last race on the card. Gimmicks similar to those which entice thousands of gaming fans in the casino could be put in place on the racing side of things quite easily. If just some advertising dollars were spent promoting horse racing, that end of the operation could also prove even more profitable for the company. Another shortfall is that, unlike at Churchill Downs, there currently is no player's betting reward card at Turfway. The truth is, live racing at today's Turfway Racecourse continues to be a "work in progress." Given Churchill's long history of change and having "an eye on the future," these problems quite likely will soon be addressed.

Conclusion

Over the past 140 years, many things have changed at Latonia/Turfway Park, Northern Kentucky's enduring premier racetrack, while other things have not. The familiar smells and sounds associated with horse racing are constants, while how they are transported and the facilities to house and train them have been updated and improved. Also, the methods and scale of wagering have evolved, allowing bettors to "hit the big one" or at least come home with more money in their pockets than with which they started. After all, that and the pageantry are the two most prominent elements sustaining Thoroughbred horse racing today.

The transformation from the "Old Latonia Racecourse" to Turfway Park Racing and Gaming and Newport Racing and Gaming is complete. Certainly, the track's long history had many ups and downs. Old Latonia, once known as "The Most Beautiful Racecourse in America," became home to the world-famous Latonia Derby. However, beginning in 1919, Matt Winn and Latonia's new owners downgraded the Latonia Derby so that the Kentucky Derby could ascend to worldwide prominence. When New Latonia opened in Florence in 1959, it had its setbacks as well. The first Spiral in 1972 drew a less-than-impressive audience and few top-quality Thoroughbreds.

New Latonia and Turfway Park eventually presented the region with one of the biggest and most anticipated events of the year. Spiral Festivals rallied community leaders and patrons from afar, and the premiere race soon grew national acclaim. Through the years, the Spiral Stakes introduced over 30 horses that would go on to win the Kentucky Derby, Belmont, Preakness, or other prestigious races. Names like *Animal Kingdom*, *Balto Star*, *Hard Spun*, *Inca Roca*, *Lil E. Tee*, *Marfa*, *Perfect Drift*, *Polar Expedition*, *Prairie Bayou*, *Rich Strike*, *Serena's Song*, *Summer Squall*, *Tabasco Cat*, and *Thunder Gulch* have a history at New Latonia/Turfway Park and helped place the racetrack amongst the top places to visit in Greater Cincinnati. As the first track to introduce the $2 bet, pick-three, pick-four, the trifecta, and other forms of wagering, the "mother" properties set the standard nationwide for horse race wagering. Turfway Park was also the first track in North America to install Polytrack and was the first to introduce Inter-track simulcasting. Jerry Carroll's "Racebook" and other innovations continue to be utilized worldwide.

While the rescue of Turfway Park by Churchill Downs has been overwhelmingly accepted, many "horsemen" seem to feel that the focus became – and will forever be – on "gaming" rather than "racing." As a result, many of them fear that the declining trend of the sport, in general, may continue into the future, and the beautiful new facility may eventually become known simply as Turfway Park Gaming.

While gaming is obviously at the forefront with Churchill Downs management, one cannot ignore the tens of millions spent on the racing side of the business. "Old Turfway" had nearly two dozen barns, most needing extensive repairs to meet state code. Leaky roofs, barn doors that would not open or close properly, and restroom accommodations so disgusting that most workers "held it" until they got home. Churchill built new dormitories, five new barns, a fully reconstructed infrastructure, the new Tapeta track, a new apron, paddock, winner's circle, and a new tote board, complete with a 45-foot-wide by 25-foot-high video screen. It should be clear to all racing fans and horsemen that Churchill Downs is fully vested in the future success of Thoroughbred horse racing in Northern Kentucky. Hopefully, the significant improvements on the backside and track will make them soon forget the old "traditional" accommodations.

The positives of the new facility outweigh the negatives a million-to-one. "Turfway Park Racing and Gaming represents the next chapter in a brighter future for horse racing in Kentucky," said Governor Andy Beshear. "I want to thank the entire team at Churchill Downs for bringing this project to fruition. We're just in the starting gate, but the race that this facility and this area is about to run will be long and successful." Maybe speaking for all horsemen, former jockey, Senior State Steward, and long-time Clerk of Scales at Turfway Park, Bill Troilo, said, "Change is inevitable. You have to adjust or get left behind. It's a new era, and we must stay positive and hope this is good for horse racing. This is our job... our love... and our life."[6]

The $145 million spent on the Turfway renovation impacted the new facility and the entire Cincinnati region. "Regional Economic Multipliers" demonstrates that dollars spent in a local business usually have an effect beyond what the recipient receives. The net impact is typically two to three times the original sale. Therefore, the $145 million received by local construction contractors and vendors significantly added to Greater Cincinnati's economy, extending across counties in Northern Kentucky, Southwestern Ohio, and Southeastern Indiana. Using IMPLAN, a financial analysis software program, the initial investment will result in a total increase in the regional economy of around $279 million, with an estimated 1,624 jobs created due to the construction of the facility (875 jobs), increased activity among the suppliers (295 jobs), and the overall increase in spending by the employees of the various firms (450 jobs). The overall result for labor income or payroll gains alone is estimated to be $106.6 million.[7]

But enough about facts and figures. Horse racing – especially in Kentucky – is all about tradition. At this new, beautiful facility, that tradition has been reborn. Like 140 years ago, a bugler, bedecked in a stylish coat, sounds "The Call to the Post." Today, jockeys, wearing colorful silks with numbers fastened to their sleeves, blend in unison with their magnificent mounts to set the stage for what is to follow. Once on the track, the horses are warmed up and prepared to enter the modern mechanical starting gate that has replaced the old-fashioned webbed barrier once used to send horses on their way. The rhythmic sounds of hooves pounding toward the finish line fuel the crowd's anticipation and excitement.

Aaron Spurlock, long-time Mutuels Manager at Turfway Park and a man in the business for more than 20 years, said, "Standing along the rail, feeling the Earth shake beneath your feet from the pounding of the horses' hooves against the ground. The sound of thunder as they come down the stretch. Hearing the horses breathe in and out like a steam locomotive and the jockeys calling out last-second orders as they hit the wire. There's nothing like it! If you could bottle that excitement and hand it out, people would never leave!"

And then it happens. The race is over. The first, second, third, and fourth-place finishers are posted on the tote board, while the other Thoroughbreds head back to their stalls to try another day. That no one can predict the outcome of any race is what makes it all so exciting and what causes fans to remain and get ready to bet on the next race. Ten years, 20 years, and even 50 years from now, people will still recall the names of these spectacular Thoroughbreds, but few will remember the name of any HRM they played.

Boldness and willingness to adjust have always been the focus propelling Latonia and Turfway Racecourses. On that sunny day in June 1883, when fans made their way to the opening day of racing at Old Latonia until November 30, 2022, when the ultra-modern racino at Turfway Park debuted, there was a palpable air of anticipation. In both cases, something new was at hand. In 1883, fans arrived on foot, in carriages, on horseback, or by train. Today, they come in cars, pick-up trucks, and even an occasional electric vehicle. The fans are dressed differently today, and their shoes are much more expensive. The age range is the same, but the neighborhoods surrounding the tracks have changed. The corner bars, small pharmacies, and grocery stores in Latonia in 1883 have been replaced in Florence by hotels, large retail stores, and a host of restaurants. The web of intersecting streets and rails that took fans to Old Latonia has been supplanted by multi-lane boulevards connecting to one of the nation's busiest interstate highways. And today, unlike at Old Latonia, the sounds of horse racing are combined with the musical sounds of historical racing machines and a steady buzz of activity in the casino portion of Turfway Park that sits alongside the racetrack.

Yes, those neighborhood kids who used to shimmy up telephone poles to watch the races at Old Latonia are gone, replaced by a new generation of race fans who come, not only to watch and bet on the ponies, but to savor in the excitement of slot-machine-style gambling, buy cheap hot dogs and beer, or perhaps arrive only to enjoy whatever local band or national talent might be playing in Turfway's incredible entertainment venue. Turfway Park Racing and Gaming and Newport Racing and Gaming are owned by a corporation that thrives on providing patrons with a pleasing gaming experience -- an experience that tips its hat to the past while also returning high-level horse racing to Northern Kentucky. A long-endearing tradition has been reborn in Northern Kentucky, and it is spectacular!

Chapter Nine Endnotes

1. Corporate New Released dated April 1, 2023, sent by Kevin Kerstein, Kentucky Racing Communications, Churchill Downs.
2. Corporate New Released dated April 1, 2023, sent by Kevin Kerstein, Kentucky Racing Communications, Churchill Downs.
3. "Kentucky Sports Betting Bill HB 551 Becomes Law," Courier-Journal (Louisville), March 30, 2023, retrieved on April 2, 2023.
4. "Answers to Kentucky Sports Betting Questions," Cincinnati.com, July 16, 2023, page 17A.
5. "T-minus two months until sports betting goes live in Kentucky, opens for NFL season," WCPO television news article, July 11, 2023, retrieved on September 13, 2023.
6.. Personal interview with Billy Troilo on November 16, 2022.
7.. Thomas Lambert, "Economic Impact of Turfway Renovation Will Reverberate Across Cincinnati Metro Area," Horse Racing News, July 19, 2021, retrieved on July 18, 2022.

Chapter Ten

*Noteworthy Owners,
Trainers, and Jockeys*

During the "Golden Age" at the Old Latonia Racetrack and the Latonia Derby, some of the world's best owners, trainers, and jockeys made their way to Northern Kentucky. Names such as William Adams, Albert Cooper, Julio Espinoza, Mack Garner, Isaac Murphy, and Jimmie Winkfield were often found in the local newspapers' sports section headlines… and were similarly seen nationwide.

At the time of this publication, a new list of horsemen can be found in the headlines. The January 2023 list of Top Thoroughbred Trainers in America shows eight names familiar to Turfway Park racing fans. D. Wayne Lukas (17th), Mark E. Casse (15th), Michael Maker (6th), William I. Mott (4th), Steven M. Asmussen (3rd), and Todd A. Pletcher (2nd). The list of Top Ten Jockeys at the time of this publication includes more names heard over the loudspeakers from the Turfway Park track announcer: John R. Velazquez (the 2012 and 2014 winner is in 18th place), Tyler Gaffalione (winner of the 2017 and 2019 events is in 4th place), and Irad Ortiz, Jr. (the 2022 Spiral winner is in the number one position). Other top-rated owners, trainers, and jockeys are featured below.

By the sheer number of career victories, more Turfway Park jockeys are listed in the top ten: Russell Baze (now retired) tops the list with 53,578 starts and 30,297 top-three finishes. Pat Day (also retired) and John Velazquez are in the top 20 (4th and 12th place, respectively). However, Perry Ouzts, still active at age 69 and a Turfway regular, is in 5th place.

While the Spiral Stakes brings in top talent from around the world (albeit for one big race on a single afternoon), it is clearly the Turfway Park "regulars" like Perry Ouzts who bring the racing fans back day after day, year after year. The following is a list of noteworthy owners, trainers, and jockeys who were/are frequent entries on the Latonia/Turfway Park racing card.

Breeders/Owners/Trainers

Abner Brothers: Brothers Walter and D.F. Abner were familiar faces at "New" Latonia Race Track and Turfway Park. From 1967, Walter Abner (1944-2013) was an avid horse trainer, first in Quarter Horse racing, then in Barrel Racing, and finally by the training of Thoroughbred horses in such notable places as Churchill Downs, Hoosier Downs, Indiana Downs, Keeneland, Latonia/Turfway Park, River Downs, and Tampa Bay Downs. His brother, D.F. Abner (1934-2011), trained horses for racing at River Downs and Turfway Park and and also ran horses at Churchill Downs, Beulah Park, Keeneland, and Waterford Park. Like his brother, D.F. started contesting with Quarter horses and eventually evolved to train Thoroughbreds. D.F. also worked at International Furniture Company in Rushville, Indiana for many years and was a bus driver for Franklin County Schools (Indiana). He was also a successful farmer. Both brothers were members of the Horsemen's Benevolence Protection Association.

- -

Elias Jackson "Lucky" Baldwin – (1828-1909): Born in Hamilton, Ohio, "Lucky" Baldwin later married and moved to California at the height of the Gold Rush. Rather than digging, he supplied food and provisions to others and amassed a large fortune. He became one of the greatest pioneers of business in the West and has many towns and parks in California named after him.

Courtesy: Wikipedia Commons

In the late 1880s, Baldwin began breeding and training Thoroughbreds and raced many of those along the east coast. One of his best filly runners was *Los Angeles*, who won the 1887 Tyro and Spinaway Stakes, plus the 1888 Monmouth Oaks and Latonia Derby. In 2018, Lucky Baldwin was voted into the National Museum of Racing and Hall of Fame as one of its esteemed "Pillars of the Turf."

- -

Mark Casse has been in the racing business since 1979. Born in Indianapolis, Indiana, Mark grew up in Florida, where he ran his father's training operation at age fifteen. He received his Kentucky trainer's license at 18 and won his first race at Keeneland in 1979. He has won 13 Sovereign awards for Outstanding Trainer in Canada, won the trainer's title at Churchill in 1988, and won four training titles at Turfway Park. He has two Triple Crown wins under his belt (2019). By 2023, Casse-trained horses had accumulated nearly 22,000 starts, resulting in over 9,000 top-three finishes.

- -

Ben Castleman, Sr. opened his regionally famous White Horse restaurant in Park Hills, Kentucky in 1936. With a tiny dining room and a single gasoline pump outside in the beginning, Castleman either remodeled or enlarged the dining room nine times over the following 22 years. In 1956, he added the "Keeneland Wing," accommodating as many as 200 guests. The White Horse was known throughout the tri-state area for its delicious food. The atmosphere was cozy and inviting, featuring a fireplace, knotty-pine paneling, and many pictures of famous racetracks and American Thoroughbred horses.

Castleman loved horses and horse racing. He bought his first horse in 1952 and purchased land for his **White Horse Acres** in Fayette County two years later. The farm's foundation mare, *Fair Charmer*, produced *My Charmer*, and one of her foals was eventually sold to partners in Seattle, Washington for $17,500. Named *Seattle Slew* by the new owners, the horse won the Triple Crown in 1977, the only undefeated horse to ever do so. Castleman then sold the broodmare who foaled *Seattle Slew* for $250,000.

- -

Louisville native **Tom Drury, Jr**. emerged on the national scene in 2020 as the trainer of *Art Collector*, winner of the Toyota Blue Grass Stakes at Keeneland. A protégé of former trainer Frank Brothers, Drury won his first race as a trainer in 1991 and built up a reputation on the Kentucky racing circuit for handling horses and caring for them during layoffs between races. He amassed an exemplary record at tracks in Kentucky and Indiana through the years. He received a big break in 2020 when owner Bruce Lunsford, a Northern Kentucky native, and successful Louisville businessman, transferred *Art Collector* to him over the winter. Drury capitalized on that good fortune as the colt developed into a leading divisional contender over the spring and summer in advance of the Kentucky Derby, which had been delayed until September due to the COVID-19 pandemic. Although *Art Collector* did not run in the 2020 Derby, he would end his career in 2022 with 20 starts, 10 wins, and over $2 million in earnings.

- -

Greg and Vicki Foley are the children of trainer **Dravo Foley**, a veteran of more than five decades in Kentucky's horse racing industry. Dravo earned his first Top Trainer Award in 1967 for the Winter/Spring Meet at Latonia. He died in March 2010. Greg and Vicki have since become quite successful in the business. Based at Churchill Downs, the two have raced several horses at Turfway Park. In 2023, Greg is known as one of the most successful trainers at Churchill Downs. His most impressive win there was when *Sconsin* won the $300,000 Eight Belles Stakes on Kentucky Derby day in 2020. Vicki has amassed more than 500 victories since taking out her training license in 1981. She earned her first stakes win with *Hotsy Totsy* in the 1983 Lieutenant Governor of Kentucky Stakes at Ellis Park. Her first multiple stakes winner was *Dusty's Darby* in 1984-1985, and she had her first Grade 1 win with *Hog Creek Hustle* on the 2020 Belmont Stakes undercard.

- -

Jeff Greenhill opened his own stable in March 1996 and saddled his first horse at age 41. Now a multiple-graded stakes winner, his first victory came with

Snappy Little Tune in the 1997 Peony Stakes at Hoosier Park. In 2023, he has more than 4,600 starts to his credit and more than 1,900 top-three finishes. A chemical engineer-turned-Thoroughbred trainer, Greenhill scored his 500th career win in December 2016 when *Stay On Shore* won the seventh race at Turfway Park. Greenhill's first career win also came at Turfway, in March 1996, with *Count Sparks*. Greenhill currently has 28 horses in his active stable, and another 10 are either turned out or training for spring debuts. In addition to his milestone 500 wins, Greenhill also has 467 seconds and 424 thirds from 3,283 starts.

An Alabama native and 1979 graduate of Auburn University, Greenhill earned a substantial income as a field engineer for the Tennessee Valley Authority in Muscle Shoals, Alabama. By 1988, he was a department manager overseeing 50 employees and a $20 million budget. At age 38, he left that life to pursue a career as a horseman. When questioned: "Why exchange a secure and profitable  career for the vagaries of Thoroughbred racing?" Greenhill, replied, "There's no winner's circle in chemical engineering. In this game, you know you're alive."

– –

Jamie Grubbs: While still looking for her first graded stakes win in 2023, Jamie has over 2,200 starts and has accumulated nearly 1,000 top-three finishes. She has career earnings of more than $3,600,000. Top Thoroughbreds include *Bless the Kitten, Can'tbetemall, Missing Sefa,* and *My Dark Secret*.

– –

Long before the Northern Kentucky Industrial Park was built at the southeast corner of what is now Industrial Road and Dixie Highway in Florence, **Highland Stock Farm** existed and produced many fine Thoroughbreds. The farm was owned by **Jerome "Rome" Respess** (1863-1939). "Rome" showed Saddlebreds at local fairs but, by the end of the 1800s, he had interests in several racetracks across the country, including Old Latonia. He began breeding and training champion Thoroughbreds at his Ohio stud farm before transplanting his operation to the property near Florence. Highland Stock Farm could house as many as 140 horses and contained nine bright-white barns. On average, there were 50 foals born yearly, and the farm was home to some of the biggest names in Thoroughbred racing during the early 20th century. Respess, after seeing his foal *Wintergreen*, boldly predicted a Kentucky Derby victory. *Wintergreen* was the 1909 Kentucky Derby winner, but his sire, *Dick Welles*, was the real star. *Dick Welles*, named after Richard H. Welles, later the father of Orson Welles, was often compared to the legendary *Man o' War* and was called the "…swiftest Thoroughbred ever seen on the American Continent" by the *Lexington Herald* in 1904. *Dick Welles'* bloodline was strong, and he is mentioned in the archives of many breeding industry organizations. Respess even erected a monument and bronze plaque on the farm to honor his achievements after his passing in 1923. When "Rome" Respess died in 1939, his widow sold the farm to the Holton family, who held it until receiving an offer to purchase from the developers of the Industrial Park. While the farm and the monument are long gone, *Dick Welles'* blood still runs strong through the veins of other championship racehorses.[1]

- -

Bobby LaRue (1938-2010): Born in Henderson, Kentucky, Bobby LaRue worked for the prominent Kentucky trainer Doug Davis, Jr. before setting out on his own in the 1960s. In the 1970s, he was a leading conditioner at Latonia and the now-defunct Miles Park in Louisville. From 1976 to 2009, he saddled 273 winners. LaRue's operation suffered two devastating setbacks in the late 2000s, however. He lost much of his equipment when a tornado swept through Ellis Park. Then, eight horses were killed in a fire at Riverside Downs near Henderson, Kentucky.

- -

D. Wayne Lukas – (1935—) was born in Antigo, Wisconsin and had a passion for horses early in his teens. Later, he earned a master's degree in educa-

Courtesy: American Quarter Horse Association

tion from the University of Wisconsin-Madison. Afterwrds, he taught high school and coached basketball. Lukas began training Quarter Horses in California in 1968, and after 10 years of success that saw him train 24 world champions, he switched to Thoroughbreds. The first trainer to earn more than $100 million in purse money, he has been the year's top money winner 14 times.

Lukas first made his mark with Thoroughbreds in 1980 when he won the Preakness Stakes with *Codex*. His horses have won the Kentucky Derby four times, the Preakness on six occasions, and have claimed victory four times in the Belmont Stakes, including winning all three of the classics in 1995 with *Thunder Gulch* (Kentucky Derby and Belmont) and *Timber Country* (Preakness), making him the first trainer to sweep the Triple Crown Classic races with two different horses in one season. He has won Breeder's Cup races a record 20 times. Other top Lukas Thoroughbreds include *Charismatic*, *Grindstone*, *Tabasco Cat*, and *Winning Colors*.

- -

Kenneth and Sarah Ramsey: Kenneth (1935—) and Sarah "Kitten" Ramsey (1939-2022) have numerous graded stakes wins, three Breeder's Cups, and have won multiple Eclipse Awards for outstanding owner and breeder. The Ramsey Farm, a 1,200-acre breeding operation near Nicholasville, Kentucky, has produced Thoroughbreds who have raced at tracks worldwide. Many of their horses' names incorporate the word "kitten," Ken's nickname for Sarah. Their leading stallion, *Kitten's Joy*, enjoyed a successful career in longer races.

The Ramseys, both from Artemus, a small town near Barbourville, Kentucky, bred a few Thoroughbreds in the 1970s and 1980s, but became serious about the sport when they purchased the former Almahurst Farm, the birthplace of the 1918 Kentucky Derby winner *Exterminator*. Over the years, the Ramseys have worked with top trainers such as Bobby Frankel, D. Wayne Lukas, Mike Maker, and Dale Romans. They have leading owner titles from Ellis Park, Gulfstream Park, Saratoga, and Turfway Park. In addition, they hold the record at Churchill Downs for most leading owner titles in the history of the track with 28 and at Keeneland with eighteen. Other top Ramsey Thoroughbreds include *Big Blue Kitten*, *Bobby's Kitten*, *Charming Kitten*, *Dean's Kitten*, *Derby Kitten*, *Oscar Nominated*, *Stephanie's Kitten*, and *We Miss Artie*.

- -

Eric Reed: In the Forego Stakes at the Latonia Race Track, *Native Drummer* provided Eric Reed with his first major win. Reed became owner of Mercury Equine Center, a 60-acre Thoroughbred training facility in Lexington, Kentucky. In 2016, a devastating fire ravaged the facility, killing dozens of horses. Several area horsemen rushed to Reed's aid and, with their tremendous support, Reed was able to rebuild his stable and continue as a trainer. Eric Reed is best known as the trainer of *Rich Strike*, who made his debut at Turfway Park and was the 2022 Kentucky Derby winner.

- -

Twin Oaks Farm was another historic breeding operation in the Northern Kentucky region. Owned by **Marvin and Alan Gaines**, the farm was located along Old Lexington Pike in Walton. The Gaines brothers' ancestors were among the first settlers in present-day Boone County. Alan also owned and managed the Walton Lumber Company for over 50 years and was president and chairman of the board of Dixie State Bank in Walton. His brother, Marvin, owned and operated the **Spring Lake Stud Farm** nearby.

The brothers teamed up in the winter of 1957, and the colt *Bally Ache* was born. His great-great-grandfather was the legendary *Man o' War*, who won 20 out of 21 races, including the Preakness and Belmont in 1920. Described as a blocky, short-backed colt with a small, choppy stride, *Bally Ache* was sold by the Gaines brothers as part of a two-horse transaction for $5,000. As a two-year-old, he won five stakes races and set a new track record at Jamaica Racetrack in New York. He won the Flamingo Stakes and the Florida Derby at age three, making him eligible for the Kentucky Derby. In the 1960 "Run for the Roses," *Venetian Way*, already beaten four times by *Bally Ache*, won, and *Bally Ache* placed. *Bally Ache* was then sold to the Turfland Racing Syndicate for $1,250,000 and went on to win the 84th running of the Preakness.[2]

‑ ‑

Lynn S. Whiting – (1939—2017): The son of jockey and trainer Lyle S. Whiting, Lynn is best known for his incredible upset win in the 1992 Kentucky Derby with *Lil E. Tee*. Born in Great Falls, Montana, Lynn chalked up a long list of major wins during his career, including Turfway Park's Clipsetta (1993), Jim Beam Stakes (1984, 1987, 1992), Fall Championship Stakes (1986), as well as the Pennsylvania Derby (1995). Besides *Lil E. Tee*, Lynn's notable horses include *At the Threshold*, *Cyber Secret*, and *Phantom on Tour*. In 6,113 starts, Whiting's horses achieved more than 3,000 top-three finishes.

Jockeys

George Edward "Eddie" Arcaro (1916-1997): Of Acaro's many wonderful nicknames, "The greatest rider since Paul Revere" was said to be his favorite. Born in Cincinnati, Ohio, but raised in Newport and Covington, Kentucky, Eddie Arcaro dropped out of school at age 13 and started galloping horses at Old Latonia. Underage, he had a few starts illegally as a jockey at Old Latonia and in Ohio in 1932. Afterward, he relocated to Tijuana, Mexico, where there were no limitations regarding age requirements. Arcaro lost 45 times before getting his first win and returned to the United States after his 18th birthday. Arcaro had great success over his 30-year career, riding 24,092 mounts with 4,779 wins, including five Kentucky Derby, six Preakness, and six Belmont victories. He remains the only two-time Triple Crown winner and has won more American Classic races than any other jockey in history.

‑ ‑

Jerry D. Bailey (1957—) had 5,893 mounts during his career. Born in Dallas, Texas, Bailey rode his first ever race in 1974 at age 17… and won! He enjoyed much success nationwide and established his presence as a rising star on the New York circuit in 1982. He

solidified his national stature with victories aboard *Hansel* in the 1991 Preakness and Belmont Stakes, won his first Kentucky Derby in 1993 with *Sea Hero*, and was inducted into the National Racing Hall of Fame two years later. Bailey won his second Kentucky Derby riding *Grindstone* in 1996, added another Preakness win in 2000 aboard *Red Bullet*, and captured the 2003 Belmont on *Empire Maker*. In 1996, he guided *Cigar*, a two-time Horse of the Year, to a 16th consecutive victory, equaling the modern era record set by the 1948 Triple Crown champion *Citation*. Bailey recorded his milestone 5,000th career win in 2001 and in 2003 became the first jockey to reach $20 million in purse earnings for a single season.

— —

Mike Bryan started his career in 1972 working at Domino Stud horse farm outside of Lexington, Kentucky. He left a good-paying job with the L&N Railroad as an electrician to learn how to ride. He soon, "...thought taking the significant cut in pay was a mistake," Bryan said. "After a year of shoveling horse manure, grooming, and walking horses, they let me break babies, which I really enjoyed. I moved to Keeneland, worked for owner J.P. Williamson, and freelanced galloping and working horses." Bryan road his first race at Common-wealth Race Track (Old Miles Park) in his hometown of Louisville in 1974. "I started riding at Latonia that same year, and trainers such as Larry Eilers, Rick Hiles, Jack Poole, D.H Skaggs, Les Wiley, and Hulon Womack helped tremen-dously at that time. D.H. Skaggs put me on more winners than anyone, including *Our Vindicator*, winner of 20 races. The best horse I ever rode was *Da White Judge*. He stood still in the gate when it opened one night at Turfway Park and still broke the track record for 5½ furlongs and was one-fifth of a second off both

6½ and 7 furlongs at Keeneland, and I never really coaxed him to run." Bryan's biggest purse was the $150,000 Budweiser Handicap at Fairmont Park on *Lieutenant Lao*. He also won a few stakes at Latonia/Turfway Park. Bryan's overall career record is 7,915 mounts, 1,039 firsts, 944 seconds, and 889 third-place finishes. Bryan recalled, "The craziest thing that ever happened at Latonia was one night, a deer ran out of the infield and caused Brian Peck to get hurt. Other animals ventured onto the track that scared horses and riders... an opossum, red fox, and geese, which were hit hard, causing feathers to fly everywhere."

- -

Patti and Donna Barton: This mother/daughter duo found great success on numerous Thoroughbred tracks across the nation. A one time barmaid turned jockey, Patti Barton was one of America's first pioneering women riders. She has over 1,000 wins, with 9,322 mounts and nearly 3,330 top-three finishes. Her daughter, Donna Barton Brothers, is one of the most decorated female riders, retiring in 1998 with 1,130 wins; she still ranks in the top five on the money list. Donna has over a dozen major victories. After retirement, she married Frank Brothers and became involved in television broadcasting. In this field, she is best known for her coverage of the Kentucky Derby and Breeder's Cup races, doing on-track interviews while on horseback.

- -

Rafael Bejarano (1982—) embarked on his professional career in 1999 while in his native country of Peru. He moved to Louisville, Kentucky in 2002 and got his first win at River Downs outside Cincinnati, Ohio. In 2004, he got his big break when he earned the title of United States Champion Jockey by wins with 455. On March 12, 2004, Rafael won seven races on a single race card at Turfway Park and ended the entire meet with a record 196 wins. In the American Classic races, he had an eighth-place finish in the 2005 Kentucky Derby, a second-place finish in that year's Belmont Stakes, and finished fourth in the 2004 Preakness.

- -

Don Brumfield (1938—) won 4,573 races during his 35-year career. He had over 33,000 mounts and won 12 riding titles at Churchill and 16 at Keeneland, including 10 in a row there. Brumfield rode *Kauai King* to victory in the Kentucky Derby (1966) and was inducted into the Hall of Fame in 1996. Born in Nicholasville, Kentucky, Brumfield won his first race at age 16 at Monmouth Park in Oceanport, New Jersey. For most of his career, Brumfield rode in the Kentucky race circuit.

-- --

Steven Mark Cauthen (1960-) was raised on the family farm in Walton, Kentucky. He began riding horses at age five and received his license to race on his 16th birthday. He began his long and successful career at Churchill Downs on May 12, 1976, riding *King of Swat* and finishing last. His first win came at River Downs on May 17, 1976, on a claimer named *Red Pipe*. He was the track's leading rider that same year with a record-setting 120 wins. Cauthen rode at numerous racetracks across the country, including Aqueduct and Santa Anita, and was the youngest jockey ever to win $6 million with fewer than 300 wins.

In 1977, Cauthen was the *Sports Illustrated* "Sportsman of the Year," the only jockey ever to earn that title. Upon *Affirmed* in 1978, he was the youngest jockey ever to win the Triple Crown. From 1979 to 1992, Cauthen rode in England and remains the only jockey to win all five major "Derby" races (Kentucky, 1978; Epsom, 1985; Irish, 1989; French, 1989; and Italian, 1992).

After retiring from riding in 1992, Cauthen established Dream Fields, an elite riding and training facility, and was a vice president of Turfway Park until 2007. In 2018, New Day NKY purchased a portion of the Dream Fields property where they provide equine-facilitated psychotherapy for high-risk youth.[3]

-- --

Patricia "P.J." Cooksey (1958-): Born in Youngstown, Ohio, Cooksey won her first race in 1979 with *Turf Advisor* at West Virginia's Waterford Park (now Mountaineer Park). A four-time "Leading Rider" at Latonia and Turfway Park, Cooksey had 2,137 wins over her 25-year career and was once the all-time leading female rider in the nation by number of victories. In 1985, she became the first female rider to ride in the Preakness Stakes.

Courtesy: America's Best Racing

Seriously injured during a race at Keeneland on April 12, 2003, she laid out nearly a year before racing again. However, suffering from persistent pain from the previous injury, she retired again in June 2004. In 2006, she became a horse-riding reporter for ESPN's coverage during the Breeder's Cup. She currently works for the Kentucky Racing Commission and resides in Georgetown, Kentucky.[4]

- -

Tommy D'Amico is a native of Ravenna, Ohio, and began his career in 1974 at Thistledown in Cleveland. He moved to the Kentucky circuit in the late 1980s. D'Amico had won nearly 3,000 races by 2004, but by then had broken his neck twice, fractured his leg, suffered a broken collarbone, and had numerous minor injuries. Despite that, he had earned a reputation as a top jockey, though he was virtually unknown outside the Midwest. He had been riding for nearly a quarter-century before he won a race worth more than $100,000.

In 2002, when trainer Ken McPeek had two colts among the four top Kentucky Derby contenders, *Harlan's Holiday* and *Repent*, both of whom had been ridden exclusively by D'Amico, McPeek had a tough decision to make. Should he bring in a nationally-known jockey with impressive credentials for classic races, or should he go with the 46-year-old unknown? McPeek replaced Tommy D'Amico with Edgar Prado on *Harlan's Holiday* in the Run for the Roses and, they finished a disappointing seventh.

D'Amico took a terrible spill at Churchill Downs in 2004. In a field of 11 horses during the 10th race on the card on October 27, D'Amico was aboard *Deep Woods* who suddenly swerved inward toward the rail and threw D'Amico in the path of the oncoming *Sally Forth*, ridden by Leslie Mawing.

- -

Patrick Alan "Pat" Day (1953—) is a four-time winner of the Eclipse Award for Outstanding Jockey and was inducted into the National Museum of Racing and Hall of Fame in 1991. Born in Brush, Colorado, Day has 8,803 career wins from his 40,305 rides. He also has more than 12,000 second- and third-place finishes. Day won nine Triple Crown races and 12 Breeder's Cup races and was a dominant rider in Kentucky, with riding records at Churchill Downs and Keeneland. Some of his top mounts were upon horses quite familiar to Turfway Park fans: *Lil E. Tee*, *Summer Squall*, and *Tabasco Cat*.

Courtesy: kyphotoarchive.com

After 30 years as an extremely successful jockey, Pat Day became a chaplain at Churchill Downs and remains a highly sought-after motivational speaker.

Courtesy: Gettyimages.com

- -

Darrell Foster was raised on a farm in Philpot, Kentucky. There, his days were spent either in a tobacco patch, hay field, or upon a tractor. He began his racing career at Ellis Park in 1977 with the mount *Skynyrd*, a horse named after the rock group Lynyrd Skynyrd. Remarkably, his first ride resulted in a win. Foster said he was extremely fortunate to be mentored by owner/trainers Shirley Greene and Charlie Hundley, two people for whom he has had a lifelong fondness. Foster's first ride at Latonia was upon *Red Ellen*, resulting in another first-place finish. Foster has ridden at tracks across the United States, including Chicago, Illinois and Hot Springs, Arkansas. He has over 8,700 starts, nearly 3,000 top-three finishes, and over $6,000,000 in career winnings. One of the jockey's fondest memories is the inaugural Queen Elizabeth II Challenge Cup at Keeneland on October 11, 1984, when the young jockey met, spoke to, and shook the hand of the late British monarch.[5] After retirement, Foster moved to Whitesville, Kentucky.

Andrew Mack Garner (1898-1936):

Mack Garner was indeed one of the greatest. With 151 wins, Garner became the nation's top rider in 1915. He won the Belmont Stakes in 1929 and 1933 and rode *Blue Larkspur* when that horse in 1929 was the greatest of the three-year-olds. Mack won the Kentucky Derby atop *Cavalcade* in 1934. Garner was a regular rider at Old Latonia and on November 11, 1923, he rode Carl Wiedemann's horse *In*

Courtesy: Descendant Rob Haney

Garner winning the 1934 KY Derby

Memoriam to victory over that year's Horse of the Year and Kentucky Derby winner, *Zev*. On October 28, 1936, he had four mounts at River Downs (with one win) but suffered a fatal heart attack at his home in Covington, Kentucky later that night. Garner enjoyed a 21-year career with 1,346 victories and more than 2,000 econd and third-place finishes. He was inducted into the Racing Hall of Fame in 1969.[6]

Ronald L. "Ronnie" Herbstreit (1946—)

began his racing career in 1962 at age sixteen. He left his home in Northern Kentucky and traveled to Wayne City, Illinois to team with Thurman Gammon, an Ellis Park mainstay and that track's leading owner/trainer during the 1950s and 1960s. In 1963, Herbstreit won his first race as an apprentice rider at the now-defunct Cahokia Downs in Illinois,

Courtesy: Wikipedia Commons

Atop *Grey Page* at River Downs

and rode successfully back when life on the racetrack was often hand-to-mouth and highly primitive by today's standards.[7] He won the Ellis Park riding title in 1965 with 34 wins and was the regular jockey for the Bob Walker-trained *King Kat*, a rags-to-riches runner and one of Ellis Park's most famous horses of that era. In September 1963, Herbstreit registered a "triple-win" at Latonia and later was a riding title winner there. Herbstreit retired in 1972, returned briefly in 1974, then spent four years cleaning tack for other riders and saddling horses in the afternoons. Afterward, he turned his attention to the "officials" side of the business. On a circuit that included Beulah Park, Latonia, and River Downs, he worked as a entry clerk, paddock judge, and placing judge. In 1979, he moved up a notch as an assistant racing secretary and became a steward at River Downs in 1985. In 1986, he became an association steward at Turfway Park. He was the Kentucky Racing Commission's Chief Racing Judge through much of the 1990s.

Courtesy: America's Best Racing

Albin Jimenez: A native of Panama, Jimenez grew up around horses and, at age 16, attended jockey training school in Panama City. He obtained his riding license in 2010 and picked up his first stakes win aboard *Aggressive Elegance* in May 2012. Jimenez guided *Lady Frog Horn* to victory in the 2016 Grade II Falls City Handicap at Churchill Downs for his first graded stakes win. He achieved his first Grade I win with *Knicks Go* in the 2018 Claiborne Breeder's Futurity at Keeneland and was aboard that colt when he ran second to *Game Winner* in the subsequent Breeder's Cup Juvenile at Churchill Downs. Jimenez rides primarily in Kentucky and Indiana,and has won six jockey titles at Turfway Park through early 2023.

Julie Krone (1963—) was born in Benton Harbor, Michigan. After spending her childhood as an accomplished show horse rider, Krone was inspired by champion rider Steve Cauthen to become a Thoroughbred jockey. She made her debut at Tampa Downs in 1981 on *Tiny Star* and won her first race there aboard *Lord Farkle*. Krone is the only female rider to ever win riding championships at Atlantic City Race Course, Belmont Park, Gulfstream, The Meadowlands, and Monmouth Park. In 1993, Krone won the Belmont Stakes aboard *Colonial Affair* and remains the only female jockey to win a Triple.

- -

Courtesy: Horse Racing Nation

Mike Manganello: rode five straight winners at Ohio's Thistledown Racecourse on June 25, 1964. His five wins in the Turfway Park Fall Championship Stakes are the most by any jockey. He rode *Dust Commander* in the 1970 Bluegrass Stakes at Keeneland, then rode the colt to a commanding five-length victory in the Kentucky Derby. He was inducted into the Italian American Sports Hall of Fame in 2017 and into the Cleveland Sports Hall of Fame in 2018. He retired in 1979 and, in 2023, resides in Lexington, Kentucky.

- -

Matt McGee (1890-1949): Born and raised in Covington, Kentucky, McGee rode *Durbar* to victory in the 1914 Epsom Derby, England's most prestigious race. He was the first jockey from the Greater Cincinnati area to ride there. McGee began his career at Old Latonia in 1908 and rode his first four years in the United States. He had his first Kentucky Derby mount in 1909 abord *Campeon*, where he finished in ninth place behind the victorious *Wintergreen*, owned by Boone County's Rome Respess. McGee died in 1949 and is buried at Latonia's Mother of God Cemetery. Interestingly, his name is often misspelled as "MacGee" in many European racing records.

- -

John McKee (1981—) was raised in an environment where horse racing was given far more importance than any other sport. His father, David, was a jockey in the United States horse racing circuit during the late 1970s and early 1980s. John got his start with Thoroughbreds at the age of 17 at Poplar Creek Farm near Bethel, Ohio where he became an exercise rider. As a jockey, he posted his first win on May 27, 2002, at Cincinnati's River Downs upon *Storm Cup*. John set a seasonal win record at River Downs for an apprentice jockey in 2002. He then found success at Oaklawn Park during the mid-2000s, leading the Hot Springs, Arkansas track in wins for its 2004 meet. McKee first gained national prominence during this time as the rider of *Lawyer Ron* early in that Thoroughbred's accomplished career. McKee won four stakes races with *Lawyer Ron* in 2006, including the Arkansas Derby. Since 2005, John McKee has been riding primarily in Indiana, Kentucky, and Ohio. Based at Turfway Park, however, McKee led that track in total earnings during its winter 2018 and winter 2019 meets. He has amassed more than 16,000 starts, with over 2,500 wins, more than 2,400 places, and over 2,300 show finishes, for a win-place-show percentage of forty-three percent. McKee returned to Turfway Park for its 2022-2023 Holiday/Winter Meet.

Isaac Burns Murphy (1861-1886): Considered one of, if not the greatest jockeys of all time, Isaac Murphy was known as the "Colored Archer," in reference to Fred Archer, a prominent white English jockey. Born in Clark County, Kentucky, Murphy won the first Hindoo Stakes at Old Latonia (1883) and would go on to win three Kentucky Derby (1884, 1890, 1891) and five Latonia Derby/ Hindoo Derby (1883, 1885, 1886, 1887, 1891) races. He also amassed four Clark Handicaps (1879, 1884, 1885, 1890) and the Kentucky Oaks (1884) at Churchill Downs. He is said to have won 628 of his first 1,412 mounts, an incredible 44 percent victory rate still never matched, and was the first jockey to be inducted into the National Museum of Racing and Hall of Fame when it opened in 1955.[8]

Thomas Peter Murray (1902-1963): In 1919, Murray became the second leading rider in the United States with 832 mounts and 157 wins. He missed the top prize by only six victories. His first win came at Old Latonia, but he rode at nearly every track in the nation and many in Canada and Cuba. After a successful 14-year career, Murray trained horses, joined the military, and died in near-poverty at a Cincinnati, Ohio hotel.[9]

Perry Wayne Ouzts (1954—): Born and raised in Arkansas, Ouzts is one of the most successful jockeys of the modern era. He started his career at Beulah Park in Grove City, Ohio, seeing his first win there in 1973. Since then, he has consistently ranked among the leading riders at tracks across the country. He has an unbelievable 35 meet titles at Cincinnati's River Downs/Belterra Park, 13 at Beulah Park, and two at Turfway. Perry's best year was 2014, when he amassed nearly $2 million in purses.

Since 1973, Perry has averaged 1,130 mounts each year, apart from 2006, when he suffered a devastating injury at Turfway Park. A regular there, he was in second place aboard *Finders Chance* when the horse suddenly collapsed. Another horse clipped his arm, snapping the bone. He also received four cracked and one crushed vertebra in the incident, requiring three surgeries and an 11-month recovery. However, Ouzts returned to racing the following year, marking one of the most incredible comebacks among athletes of any sport. Over the years, Outzs has broken his back, jaw, collarbone, arm, and nose and has metal plates around his eye socket and mouth.

In 2012, when he crossed the 6,000-win mark, Hall of Fame jockey Steve Cauthen said, "Perry is a straight-shooter. I learned a lot from him that I carried on throughout my career." While eligible for the National Museum of

Perry Ouzts after his 7,000th victory

Courtesy: Horse Racing Nation

Racing and Hall of Fame since the early 2000s, many jockeys who ride at less prestigious tracks never make it there.

On September 21, 2018, Perry rode *Emmy's Candy* to victory at Cincinnati's Belterra Park, marking his 7,000th career win, only the ninth jockey ever to reach that pinnacle. He often told reporters that he would retire after 7,000 wins, but the mounts and the victories are still coming. With over 53,000 mounts, the only jockey with more starts is Russell Baze, a now-retired rider out of California. At 69 years old in 2023, Ouzts seems to have no plans to slow down. He returned to Turfway Park for another season, arriving each morning at around 7:00 to gallop horses, only to return in the evening to ride as many as six races on an eight-race card. He currently ranks fifth in all-time wins in the United States and Canada and number 10 worldwide.[10]

Rodney Prescott is another Turfway Park regular, with over 31,000 mounts as of the end of 2022. He has amassed over 4,000 wins, 4,000 place finishes, and 3,700 shows. He is a three-time leading jockey at Indiana Grand (2004, 2005, 2018) and shares the title of most wins on a card there with six. Prescott also ranks number four of all-time as a Quarter Horse jockey. A native of Portland, Indiana, Prescott began riding in 1994 and has several riding titles at River Downs and Turfway Park.

Courtesy: Shelbyvillenews.com

Michael Francis Rowland (1963-2004): Born in Saratoga Springs, New York, Rowland enjoyed great success across the nation and had amassed 3,997 wins by February 4, 2004. Management at Turfway Park had planned a wonderful celebration once Rowland reached the 4,000-victory milestone. In anticipation, a large sign with orange and blue lettering lay in a conference room: "Congratulations, Mike Rowland – 4,000 wins." Rowland rode in two races on the card that night without a victory. In the seventh race, he was atop *World Trade* when his mount suffered a devastating breakdown, throwing the promising jockey to the dirt. Other riders were unable to avoid a collision with the fallen jockey. Rowland suffered severe injuries, including massive head trauma, and was taken to Cincinnati's University Hospital. Having never regained consciousness four days after the incident, Rowland was taken off life support.

- -

Mike Smith began riding in his native New Mexico and started breaking horses at age eight. He dropped out of school in the ninth grade and, accompanied by his paternal grandparents, began his riding career in a Midwestern circuit.

Courtesy: Blood Horse Magazine

Since then, he has been one of the leading riders in the United States and was inducted into the National Museum of Racing and Hall of Fame in 2003. Smith has won the most Breeder's Cup races of any jockey, with 27. In 2005, he rode 50-1 longshot *Giacomo* to victory in the Kentucky Derby. In 2018, at age 52, he rode *Justify* to victories in the Triple Crown, becoming the oldest jockey to do so. In 2023, Smith has accumulated more than 34,000 starts with nearly 15,000 top-three finishes. He has amassed more than $343 million in earnings.

At Turfway Park, Smith road *Prairie Bayou* to victory in the 1993 Spiral Stakes before going on to win the Blue Grass Stakes with him at Keeneland. He found his way to a second-place finish behind *Sea Hero* in the 1993 Kentucky Derby. Upon *Roar*, Smith won the 1995 Kentucky Cup Juvenile and the 1996 Spiral Stakes. In 2002, Smith had the irons with *Pure Prize*, winner of the Kentucky Cup Classic at Turfway Park.

Smith may be best remembered as the jockey of *Zenyatta*, the 2010 Horse of the Year. Smith rode the superstar mare in 17 of her 20 races, winning all but one, with their only loss being a second-place finish in the 2010 Breeder's Cup Classic, *Zenyatta's* last race.

- -

Gary Stevens (1963—) became a professional jockey in 1979 and amassed three Kentucky Derby winners in his career (1988, 1995, 1997). He had nine wins in Triple Crown races, winning the Preakness (1997, 2001, 2013), Belmont (1995, 1998, 2001), and 10 Breeder's Cup races. He won over 5,000 races and, in 1997, was inducted into the Hall of Fame. Some of Stevens' top mounts include *Thunder Gulch*, *Silver Charm*, and *Serena's Song*. Stevens even had an acting role as jockey George Woolf in the film *Seabiscuit* and, in 2023, is a race analyst on television for FOX Sports.

- -

Philadelphia native **Bill Troilo** became a professional jockey in 1982 and has ridden 2,514 winners in his 27-year career. He had his first graded stakes win in 2009 at Churchill aboard *Karelian*. After high school, where Bill successfully played ice hockey, he found himself in Lexington, Kentucky with trainer George Arnold, learning how to ride Thoroughbred horses. A regular at Turfway, Troilo retired on April 2, 2009, after winning more than $27 million in purse money. In his long career,

Courtesy: Tina Hines

he amassed more than 20,000 starts, 2,514 wins, 2,294 places, and 2,379 shows.

After retirement, Troilo wanted to be a racetrack steward. In a post-retirement interview, he described that occupation as "…the sport's police officers. People who watch the races to ensure they are played fairly and dish out disqualifications if necessary."[11] Troilo became a Steward in 2011 and has been the Senior State Steward in Kentucky since 2018. At Turfway Park, Bill serves as the Clerk of Scales, a position he has held since 2011.

_ _

Melinda Vest: As a jockey, the former Melinda Spickard was described as "aggressive... not one to take any sap" by J.L. "Buck" Wheat, a former trainer. "She doesn't let anybody intimidate her. She knows the tricks of the trade."[12] Spickard raced mainly at Latonia and River Downs, with some appearances at Churchill Downs and elsewhere. In 1981, she became the first woman to ride three winners on a card at Churchill. In 1984, she won 95 races to finish 5th nationally among female riders. Her mounts' earnings that year exceeded $475,000, ranking her seventh. A jockey from 1980-1988, she won 402 races from 4,707 mounts while competing on the Kentucky-Ohio racing circuit.

Vest grew up in Louisville and was determined to be around horses after graduating high school. She enrolled in an equine program at the Kentucky Horse Park in Lexington. There, she learned horsemanship and advanced riding, which led to her first job as an exercise rider at Keeneland. She galloped horses there and at Churchill for five years before racing competitively. Her first win was aboard *Big Red Chief* at Ellis Park in Henderson, Kentucky in 1980. In 1986, she won the day's feature race at Latonia upon *Colorful Countess*.

After retiring as a jockey, Vest became an "identifier." In that role, she receives a most unusual view of horses. When they arrive in the paddock before each race, Vest turns their upper lips inside out to read the numbers tattooed there. The procedure ensures that the name in the program matches the animal standing before her. In some cases, Vest knows exactly who a horse is, but she still needs to check the tattoo. "I almost feel silly checking their tattoos, and I apologize because I know the horse is the right one," she said. "When I checked *American Pharoah's* tattoo before he won the 2015 Breeders' Cup Classic at Keeneland, of course, I knew he really was *American Pharoah,* but I still had to do my job." [As a footnote: just a couple of years ago, a 90 to

1 long shot won easily in a race at Charles Town after which it was discovered, he was a much higher class horse who's identity tattoo had been altered.]

– –

Charlie Woods: In a career that began in early 1974 at Oaklawn Park in Hot Springs, Arkansas, Woods won 2,857 times in 21,047 races, with his mounts earning more than $36.6 million. A native of Louisville, Woods was a mainstay of the Kentucky circuit and endeared himself to racing fans within the state. Although he regularly rode at Ellis Park and Keeneland, he enjoyed greater success at Churchill and Turfway. At Churchill, where he was the leading rider at the 1985 Spring Meet, he won 748 races, placing him fifth behind Pat Day, Don Brumfield, Jim McKnight, and Larry Melancon. At Turfway, he won a remarkable eight riding titles.

Top: The jockeys riding in the 46th running of the Jack Cincinnati Casino Spiral Stakes at Turfway Park;

Above, left: Julie Krone, a Turfway Park regular, featured on the cover of Sports Illustrated in 1989;

Center: England-born Sophie Doyle, one of the top female riders at Turfway Park;

Right: Robert A. "Cowboy" Jones. Cowboy rode his first win in 1959 and had victories in six decades. He passed away in 2022.

Appendix

Kentucky Derby winners who first ran at Latonia/Turfway Park

1883: *Leonatus* and *Buchanan*

1885: *Joe Cotton*

1887: *Montrose*

1888: *Macbeth II* and *Spokane*

1890: *Riley*

1891: *Kingman*

1896: *Ben Brush*

1898: *Plaudit*

1900: *Lieutenant Gibson*

1903: *Judge Himes*

1904: *Elwood*

1906: *Sir Huron*

1907: *Pink Star*

1909: *Wintergreen*

1910: *Donau*

1911: *Meridian*

1912: *Worth*

1913: *Donerail*

1914: *Old Rosebud*

1916: *George Smith*

1918: *Exterminator*

1919: *Sir Barton*

1923: *Zev*

1924: *Black Gold*

1929: *Clyde Van Dusen*

1992: *Lil E. Tee*

2011: *Animal Kingdom*

2022: *Rich Strike*

Spiral Stakes Winners

1972 – *Big Dot*

1973 – *Bootlegger's Pet*

1974 – *Jacks Chevron, Aglorite,*
            King of Rome

1975 – *Naughty Jake,*
            Ambassador's Image

1976 – *Inca Roma*

1977 – *Smiley's Dream, Bob's Dusty*

1978 – *Five Star General*

1978 – *Raymond Earl*

1979 – *Lot o' Gold*

1980 – *Major Run, Spruce Needles*

1981 – *Mythical Runner*

Jim Beam Stakes Winners

1982 – *Good N' Dusty*

1983 – *Marfa*

1984 – *At the Threshold*

1985 – *Banner Bob*

1986 – *Broad Brush*

1987 – *J.T.'s Pet*

1988 – *Kingpost*

1989 – *Western Playboy*

1990 – *Summer Squall*

1991 – *Hansel*

1992 – *Lil E. Tee*

1993 – *Prairie Bayou*

1994 – *Polar Expedition*

1995 – *Serena's Song*

1996 – *Roar*

1997 – *Concerto*

1998 – *Event of The Year*

GalleryFurniture.com Stakes

1999 – *Stephen Got Even*

Spiral Stakes

2000 -- *Globalize*

2001 – *Balto Star*

Lanes End Stakes

2002 – *Perfect Drift*

2003 – *New York Hero*

2004 – *Sinister G*

2005 – *Flower Alley*

2006 – *With A City*

2007 – *Hard Spun*

2008 – *Adriano*

2009 – *Hole Me Back*

2010 – *Dean's Kitten*

Vinery Racing Stakes

2011 – *Animal Kingdom*

2012 – *Went the Day Well*

Horseshoe Casino Spiral Stakes

2013 – *Black Onyx*

2014 – *We Miss Artie*

2015 – *Dubai Sky*

Jack Casino Spiral Stakes

2016 – *Oscar Nominated*

2017 – *Fast and Accurate*

Jeff Ruby Steaks

2018 – *Blended Citizen*

2019 – *Somelikeithotbrown*

2020 – *Field Pass*

2021 – *Like the King*

2022 – *Tiz the Bomb*

2023 – *Two Phil's*

Hindoo Stakes/Latonia Derby/
Latonia Championship Winners

Hindoo Stakes

1883 – *Leonatus*

1884 – *Audrain*

1885 – *Bersan*

1886 – *Silver Cloud*

1887 – *Libretto*

Latonia Derby

1888 – *Los Angeles*

1889 – *Hindoocraft*

1890 – *Bill Letcher*

1891 – *Kingman*

1892 – *Newton*

1893 – *Buck McCann*

1894 – *Lazzarone*

1895 – *Halma*

1896 – *Ben Brush*

1897 – *Ornament*

1898 – *Han d'Or*

1899 – *Prince McClurg*

1900 – *Lieutenant Gibson*

1901 – *Hernando*

1902 – *Harry New*

1903 – *Woodlake*

1904 – *Elwood*

1905 – *The Foreman*

1906 – *Sir Huon*

1907 – *The Abbot*

1908 – *Pinkola*

1909 – *Olambala*

1910 – *Joe Morris*

1911 – *Governor Gray*

1912 – *Free Lance*

1913 – *Gowell*

1914 – *John Gund*

1915 – *Royal*

1916 – *Dodge*

1917 – *Liberty Loan*

1918 – *Johren*

Latonia Championship

1919 – *Be Frank*

1920 – *Upset*

1921 – *Brother Batch*

1922 – *Thibodaux*

1923 – *The Clown*

1924 – *Chilhowee*

1925 – *Broadway Jones*

1926 – *Bagenbaggage*

1927 – *Handy Mandy*

1928 – *Toro*

1929 – *Buddy Basil*

1930 – *Gallant Knight*

1931 – *Spanish Play*

1932 – *Stepenfetchit*

1933 – *Gold Basis*

1934 – *Fiji*

1935 – *Tearout*

1936 – *Rushaway*

1937 – *Reaping Reward*

Kentucky Cup
Classic Stakes

1994 – *Tabasco Cat*

1995 – *Thunder Gulch*

1996 – *Atticus*

1997 – *Semoran*

1998 – *Wild Rush/Silver Charm*
   (Dead Heat)

1999 – *Da Devil*

2000 – *Captain Steve*

2001 – *Guided Tour*

2002 – *Pure Prize*

2003 – *Perfect Drift*

2004 – *Roses in May*

2005 – *Shaniko*

2006 – *Ball Four*

2007 – *Hard Spun*

2008 – *Zanjero*

2009 – *Furthest Land*

2010 – (No Race)

2011 – *Future Prospect*

2012 through 2017 – (No Race)

2018 – *Camelot Kitten*

2019 – *Nun the Less*

2020 – *Nun the Less*

2021 – *Visitant*

2022 – *King Cause*

2023 – *Wolfie's Dynaghost*

Chapter Ten Endnotes

1. "Horse racing in Northern Kentucky," Robert D. Webster with James C. Claypool, *Northern Kentucky Heritage Magazine, Vol. XXVIII, No. 2.*

2. *Ibid.*

3. *Ibid.*

4. *Ibid.*

5. "Memorable Minute—Former Whitesville jockey recalls encounter with queen," *Messenger-Inquirer* (Whitesville, Ohio), October 27, 2022, retrieved on November 8, 2022.

6. Webster/Claypool.

7. "Herbstreit's path to the top wasn't paved in gold," *Evansville Courier and Press* (Evansville, Indiana), August 6, 2000, retrieved on November 8, 2022.

8. Webster/Claypool.

9. *Ibid.*

10. Tina Bovenzi, "Decorated Jockey Perry Ouzts Still Rides Strong at 67 Years Old," Spectrumnews1. com, retrieved on June 17, 2022.

11. "Going to Great Lengths," *South Philly Review*, April 30, 2009, retrieved on October 27, 2022.

12. "Spikard making a run at being a jockey," *The Messenger,* January 23, 1986, page 12.

Index